C000162103

DAVID
Waddington

DAVID
Waddington

MEMOIRS

Dispatches from Margaret Thatcher's Last Home Secretary

Biteback Publishing

First published in Great Britain in 2012 by
Biteback Publishing Ltd
Westminster Tower
3 Albert Embankment
London SE1 7SP
Copyright © David Waddington 2012

ISBN 978-1-84954-319-4

10 9 8 7 6 5 4 3 2 1

A CIP catalogue record for this book is available from the British Library.

Set in Adobe Garamond Pro

Printed and bound in Great Britain by
CPI Group (UK) Ltd, Croydon CR0 4YY

To my parents, whose love and support never faltered.

Contents

Acknowledgements

A friend of mine wrote a book about his life and forgot to make any mention of his wife. I have not fallen into that error and Gilly appears on page after page, not in order to buy peace at home but because she has played a central part in the story. Without her I would have got nowhere. So thank you, Gilly, from the bottom of my heart.

I am also enormously grateful to my children for putting up with all the inconveniences which come from having a politician for a father and for making me so proud of them.

I hope all those others who appear in the story feel I have done them justice. I think I have been very lucky to know them and I have received many kindnesses from them.

I give my heartfelt thanks to Jane Wilson, my secretary, without whom none of this would have been possible. In writing the book I have not had any diaries to rely on. Much of the content is based on memory. So if I have got the odd date wrong I hope I may be forgiven.

CHAPTER ONE

Early Days

I was born in Burnley, Lancashire, as were both my parents. My mother came from a cotton-manufacturing family. Her grandfather, Robert Pickles, born in 1816, worked for many years as weaver before, in 1859, going into business on his own. Once a month he walked to Manchester – a round trip of fifty-four miles – to buy his yarn and sell his cloth, and he prospered. He was an inventor of some note and devised the check-strap which allowed looms to run at twice the speed which had previously been possible. My mother's father was his eldest son Thomas, who greatly expanded the business which eventually included a linen mill in Belfast.

The family had a house in Wigtownshire called Tonderghie and Thomas fell in love with and married one of the girls who worked in the house, the daughter of a local farmer. The Pickles family thought he had married below his station, but you would not have thought so from family photographs. In those Thomas's wife looks dignified, indeed rather imperious, and I was the only person who suffered from the union, being required as a little boy to wear a kilt at parties. We once visited a house in Wigtownshire to meet a Scottish relation and the son of the house on meeting us uttered only one word: 'Scram!' This enabled me many years later to face Scottish devolution with equanimity.

My mother, the youngest of seven children, spent most of her childhood at Tonderghie. She went there with her mother in the spring and did not return to Burnley until the autumn. As a result she only went to school for a few months each year, which seemed to do her no harm at all. When she told her mother she had received a proposal of marriage from Charlie Waddington, her mother said 'Oh no! Not one of the wild Waddingtons.'

The Waddington grandparents lived in a house called Westwood in Padiham Road, Burnley. There was a grand piano in the drawing room and when seeking to ascertain what went on underneath it my sister Zoe and I discovered that, suspended from a hook screwed into the back of the instrument, was a string bag full of currant buns.

Grandma assumed, no doubt rightly, that there was little chance of the maids dusting below waist level and that there was no better place to store emergency rations. My mother thought Grandma rather mean because it was only after a lot of coaxing that she was prevailed upon to produce her handbag and cough up half crowns for the children on their birthdays; but when the butcher's boy ran into her on his delivery bicycle she gave him half a crown for his trouble. Two hours before my grandfather's death in 1935 she decided he needed cheering up and went to the butcher's to buy him a pork chop. She could not decide which of two chops was the more toothsome so she asked the butcher if she could take both home on approval. When she dangled them in front of Grandpa's nose, he expired. After the funeral the family and one or two others went back to Westwood to 'bury him with ham'. The vicar got carried away and said 'Mr Charles, this calls for an oration'. 'Two minutes, Mr Veale,' said my father.

Grandpa's father had been in the cotton industry, eventually owning Bridge End Mill and Orchard Mill in Padiham; and after the First World War Grandpa decided that he also would try to make some money out of cotton and acquired two other mills in

Padiham. But he was first and foremost a solicitor and a very good one at that, having passed out top in the Solicitors' Finals. For a time he was an ardent Liberal, being election agent for Mr Jabez Spencer Balfour when he won Burnley for the Liberals in the 1892 general election, but it does not seem that he was ever minded to make a career of politics and he soon had a flourishing law practice. He was a great worker and anyone coming down Manchester Road, Burnley at dead of night was likely to see a light still burning in his office in Imperial Chambers. Some said he worked late because he was a perfectionist and no case placed in his hands received other than the most meticulous attention. Others less charitable assumed he was there to escape from his wife, but there is no doubt that the business was run with great efficiency. He was on the doorstep at ten to nine in the morning to remind those arriving on the hour that by then they should already be at their desks – and without lipstick, which he believed had no place in an office. Somehow or other he found time not only to run the office but to look after his mills. He also bought and took a close interest in the running of a number of farms including two in the village of Read, six miles from Burnley, where my parents in 1931 bought The Old Vicarage. J.C. (as my grandfather was known) excelled in farming as in the law. He kept some of the best shire horses, had a magnificent dairy herd and was a breeder of Wensleydale sheep.

My sister Nancy, now going on for ninety, remembers J.C. as being very strict, particularly when it came to good manners at Sunday lunch. 'All joints on the table will be carved' was his favourite saying; but once when Nancy, sitting on his knee, smashed to pieces one of the best dinner plates with her spoon, all Grandpa could think to say was 'If you do that again you will find yourself in the "Tounty Tourt".' I certainly do not remember him as being at all fearsome, but rather a nice old chap who clearly meant no harm when he insisted on my following him round his greenhouses.

When he died Grandma went to live in a hotel at Blackpool. She said she never wanted to see Burnley again, but luckily for her no one believed her and when, at the beginning of the War, she decided to come back to Burnley, her old house Westwood was there waiting for her with nothing changed. She died during the War; my father learned of the event when his sister, Aunt Dot, rang him at the office. She said 'Mother's dead, but just hang on a moment while I run upstairs to make sure.'

My father was one of five children and the second of three brothers. He was sent away to the preparatory school at Sedbergh and there made the painful discovery that his eldest brother George was the school bully. From Sedbergh he was sent first to Skipton Grammar School and then to Kelly College, Tavistock. In 1913 he went to Oxford where he enjoyed such a boisterous first year that he failed Divinity Moderations. Early in 1914, however, he had joined the Territorial Army, and the outbreak of War and a posting to France enabled him to escape his father's wrath.

My father was very lucky to survive the War. He was loath to talk about those years, but on a visit to the battlefields of Flanders in 2010 I met a man who was willing to do some research, and the record which follows was found in the National Archives.

On 15 August 1914 Charles Waddington was commissioned as a second lieutenant in the 3rd battalion East Lancashire Regiment. On 5 January 1915 he went to France and fought in the second battle of Ypres. On 7 July he was wounded in the fighting in Boesinghe and evacuated to a hospital in Boulogne before being sent back to England.

(He lost a chunk of his right foot which, in the Second World War, would almost certainly have resulted in his being invalided out of the army.)

In March 1916 he returned to France, was promoted to captain and served on the Somme front. At one time he was in temporary command of the battalion and took part in the attack on Redan Ridge. The attack was a costly failure with heavy casualties – some 5,752 officers and men were killed or wounded. With such heavy losses the division was moved up to the Ypres Salient for a 'rest' and to refit with drafts from England. However, they were soon back on the Somme, in time to fight in the Battle of Le Transloy Ridge in October 1916. On 17 October the ground was in an appalling condition. Heavy rain had fallen for weeks, and in front of the British trenches there was a vast lake of mud, pitted with shell-holes. For this reason a postponement of the attack was requested by the Brigade commanders, but the request was refused.

The night was pitch black and the enemy's line was extremely vague. German trench maps had been issued but they were of little use as the German line really consisted of detached machine guns in shell-holes. At zero hour a barrage was put down on one of the objectives, Dewdrop trench. The battalion then began to flounder in no man's land. The men, wearing full equipment and carrying extra bombs, were utterly exhausted and were shot down, drowned in shell-holes or rounded up by the Germans. Eventually the remnants were withdrawn to the original front-line trenches.

After dark on the 18th the attack was resumed, but 'casualties were heavy' says the report and included all the officers in the two leading companies. 'In "C" company 2nd Lt E.W. Graham was killed, and Captain Waddington (O.C. Company), 2nd Lt Quayle and Wilks captured. CSM Ashcroft and Cunliffe were killed, CSM Vaughan made prisoner; the total casualties in the other ranks were killed twelve, wounded fifty-eight, missing 292.'

That is the end of the official report, but in his own report made after his release from a prisoner of war camp in November 1918 my father explained how, when the attack started in pitch dark at 3.30 a.m., the line was not maintained and the men went forward in bunches, and with a few men he must have gone right through the

German lines. After realising he had gone too far he decided to dig in. At dawn he saw no sign of trenches, but Germans walking about the place as bold as brass and some British soldiers being marched away as prisoners. He decided to lie low and await developments, but eventually he and the others were discovered. His parents got a telegram saying he was missing believed killed, but some months later, they were told that he was in a prisoner of war camp.

In the camp Pa got into trouble for failing to spring to attention when a German officer entered the barrack room while he was shaving. The officer said he was under arrest, but my father asserted that under the Geneva Convention no officer could be placed under arrest without an escort of two soldiers with fixed bayonets. This threw the Germans off balance and they retired in disorder. Months went by and my father had entirely forgotten the incident when at six o'clock one morning two soldiers with fixed bayonets arrived to take him before the Camp Commandant. The Commandant, having awarded him twenty-eight days' detention, went on to say that all the cells were full of other British officers serving punishment and my father would have to wait his turn. After more months had gone by two soldiers with fixed bayonets again turned up – a vacant cell was waiting.

After the War my father decided not to go back to Oxford but to become articled to my grandfather so that he could qualify as a solicitor in the shortest time possible. In a year or so he married my mother and the two of them went down to London and lived in lodgings in Notting Hill Gate while he studied at Gibson & Weldons, the law crammers who were still in business when I read for the Bar thirty years later.

My mother's and father's relations gave my sisters and me much innocent amusement; the game being to award points for sanity to each uncle and aunt and, by this quite scientific means, determine which family was dafter than the other. It was usually a very close-run thing. Aunt Edith, one of my father's sisters, may have been unfairly marked down because of the unpopularity of her husband, Donald Harris. At a Christmas party, he turned on one of my sisters and shouted: 'Don't call me Uncle Donald. You all think I'm beastly so call me Uncle Beastly.' And from that day forward Uncle Beastly was his name.

Our favourites were aunties Gertrude and Isaline (Robinson) who were, in fact, my father's cousins, and were by then living at Sunnyside, Simonstone. One of my family relics is a caution written in his own hand by the Chief Constable of Burnley following Auntie Isaline's apprehension for riding her pedal cycle without lights. They were, I imagine, typical of many women who would have married but for the death of tens of thousands of men of their generation in the Great War. Instead, they gave their lives to caring for their father and they made a particularly good job of it. At the age of eighty-two Doctor Robinson, known to us as 'Uncle', was forced to retire as Medical Officer of Health for Burnley. He claimed that there was a war on and his country needed him, but his pleas fell on deaf ears. He then lived on until nine days short of his 102nd birthday.

The other great friend of the family was my godfather, Harold Parkinson, known to us all as Nunky. After marrying Evelyn Green, the only daughter of a wealthy cotton manufacturer, he was soon running the Green business and made a great success of it; and just before the Second World War he bought Hornby Castle, outside Lancaster, and much land round it. During the War he became first a colonel in the Home Guard and then vice-chairman of the National Savings Movement, a job which eventually earned him a KBE.

My parents had moved to Read in 1931. The Old Vicarage was a long, ivy-covered house which stood directly on the side of a quiet lane overlooking the church. So quiet indeed was the lane that on summer evenings we used it for cricket and, throughout the year, for hockey on bicycles; and only very rarely were our activities disturbed by passing traffic. If cars did come along, the drivers waited politely for half time or the fall of a wicket.

We all loved the Old Vicarage, but it was not a particularly comfortable home. The room known as the nursery, in which we spent our time during our school years, and which my parents also used during the War because it was easier to keep warm than the drawing room, had a floor covering of linoleum: so had the kitchen in which we normally ate. The scullery housing the gas cooker and sink had a concrete floor and in winter was appallingly cold. In one corner of the pantry, which was even colder ,there was, during the War, an earthenware vat to hold pickled eggs and on the stone slab were arrayed dozens of tins of mixed vegetables, obtainable off the ration because of their unpopularity. There was no refrigerator; on winter nights my father put a saucer of water out in the backyard in the hope that the temperature would drop below freezing point and there would be ice for his cocktail.

One oddity upstairs was that the bath in the family bathroom was in the middle of the floor; and when my father was required to administer punishment, the bathroom was the place where the deed was done. The dignity of the occasion was, however, sometimes marred when the offender sought to escape by running round the bath and my father had to set off in pursuit, vainly trying to bring the back of the hair brush into contact with the sinner's behind. There was a second bathroom for Gladys the cook and Rhona the maid but this was commandeered for use as an operating theatre when tonsils had to be removed and other minor operations performed.

We were always surrounded by dogs, cats, ponies and poultry, my father being particularly keen on guinea fowl. One night the guinea fowls flew off into the top of an oak tree and we spent an hour or two trying to coax them down. It was very cold and they stayed there until they dropped off the branches frozen stiff. My sister Zoe once took some photographs of the hens, no doubt thinking it would give my father great pleasure to see his birds on film, but she got a gigantic rocket for wasting money.

I was the youngest of five children and the only boy. I was not spoiled by my sisters. When it came to housework, I had to do as much as the others. Although my parents had a maid and, until the outbreak of War, a cook, we all had to make our beds and sweep and dust our bedrooms, and then set about peeling the potatoes. In those days before television we never seemed to have much difficulty entertaining ourselves, but we were very lucky living in the country. At weekends and during school holidays we were not allowed to stay inside the house unless it was pelting down and we roamed the surrounding fields and haunted the farm where the tenant, Dick Earnshaw, treated us with great forbearance. All he got in return was help with hay-making when two or three Irish labourers also turned up to lend a hand and lived in the barn.

Being a large family we were very self-sufficient. Occasionally, school friends were asked back for tea but, after being subjected to various ordeals to establish their courage and physical fitness – all guests were required to swing on a rope from one side of the barn to the other – some did not come a second time.

On Fridays in the school holidays we used to get the bus to Burnley to do the shopping. Sometimes my sister Zoe and I stayed on in Burnley and went to see Aunt Dot who lived on Manchester Road. Once we used our pocket money to buy a budgerigar. The shop keeper popped it into a paper bag and when we presented bag and bird to my mother and asked her to carry it home on the bus in her shopping basket she was most indignant but complied.

I was born in 1929. I cannot put a date to many early memories, but I do remember sitting on a wall to watch King George V and

Queen Mary go past on their way to open the Mersey Tunnel. That, I find, took place on 18 July 1934. I then have a very clear memory of the Silver Jubilee in 1935. We were all in bed with measles and every few minutes, or so it seemed, God Save the King was played, and every few minutes we leapt out of bed and stood to attention. Before the abdication in 1936 I remember being taught some rude rhymes about Mrs Simpson and, on the day of the coronation in 1937, I planted a tree to mark the occasion.

When five I went to Sunnybank School in Manchester Road. We were taken there each morning by my father and usually we were late. Martyn Noble, who started at Sunnybank at the same time, used to help me do up my shoe laces but otherwise I was well ahead of the other children, having been taught by my sisters to read, write and do some arithmetic.

One day on arriving at school I took off my mackintosh in the cloakroom and was horrified to find that before leaving home I had failed to put on my jacket. The Headmistress, Miss Farrer, was disgusted to see me displaying my braces and rang up my mother to tell her I was improperly dressed. Rhona, our maid, came to the rescue and sped to Burnley on her Francis Barnett motorbike carrying the missing jacket.

I was never allowed to forget this event, any more than I was ever allowed to forget the time when we were out for the day in the car and I lost my purse with all my pocket money in it. My father stopped the car to allow it to be searched, but of the purse there was no trace. Bitter tears were shed. And then a mile or two down the road I took off my school cap and, lo and behold, my purse was sitting on my head where I had very sensibly placed it for safekeeping.

At Sunnybank there were brass studs on the bannisters to stop us sliding down them and Miss Farrer had a bad-tempered Scottish terrier which took a big piece out of Cynthia Forsyth's face. In time the scar disappeared and all that was left was a pretty dimple but it was a very bloody business.

My father's office was above Barclays Bank in Burnley, and if he wanted to see the manager, Mr Shutt, he walked down the stairs and straight in by the inside door. Once I was with him and he stormed in saying that he wanted to borrow quite a big sum of money and that he had not the slightest intention of providing any security. Mr Shutt replied: 'Calm yourself, Mr Charles. Of course I don't need security.' Banking seems to have changed a bit since those days, and not in the interests of the customer. My father could be peppery, as he was on this memorable occasion, but he was very kind to me and rarely complained about my behaviour, even when sorely tried. He seldom gave me any advice, but he did tell me that there were only three things to avoid in life – calling the fire brigade, playing cards with men on trains and questioning the decisions of magistrates; and I would have saved myself much trouble had I accepted his advice on the first two counts. When I was old enough to know better I was accosted by an Irishman on the train from Manchester to Llandudno. He invited me to find the lady, which I did with great ease, until the moment came when I agreed to back my judgement with a five-pound note. And after marrying I had a minor fire at home which the local fire brigade attacked with enormous ferocity, doing great damage to the fabric of the building. The reason for my father's advice regarding magistrates was that he had on one occasion appeared before a particularly crowded bench and after a long retirement the chairman returned to say they were equally divided. 'But how', said my father, 'can you be equally divided when there are nine of you?' 'Very well Mr Waddington,' said the chairman, 'in that case we find against you.'

Pa suffered great provocation at the hands of my sisters Ann and Mary who used to get the most appalling school reports. My mother was so afraid of the effect that they might have on Pa were he to see them at breakfast-time, that she used to intercept the post and secrete the inflammatory literature until before dinner when he had settled down in his armchair with a large drink in his hand. Once, and only once, did Ma's plan come unstuck and a report did fall in to Pa's hands at breakfast. There was a major explosion after which Ann and Mary summoned Zoe and myself to a council of war in the dog kennel. They said we all had to run away to teach Pa a lesson. Happily, however, the scheme never got off the ground because of a shortage of rations for the journey.

Once Ma and Pa were summoned to Cheltenham and arraigned before the Headmistress, the terrible Miss Popham, who told them of Ann and Mary's manifold sins and wickednesses. 'But,' said my mother, 'they are very happy here.' 'Happy?!' said Miss Popham. 'That's the whole trouble.'

My mother used to spend a lot of time railing against the weather – 'Call this flaming June? It ought to be ashamed of itself', 'You would have thought it had more sense', etc. It always seemed to me a somewhat exaggerated reaction as almost permanent rain seemed our lot in east Lancashire. Indeed we were told that it was because of the rain that the cotton industry had gone there in the first place and given us all a living.

As a child I spent a lot of time praying that there would not be another war. My parents spoke about the horrors of the Great War and their fears that another one would soon be on us. 'Is it the crack of doom?' my sister Mary asked when income tax went up in the 1938 budget; and in spite of the merry times, doom did not seem far away. I remember the eerie silence when all the traffic in Manchester Road stopped for the two-minute silence on each Armistice Day. It was as if the world was standing still. Then trenches were dug in Scott Park where the school went for its midday walk, and gas mask practices were held in the school yard. This was in the summer of 1938 and, although a month or two later Chamberlain came back from Germany saying there would be peace in our time, my parents did not believe a word of it.

In August 1939 we had our last family holiday together, staying at the Monreith Arms, Port William, in Wigtownshire. I travelled in my godfather Nunky's new Rolls-Royce which was towing a trailer carrying the family bicycles. On the car wireless, the first I had ever seen, there were repeated renderings of 'Roll out the barrel' and 'He was a handsome territorial'. At nearby Burrow Head an anti-aircraft unit was in training and on most days a target was towed overhead. We did not often see a hit. It was while we were in Scotland that the Molotov–Ribbentrop Pact was signed and we all knew then that war was certain. On Friday 1 September, the day on which Poland was invaded, I went on the bus to Burnley with my mother and she bought black-out material from a little draper's shop against the side of the very distinguished Market Hall, which was not destroyed by Hitler but by developers in the 1960s. On Sunday 3 September my father and I went down to the Mill in Padiham and we switched on the wireless on the board room table to hear Chamberlain say that there had been no reply to our ultimatum and we were at war.

CHAPTER TWO

Away at School

Two weeks later I arrived at Cressbrook, a preparatory school in Kirkby Lonsdale. I was terribly homesick and wished I could die. The pain seemed never to leave me. It was there in the classroom, at play and, most of all, at night. I had a model aeroplane which was shot down by a boy armed with a spear. The event coincided with a visit from Nunky who in due course sent me a new plane, but it did not help the sickness. Things got a bit better as the weeks went by, but it was years before going back to school at the beginning of term did not reduce me to tears. In spite of all this I still remember sunny times and I made some very good friends. It is surprising that a few of us did not finish up in the mortuary for we spent our play time capering around on the school roof, throwing spears and lumps of lead at each other and swinging from the branches of trees. One particularly sensational exploit involved our leaping off the terrace, hoping that the home-made parachutes strapped to our backs would ease our landing. They did not.

Every Sunday we had to learn the collect for the day and many have stuck in my mind ever since, particularly 'Stir up, we beseech thee, O Lord, the wills of thy faithful people; that they, plenteously bringing forth the fruits of good works, may of thee be plenteously rewarded.' This was learned on 'Stir-up Sunday' and after church we all went into the kitchen and stirred the

Christmas Pudding. Most of our thoughts centred on food. They were hungry times and one boy with great strength of mind built a splendid stamp collection by swapping his tea-time buns for my Mozambique triangulars. If we were feeling ill we were sent up to the sick room and always received the same treatment – starvation. It was amazing how soon we got better.

In 1939 and for the first few months of 1940 the War did not impinge on our lives to any great extent, except that we were required to knit balaclava helmets for the Finns after Russia's attack on that unfortunate country. I doubt whether my misshapen effort brought much delight to its Finnish recipient.

In the summer of 1940 we sat in the headmaster's study listening to news of the evacuation from Dunkirk and the following winter we lay in bed hearing German bombers flying overhead on their way to the shipyards in Barrow. Back home for the Christmas holidays the passage running along the back of the house had been turned into an air raid shelter, and the valley between Blackburn and Burnley was embellished with barrage balloons, each of which was given a nickname leading to questions such as 'Why isn't Dickie up, today?' An Ack-Ack battery was stationed at Simonstone and we had a few noisy nights during the Manchester blitz when the sky was red with the fires of Manchester and Salford, and shrapnel, presumably from anti-aircraft shells, fell on the barn roof. Pa had joined the Home Guard and was enjoying himself enormously, walking up and down outside the house wearing his tin hat and imagining he was back in the trenches.

Once a week Pa had to perform guard duty at the barracks in Burnley. Before leaving home my mother stuffed him full of raw carrots in the belief that it would help him see in the dark. The blackout meant that cars had virtually no lights, drivers being required, at that stage of the War, to cover almost all their headlights with cardboard.

When Hitler invaded Russia, Sykie, Cressbrook's deputy head, told us to rejoice. Hitler would suffer the same fate as Napoleon and lose the War. I suppose he also told us that Japan's attack on Pearl Harbor on 7 December 1941 was good news, but all I can remember about the end of 1941 and the beginning of 1942 was the sinking of the *Prince of Wales* and the *Repulse* off the east coast of Malaya and the fall of Singapore. They were disasters of enormous proportions and, although none of us doubted ultimate victory, we could not see it happening for many years.

Before I went away to school my sister Zoe and I used to quarrel a lot. But separation made the heart grow fonder and after I had gone away to Cressbrook the holidays found us inseparable. Once Zoe was so pleased I was coming home for the holidays she jumped into the air while running along the upstairs landing, hit the ceiling and knocked herself out.

My father bought a bicycle and together we cycled from Cressbrook to Sedbergh to see what was going to be my next school. I did not much like what I saw. I should have gone to Sedbergh in September 1943 but I fell off my bicycle and broke my leg so I did not arrive until January 1944. This turned out to be a considerable misfortune because seniority based on length of time at the school counted for a great deal and the chances of getting in to a senior position after only three years in the place were slight. I was faced with another more immediate problem. I was very well aware that my parents were hard up. They had sent all my sisters to Cheltenham Ladies' College and my youngest sister Zoe was still there. So I had insisted on taking the scholarship to Sedbergh. The papers, however, turned out to be beyond my comprehension. (One of the questions I remember was 'What is surrealism?') I did so badly in the scholarship papers that when I arrived at Sedbergh I found I had been placed in the third form doing work which to me was infantile. Eventually I plucked up courage and told the form master, who was old, crusty and frightening, what I thought; and he was so amazed and amused at my temerity that he sent me round to the Headmaster. He was equally amused and promptly transferred me to lower fourth classical where I blossomed and was then swiftly transferred to the fifth form. It was very important to me because I had worked out exactly where I had to get to in order to take Higher School Certificate at seventeen and leave school before I was eighteen.

Sedbergh went in for cold baths and running up hills and had a discouraging motto 'DURA VIRUM NUTRIX' (A Hard Nurse of Men). Winder House faced Winder the hill which, towering above the town, was attacked almost daily by hundreds of boys. A friend told me the other day that he had been back to Sedbergh recently and at first could not grasp why the place looked so different. Eventually he realised that it was because Winder was covered in heather. In our day any heather was removed by boys' bottoms as they slid down from the summit school-ward bound.

But in spite of the running and emphasis on sport, and in spite of the fact that I was once beaten for forgetting to bring a rugger ball back from the field and threatened with another beating for reading a history book by the side of the cricket pitch when I should have been watching the game, Sedbergh was certainly not 'one of the more pointlessly sadistic public schools' as it was described by *The Observer* in 1994. Headmaster John Bruce-Lockhart was quite forward-thinking and, recognising that there was excessive emphasis on prowess at games, particularly rugger where he himself and his sons had excelled, introduced school colours for music.

I enjoyed music at school, playing the piano and then the violin and the viola in the school orchestra. I transferred to the viola because it meant promotion of a sort – from second violin to first viola. A friend, Brian Hurst, played the cello. One night the bridge on his instrument broke with an awful report. Brian suffered from the schoolboy equivalent of shell shock.

Everybody had to join the JTC (Junior Training Corps) which was the old OTC (Officers' Training Corps), renamed to bring it more in tune with the egalitarianism by then in vogue. I have a certificate to prove that I passed the examination for War Certificate A. I cannot think why because the examination was a nightmare. I was told to reassemble a Sten gun which lay in pieces at my feet. I thought the parts were a bit stiff or the barrel a bit thin but by standing on the butt I managed to apply sufficient extra pressure to force the breech block into place. I had achieved the almost impossible. The breech block was in the wrong way round.

VE Day plus one was a very special family occasion. It was the day of my sister Nancy's marriage to an RAMC captain whom she had met as a nursing sister in Normandy very shortly after D-day. She had crossed the English Channel in an American ship, docking at Mulberry Harbour, and had then had a dangerous journey by lorry to Bayeux. It must have been very exciting but also very terrifying for a 22-year-old trained at Victoria Hospital, Burnley, who had known precious little of the world before becoming a nursing sister in the QAs.

In August 1945 my mother took Zoe and myself to London and we were there on VJ Day mingling in the enormous crowd outside Buckingham Palace. The Goring Hotel's scrambled egg made from egg powder did not impress, but we relished seeing the King and Queen arrive at Parliament for the State Opening. Our London visit ended with a performance of 'Perchance to Dream' by Ivor Novello and not only did we sing 'We'll gather lilacs' all the way home, we played it for months afterwards – Zoe on the squeeze-box, Ma on the piano and myself on the violin.

Back to Sedbergh where in 1946 we had a day off to enjoy the end of the War. The headmaster announced that we could go anywhere we wanted provided we did not use motor car, train or bus. It did not seem much of a bargain. Sedbergh, after all, was the back of beyond; twelve miles from Kendal, the nearest place with a cinema.

Plans were laid, and four of us walked to Sedbergh railway station, which was well outside the town, and boarded a waiting taxi. In Kendal we went into a pub and bought a pint of beer each and twenty cigarettes, and then proceeded to a picture house where we found four girls who were prepared to sit in the back row with us and let us have a few kisses. The taxi then whisked us back to where we had started, and from there we ran back to Winder House well pleased with ourselves. Unfortunately, one of our party decided to finish off his packet of Players in the boiler room. The packet and a few fag-ends were discovered by the man who did the stoking, and we were all for the high jump.

I had decided that the next year was to be my last at Sedbergh and was determined to do my best to get up to Oxford to read law. So it worked out. I was accepted by my father's old college, Hertford, and found my way there in October 1947.

CHAPTER THREE

Happy Times at Oxford

I do not know why I was so confident I would get in to Oxford that year. Men who had fought in the War were still coming home and were entitled to priority, and my sister Zoe had had a real struggle the previous year before, eventually getting a place to read medicine at Queen's University, Belfast. But I felt in my bones that everything would turn out all right, and so it did. So at the beginning of October 1947 I caught a train to Oxford and on arriving at Hertford was directed to a gloomy set of rooms in the shadow of the bridge across New College Lane. There I met my roommate, Peter Nicholls, who for a year had, I fear, a lot to put up with from me.

Before long there was a knock on the door and I was recruited to play squash next day; another knock and I was joining OUCA (the Oxford University Conservative Association) and so it went on. It was the beginning of a time in my life when every day seemed to bring new excitements.

Over the years I learned to love north-east Lancashire but in 1947 it was rather shabby, dismal and damp and certainly not very exciting. By contrast, Oxford seemed bright and clean, warm and friendly and bustling with life and interest.

My studies were not demanding. I had to see my tutor once a week, read him an essay and go to one or two lectures, and that left plenty of time for politics and many other delights.

I am not sure whether I went up to Oxford determined to get involved in politics or whether it was something that happened after I arrived. At school I had been interested in public affairs and my house tutor, realising I was a voracious reader, had set me to keeping up to date his edition of Keesing's Contemporary Archives, an enormous work on world events. But my parents were not over-concerned with politics and, although suitably shocked when the Clitheroe constituency went Labour in 1945, they rather disapproved of the Conservative candidate, mainly because he had absent-mindedly shaken hands with them twice in one afternoon.

I was very shy and terrified at the idea of speaking in public but I persuaded myself that I had to conquer conquer my fears. I went, therefore, to speaking classes and spoke in the Union. Too well as it turned out because my speech based on *The Road to Serfdom* by the relatively unknown Professor Hayek attracted the attention of the President, Sir Edward Boyle Bt, who promptly invited me to be one of the main speakers the following week. The result was a disaster. I cannot now remember the subject of the debate in which I was to take part, but when I told a friend that I had no idea what to say he suggested that we should go punting on the Cherwell and something would come to me. Nothing did and after a dismal performance I then had to endure the shame of dining with the other debaters whose eyes I felt never left me. Most of all, I was deeply ashamed that I had let myself down and, in later years, I often suffered greatly from a realisation that again I had done just that. It was a while before I summoned the courage to have another try in the Union, and when I did, and in similar situations in later life, I made sure that I knew as much about the subject to be discussed as anyone I was likely to encounter.

In those days the Union was a thriving institution and many of those taking part were later to make their mark in public life – Edward Boyle, Anthony Wedgwood Benn, Robin Day, Ludovic Kennedy and many more.

I cannot think why I persevered with public speaking when it made me so miserable, but persevere I did, and eventually I was twice rewarded. I got a career in politics and the law, and I got a wife. In those days OUCA used to send teams of speakers to help Conservative candidates in various parts of the country, and at Christmas 1947 I joined a team bound for Nelson & Colne because the constituency was close to my home. I lived at home but caught the first bus in the morning and joined the others in Nelson. During the day we held street corner meetings and harangued people at works' gates. For the most part we were treated with good humour and nothing was thrown at us. At 5.30 p.m. we had high tea at the Lord Nelson Hotel and then repaired to one of the many conservative clubs to bore the beer drinkers and snooker players. The club secretary would call for silence and then ask the assembled company to give a hearing to some young gentlemen who had come all the way from Oxford to speak to them. Ninety-nine percent of the congregation was there for the beer and in no mood to be interrupted by the likes of us, and they were no more appreciative of our efforts than the weavers. But at the Brierfield Club I met the Conservative candidate Alan Green and his wife, and years later I met, first, their eldest daughter Hilary and then their second daughter Gill who, after a decent interval, I proceeded to marry. I then myself became the candidate for Nelson & Colne and by 1968 was the Member of Parliament. But more of that later.

Back to Oxford, and in January 1948 I was persuaded to take up rowing. Sitting in a boat on the Thames in the freezing cold was not a pleasurable experience but it was good to get some exercise, and I made some great friends outside politics. In the summer term I rowed in Eights Week and at Marlow Regatta and had a fine time.

In the summer of 1948 I went off to France with Nicholas Coleridge. We went by train to Paris and our party (it was a tour organised by the National Union of Students) went to a university refectory to get an evening meal. We were given a coupon which we exchanged for soup and black bread and then took the metro to the Gare de Lyon. The journey south overnight was very uncomfortable. The lucky ones were in very old first-class carriages sitting six instead of three a side; the less lucky lay down in the corridor. After a sleepless night we arrived in Marseilles, after which the train travelled along the coast to our destination in heat the like of which I had never before experienced. St-Aygulf was then a small village waiting to be rebuilt after suffering much damage when the Americans landed in the south of France in the summer of 1944. We slept in one of the buildings which had been shelled and were given a hunk of black bread for breakfast in a barn without a roof. A nice girl said that what we needed was 'onny', which when translated was 'honey', and we bought a communal pot which made the bread nearly edible.

In my second year at Oxford I had a room to myself and decided to throw a party. It was a big mistake. When everyone had settled down to drink and have food, I announced that I had to slip round to Oriel to see my friend John Morrison who was also having a party. I returned an hour or two later to find my party was still going strong but the room looked somewhat bare. It took me a moment or two to realise that several large pieces of furniture had been thrown through the window into Catte Street. The next day I was summoned before the Dean, John Armstrong. He had a very soft voice but his dulcet tones did not disguise the message. I would be sent down if I erred again.

At about this time Peter Emery, who had been on the Nelson & Colne tour, asked me if I would like to stand for the OUCA committee. He said that if I was interested he would look after my campaign. Canvassing was strictly forbidden so I did not see what campaigning needed to be done; but I said, rather weakly, that I was prepared to leave matters in his hands. I was mortified when the result was announced: Brown 14, Collins 15, Jones 23, Snooks 4, Taylor 3, Waddington 148. Nowadays it would be called 'overkill'.

Years later Peter entertained me most generously both in London and in his constituency, Honiton, where I went to speak for him. But I was a bit disappointed with his hospitality in Oxford. He invited me out to lunch and took me to the BR (British Restaurant) in Gloucester Green. The BR, which was located in a Nissen hut, provided meagre meals for less than a shilling, helping people to eke out their rations.

In those days Gloucester Green was a rather seedy part of Oxford and home to the bus station. There was a pub there with a bad reputation which was frequently raided by the proctors. John Addleshaw, head of the Manchester chambers which I was later to join, told me that when he was an undergraduate he was in the pub when one of these raids took place; and the landlord's wife invited him to hide under her skirts. He accepted the invitation but the experience persuaded him never to marry.

I decided fairly early on in my time at Oxford that I was going to become a barrister, mainly because a career at the Bar could, I thought, be more easily reconciled with being an MP than life as a solicitor. So when my father rang me to say he was giving up his solicitor's practice in Burnley to become county court registrar and wanted to know whether on the sale of his practice he should make provision for me to become a partner in the firm, I told him he had no need do so.

My father treated his former partners generously and they in their turn were very helpful to me. By a gentleman's agreement they undertook to provide me and my family with free legal services and they honoured that promise punctiliously, as have their successors in the practice. I am immensely grateful to them.

At about this time I joined the Pullen Society, named after Josiah Pullen, a particularly undistinguished former principal of Hertford whose only claim to fame was that the Pullen Tree on the outskirts of Oxford had been named after him. The society was open to members who did not blow their own trumpets.

It was the done thing to keep a little drink in one's room for the entertainment of callers and this was invariably South African sherry which one could buy from the college buttery for five shillings a bottle. The food in college was poor but when in training the rowing eight received sumptuous fare. After one boat club dinner we tried to hit golf balls from the front quad at Hertford over the library in to All Souls. We weren't entirely successful.

A term was wasted because I fell in love. All I could do was sit on my window-sill looking down onto Catte Street hoping for Marigold to go by. My friends called her Poppy. It was rather an involved joke connected with her very beautiful dark complexion. My mother only made one visit to Oxford when I was there, and when I was escorting her across the high street I spotted Marigold about 150 yards away. I could not resist pointing her out to my mother and was very offended when she sniffed and said: 'It looks to me as if she could do with a good wash.'

Eventually I became President of OUCA and at the end of my Presidential term was responsible for the proper conduct of the election of my successor, and of the other officers and committee. The result of the presidential election was surprising. While all the well-known candidates had obtained only a modest number of votes, a Mr Christopher Vere Tombs of Oriel College got 220. That would not have mattered greatly had it not transpired that Mr Tombs, proposed by Cranley Onslow and seconded by John Morrison, was the statue in the front quad at Oriel. Cranley later became chairman of the 1922 Committee. John, the second Viscount Dunrossil, was one of my predecessors as Governor of Bermuda.

Looking back on my time in Oxford I can remember sitting up into the middle of the night debating the ills of the world and the shortcomings of the Labour government, which seemed to be making a mess of everything it touched. Countries which had suffered defeat and occupation were already well on the way to economic recovery while we remained enmeshed in a web of controls designed to make life as uncomfortable as it had been in the middle of the War. Those who dared attack the accepted wisdom of the day – that the man in Whitehall knew best – were derided, insulted and referred to as vermin. The patronising arrogance of some of the Labour politicians was beyond belief. When the Minister of Food, Dr Edith Summerskill, was asked in the House of Commons why there was no Stilton in the shops she replied: 'The function of the Ministry of Food is not to pander to an acquired taste but to ensure that the people who have never had time to acquire these tastes are suitably fed.' No wonder we laughed when, after she had challenged an undergraduate called Prentice to tell the difference between a piece of margarine and a pat of butter, a special tasting was arranged and Prentice emerged triumphant. No wonder many of that generation grew up with an abiding hatred of socialism, with all its bossy advocates, and took a great delight in cutting down to size people like Hugh Dalton who, on a visit to Oxford, was reminded by an impious undergraduate that at Eton he had been known as 'Crab' Dalton because he always had to cling to the nearest wall to avoid being kicked in the backside.

About this time Lord Woolton made a broadcast in which he said he wanted the day to return when a chap could buy his girl a box of sweets. When a Labour politician criticised the speech in a Union debate, saying that *his* father had had eight children and their family had never been able to afford a box of sweets, he was told by another irreverent student that no doubt his father could have afforded sweets if he had not kept his brains in his balls and he could not blame Woolton for that.

I do not know which of the visiting Conservative politicians-made the greatest impression on me. I know who made me laugh the most – Lady Astor. In one speech she set out to illustrate the point that all of us are born different with different intelligences; and that equality was, therefore, unachievable. 'I have two sons,' she said. 'Put one down in darkest Africa and he will come out leading the natives. Put the other down in Piccadilly Circus and he can't find his way home – and I only live round the corner.'

Bob Boothby was one of our favourites. His support for a united Europe which would never again tear itself apart in war gave us an idealistic theme when we were bored of just thumping Labour for its arrogant incompetence. We looked forward to France, Germany, the Benelux countries and Italy forming a close federation with their industries so intertwined they could not make war against each other – however much they wanted to do so. Britain would help them with their endeavours and would be the bridge between Europe, the Commonwealth and America. We never thought for one moment that Britain should become a member of a united Europe at the cost of abandoning her Commonwealth and world-wide commitments. Anyone who had suggested anything of the sort would have been thought to have taken leave of his senses.

I had an impressive list of speakers for my term as president. The great disappointment was Viscount Simon who afterwards complained bitterly that he had been questioned by members of the audience about his past. In fact, the audience had been very restrained and I could not understand how someone in his position could resent being questioned about the years of appeasement and his actions at that time.

CHAPTER FOUR

Life in the Army

In the summer of 1950 I went on holiday to Corsica and Italy and arrived home to find that my Bar final course at Gibson & Weldons had already started. I set off for London and found lodgings in Notting Hill. Then I fell on my feet. John Morrison's father, Shakes Morrison, who became Speaker of the House of Commons before being elevated to the peerage as Viscount Dunrossil, offered me the use of his flat in the Inner Temple. My fellow lodgers in Notting Hill could hardly believe their eyes when I showed them my new 'digs'.

Rationing was, however, still very severe and one person living alone had to use a great deal of ingenuity to avoid going hungry. The weekly meat ration from a butcher in Fetter Lane provided one good meal. I used to enjoy fried onions – just fried onions – for one or two other meals.

I took the Bar finals examination in December 1950 and it could not have been very testing because I passed with little difficulty. But when, wanting to get my national service over as quickly as possible, I tried to get called up for the army, I found no one in any great hurry to have me. Eventually, after a frustrating wait, I was ordered to attend an interview at Preston in the course of which I was asked which part of the army I wanted to join. I found it very difficult to answer given my rudimentary grasp of matters military, but I did not fancy walking, so murmured something about the Armoured Corps. 'The Royal Armoured Corps, please' said the officer rather testily and a few weeks later I received a rail warrant and orders to report to the 67th Training Regiment, RAC, Hadrian's Camp, Carlisle.

In time I came to enjoy the army but the first few weeks brought no merriment. All day long we were marched up and down the barracks square and bawled at by terrifying sergeants. I longed for the occasional smoke break spent propped up against the nearest building. One day we were taken to the gym where the instructor paired us off according to size and told us to get boxing. I took a swing at my opponent, who promptly turned his back on me and trotted off round the edge of the ring. For the next two minutes I was hot in pursuit, flailing at his fleeing figure. Eventually we were deemed trained, after which those of who were considered potential officers were sent to a hut of our own to await a summons to WOSB (War Office Selection Board) at Barton Stacey.

While queuing up to get my paybook on my first day in the army I had got into conversation with a fellow recruit called Geoffrey Wheeler who asked me what regiment I was going to join. He, it appeared, had already applied for the XII Royal Lancers and I, having no knowledge of that, or for that matter any other regiment, thought I might as well apply for the 12th as well. The upshot was that a few weeks later the two of us were in a 15 cwt truck heading for Barnard Castle where the regiment was stationed. I thought we were going for an interview but instead we were invited to lunch in the officers' mess during which we were asked a few questions and our table manners observed. We were then told that if commissioned we would be welcome as members of the regiment.

I then continued my life of ease in the potential officers' hut. No one took any notice of us and we kept ourselves to ourselves lest anyone should come along and give us anything strenuous to do. One Sunday I decided to go to the pictures in Carlisle –

Mammy starring Al Jolson. Some hours later I walked back to the camp and when passing the Orderly Room was put under close arrest. I, along with five other potential officers had, unbeknown to ourselves, been detailed for guard duty. The next day we appeared before the squadron leader and were given seven days CB.

There then followed one of the more unpleasant weeks in my life. CB, I discovered, involved a lot more than being 'confined to barracks'. It involved parading in full kit every hour or two with the threat of further days CB for any lapses such as dirty webbing, imperfectly shined boots or the like. Terrified that I would spend the rest of my days on 'jankers' I worked unceasingly on my outfit and eventually, to my intense embarrassment, was paraded before everyone else serving punishment as a model 'jankers' man.

Our first parade was at 5 a.m. after which we had to carry out various fatigues. One morning I was given the best job of all, cleaning the Adjutant's office; and while doing so I took advantage of one of the perks of the job, access to the Adjutant's in-tray. There I read a memorandum commenting on the fact that some potential officers had been awarded CB and that never again should young soldiers who had undergone punishment be allowed to go forward to WOSB.

When still waiting for WOSB, I went to the same squadron leader who had awarded me CB and asked for compassionate leave to go to London to be called to the Bar. In retrospect I can see it was pretty cheeky and so thought the squadron leader. I do not think he believed a word I was saying. But eventually he said I could go on the understanding that if I did not return with the clearest possible evidence that I had indeed been called to the Bar, the most appalling consequences would follow.

A few days later I took the train to London and I went to see the under-treasurer of Gray's Inn, Mr O. Terry, who looked at me as if I had crawled out from under a stone and said that he had never heard a more ridiculous proposition than that I should be called to the Bar the following night. For a start I had to be sponsored by two Masters of the Bench and there was not a chance of my getting two benchers to do so in the few hours remaining before the ceremony was to take place.

I had visions of months, if not years, in the guardroom at Carlisle, polishing my boots and webbing until I was old and bald, and, in despair, I rang my father. He said that he did not know what to advise, but Mr Justice Ormerod might be able to help. Ben Ormerod was an old boy of Blackburn Grammar School and had been a county court judge in the Blackburn and Burnley area before promotion to the High Court. He was the local boy made good and my last hope. I looked up Ormerod in the telephone book and set out in my battle dress and beret to see the great man. On the doorstep I explained who I was and what I wanted, and the judge said that he could not sponsor me because he was not a bencher of Gray's Inn, but his friend, Hubert Wallington, was a Gray's Inn man and he would give him a ring. Mr Justice Wallington invited me to call round at his home and within the hour I had one of the signatures I needed and an introduction to Master Salt who, before the night was out, had provided me with the other one. My visit must have greatly impressed Mr Justice Wallington because two years later, when I started practising in Manchester and he was one of the High Court judges who regularly came there on Assize, he kept inviting me to lunch at the judges' lodgings. This was a rare mark of favour which greatly impressed other beginners at the Bar and it later turned out that the old boy had, right at the outset, misheard my name and had been proceeding on the assumption that I was the eldest son of his dear sister Emily.

The next morning I returned to Gray's Inn in triumph, but my troubles were not over. Mr O. Terry tried to erect various new obstacles to my being called, such as the absence of a dinner jacket, but nothing was going to stop me now. I had got my signatures and called I was going to be; and called I was. Then, as now, students and barristers sat down for dinner in messes of four and at the appropriate time each member of the mess had to toast the three other members by name. For years I kept the piece of paper on which I had written the names of the members of my mess. Each name except mine was completely unpronounceable. My three companions all came from West Africa where I suppose they returned in due course to be Prime Minister or shot for treason – or both.

In those days the call ceremony was not very impressive. The hall and chapel at Gray's Inn had both been destroyed in the Blitz and I had eaten my dinners to qualify for call in a bare lecture room with trestle tables. In that same room I was now called as an 'Utter Barrister'. The next morning I wrung out of Terry a certificate evidencing what had happened and back in Carlisle presented it to a very surprised squadron leader.

Shortly after this episode I attended WOSB. I was required to climb a few ropes, negotiate an obstacle course and be interviewed about my hobbies and ambitions. I was then told that I had passed and would be going to Mons Officer Cadet School at Aldershot with a view to being commissioned in the cavalry.

At Mons, RSM Brittain was responsible for licking us in to shape. He not only had the loudest voice in the British Army, he also had an eagle eye. Once, when we were rehearsing for the passing out parade of the squad immediately senior to ours, he spotted something seriously amiss in the mass of soldiery before him. 'You,' he bellowed, 'third man from the left in the second rank – your rifle's cocked – pull the trigger.' The man in question was a scruffy individual called Simon Plunkett. He was a Walter Mitty type character who had spread the rumour that he had flown in the RAF and that he was the brother of Shaun Plunkett, a much admired model.

Simon pondered for a moment but another bellow from Brittain convinced him there was no way out. He pulled the trigger. There was a loud bang. The Sergeant closest to Plunkett was temporarily deafened and at first could not hear Brittain bawling that Plunkett be put under close arrest, but eventually a posse of other NCOs descended on him and he was marched away to the Guard Room.

This incident, and another round about that time, convinced me that whatever I was I was not a member of the upper classes. For some weeks the weather had been cold and we were being drilled each morning in full battle dress. Then quite suddenly the weather improved and on the barrack square the Drill Sergeant's first command was 'shirt sleeve order'. We set about taking off our battle dress tops and rolling up our shirt sleeves and the operation proceeded calmly until the drill sergeant's eyes lighted on Viscount Lumley. 'Dirty elbows, Mr Lumley, Sir.' Viscount Lumley later became the Earl of Scarborough and performed with great dignity numerous high offices, but never with bare arms.

Eventually the time drew near when, if all went well, I would pass out from Mons and become a commissioned officer, but I had no great confidence in my abilities and whenever anyone was RTU'd (returned to unit) I thought 'there but for the grace of God go I'. It was in this frame of mind that I conveyed to my parents an invitation to attend the passing out parade but accompanied it with a warning that my own chances of passing out were not great. It was, therefore, with some embarrassment that I told them on their arrival at Aldershot that, not only was I to pass out, I was to be awarded the Stick as best cadet.

The night before the parade RSM Brittain drilled me personally, teaching me how I was to walk up the steps in slow time and take the Stick from the Field Marshal. He was not enthusiastic about my performance, at one point crying out in desperation 'your bottom waggles, sir.' But the next day all went reasonably well until after the parade was over when I was told that I had to introduce my parents to the Field Marshal.

There was one immediate problem. I was not sure how I should handle my rifle in this more informal setting; in particular I had not the faintest idea whether I should or should not present arms. So with great presence of mind I hid my rifle under a bush growing conveniently close to the top of the steps where the Field Marshal was still standing. I then joined my parents and took them up to the Field Marshal. He was very friendly and said to my father: 'I do hope your son will consider making the army his career.' 'Not on your life,' said my father, 'he has cost me a fortune studying for the Bar and to the Bar he is going.'

The next stop was Bovington in Dorset, the headquarters of the Royal Armoured Corps, and after that came the excitement of getting measured for my uniform in London. The 'warm weather' mess dress was a very fetching white jacket and shirt with scarlet cummerbund, overalls with a double yellow stripe down the side and black boots with spurs. There was also a flat hat and a side hat of scarlet with gold piping.

Embarkation leave ended with my parents taking me by taxi to Liverpool where the following day I was to board the *Empress of Australia*, bound for Singapore. But then came a most terrible humiliation. The ship cast off, slewed across the dock and hit the other side, seriously damaging a propeller. Two thousand soldiers who had just embarked had then to disembark and be dispatched to various camps in the north-west while the damage was repaired. I went to Saighton Camp near Chester. A fortnight of route marches followed, by which time it was plain that it was still going to be weeks before the propeller was ready. So we were sent home with our tails between our legs.

I got my trunk as far as Manchester, crossed from London Road to Victoria Station with it, put it in the luggage van on the train to Burnley and settled down in the compartment next door. I arrived at Burnley to find the trunk had gone. Apparently someone had concluded that Burnley via Bury and Ramsbottom was not the quickest route to Singapore, the destination for which the trunk was labelled. It took a few weeks to sort out that little problem, by which time the ship was ready to sail; so to Liverpool I returned.

I was responsible for a troop deck which was home for 130 men. There were long tables across the floor at which they were to eat and hooks in the ceiling from which they were to hang their hammocks. In the best of conditions it would have taken the men a while to get used to sleeping in hammocks, but a day out from Liverpool we ran into a storm and by the time we got to the Bay of Biscay there was not a man capable of carrying out any duties, and conditions on the troop deck were squalid beyond belief. But at last the ship rounded Cape St Vincent, and soon we were in good order and in a holiday mood.

The ship was to have refuelled at Port Said but at the end of 1951 Britain was coping with the first Suez crisis and it was decided to stop at Algiers instead. I remember how beautiful were the gardens facing the quay and how immaculate and prosperous-looking was the centre of the city. (I returned in 1968 as an MP to find it had changed out of all recognition – dirty, drab and squalid.) Orders went out that no one was to enter the Casbah in the interests of their own safety. Two hours later the place was full of soldiers. I know. I saw it for myself.

The Suez Canal was not a pretty sight, the banks being lined by masturbating Egyptians – a very exhausting form of political protest which I have never seen repeated. An enterprising subaltern dressed up as an Arabian potentate entered the ship's dining room. He was announced gravely as the Ding of Dong, and proceeded to the Captain's table. There the Captain politely gave up his chair to him and stood blushing like a bride while The Ding (otherwise 2nd Lt Piers Dennis) ate his turkey.

Next stop was Aden where we had another day's shore leave. I took a fancy to a dinner service, bought it and arranged for it to be sent to my parents as a present. It was not a good move and led to my father complaining bitterly that he had to pay a large sum as demurrage because of the consignment languishing for some weeks on Liverpool Docks. When I arrived home a year and a half later I found the dinner service unused, at the back of a bedroom cupboard, and a few years after that it was given back to me as a wedding present.

On Christmas Day 1951 we arrived at Colombo and I met my first snake charmer sitting on his haunches outside the Galle Face Hotel. On New Year's Day 1952 we sailed into Singapore harbour through a veil of rain but, before docking, ran in to a bit of trouble. OC Troops had ordered all baggage to be brought up on deck and put on the port side, but this led to the ship leaning over in that direction and being unable to get alongside in an orderly fashion. An exasperated captain then countermanded the order and after half the baggage had been moved to starboard we tied up and went ashore. A few hours later, after being issued with a side-arm, I was on a train bound for Ipoh in Penang.

We were in Malaya to take part in a fight against a communist insurgency which had begun not long after Britain, the colonial power, had arrived back on the Malayan peninsular at the end of the War. A plan had been laid for Malaya to be retaken by ground forces in 1945, but the collapse of Japan after the destruction of Hiroshima and Nagasaki by atom bombs meant that the British did not re-enter Malaya as conquerors but as representatives of a recently defeated colonial power. Many Chinese (the Chinese forming a large minority of the population) had fought the Japanese throughout the War from their jungle hide-outs and soon there was a communist-led movement, the Malayan National Liberation Army (MNLA) determined to seize power from the British by force. By 1950 there were about 40,000 British and Commonwealth troops in the country, and we had come to join them. The British Army had enough on its hands with war in Korea so there was a fair chance of anyone being called up in 1951 seeing some action. I felt extremely lucky: I had already seen parts of the world which I had never in my wildest dreams thought I would be able to visit. No one then thought that world travel would soon be commonplace, and I felt truly privileged to be visiting countries which I thought few others would ever have a chance of seeing.

The time came for the train to leave Singapore and we set off into the darkness with armed guards on the platform at the end of each carriage, peering into the surrounding jungle and longing for a burst of fire as the prelude to a pitched battle and the winning of much glory. But on this occasion, as on so many others, the opportunity for glory never came: and at two in the morning we arrived at Ipoh. Transport was there to take us to the 12th Royal Lancers RHQ. There I was taken to a room in a straw-roofed hut and as I arrived a young subaltern sat up in one of the two beds and said: 'I am David Duckworth and you're the fellow who stuck a compass in my sister's bottom at Sunnybank School, Burnley!' I had forgotten the incident but at the time it had led to fearsome punishment, and it ought to have stuck in my mind as the point of the compass had stuck in Rachel's posterior. She was a nice girl and at the time I felt she should have taken my attentions as a compliment.

I did not stay in Ipoh long – but long enough to learn something of the eccentricities of the Commanding Officer, Lt Col Horsburgh-Porter. On mess nights, subalterns were required to perform feats of bravery like jumping off the first floor terrace and grasping the trunk of a nearby tree to slow their descent to the ground. In calmer moments we were set the almost impossible task of dislodging lizards from the ceiling of the mess with the end of a long brush and catching them in free fall. The regiment had arrived in Singapore in August 1951 and consisted of twenty-five officers and 470 other ranks, 35 per cent of whom were National Servicemen conscripted for two years. It was deployed in three principal locations – Ipoh, Taiping and Raub, with a detached troop at Kuantan and another up in the Cameron Highlands.

After a week or two I set off to join 'B' Squadron at Raub and there served happily under the squadron leader, John Clark Kennedy. The officers were housed in the government Rest House, and a fellow subaltern was John Lang, later Dean of Lichfield. Then I went to Kuantan for a few weeks. It was off Kuantan that the *Prince of Wales* and the *Repulse* had been sunk on 10 December 1941 and it was on the padang at Kuantan that in February 1952 we paraded for the funeral of King George VI. The Sultan's palace was at Pekan and we were summoned there one night to hear his complaint that his polo ponies had been blown up by a landmine on the road to Ipoh.

Back in Raub one of my jobs was taking consignments of gold from the local mine to Kuala Lumpur. The officer in command travelled in a Daimler armoured car with a driver and gunner and we were accompanied by an armoured personnel carrier with a driver and about half a dozen men. Once, on arriving in KL, we drove into the car park adjoining the NAAFI and, with a breezy 'carry on sergeant', I nipped across the road to the railway station to have a drink. When I returned I found the whole troop under arrest. They had abandoned the vehicles without a guard and had themselves gone for a drink. I felt entirely responsible and on returning to HQ made this absolutely plain to the commanding officer. Not for the first time, I found that the army mind did not work quite as mine. I was told in no uncertain terms that the day for my martyrdom had not arrived and that in the colonel's view

I was in no way to blame for what had occurred. If a sergeant was told to carry on, that meant that or, rather, it meant the opposite of that. He had not to carry on. He had to stop carrying on and do his duty even if that meant denying himself a drink, etc., etc.

'B' Squadron then returned to Ipoh and the routine was dawn patrols along the roads surrounding the town. A few days later Julian Brougham was orderly officer and said he didn't feel well. I said I'd relieve him if he didn't improve and an hour or two later when I went to see him he was so obviously ill I called the doctor. The next day he died of polio. A short time later I was on guard duty and had to wake a fellow officer to tell him that his wife had also died from the same cause.

In October 1951 Sir Henry, the High Commissioner, had been murdered by communist bandits, and Sir Gerald Templar had been sent out to replace him. Already, vigorous policies launched before his arrival were beginning to bear fruit. Isolated villages were being shut down and the inhabitants moved lock, stock and barrel to newly built villages surrounded with barbed wire and watch towers. In this way the terrorists were prevented from preying on the villagers and demanding food and other supplies from them. But descending on a village at dawn and herding terrified men and sobbing women and children into lorries with only what they could carry was not a pleasant task.

The new High Commissioner soon began to make his mark. He set about seeing that the police were reorganised and retrained, took steps to see that intelligence was properly coordinated and that the information services were smartened up so that people knew what was going on and why. Gerald Templar was very popular with all who had dealings with him. He was particularly nice to junior officers, full of enquiries about their families, careers and ambitions. On one occasion I was responsible for providing an escort for him and, over a meal in a village hall, engaged him in conversation.

He was limping badly and I asked him at what stage in the War he had been wounded. 'Wounded?' he said. 'I was getting a grand piano out of the mess at Naples ready for our move up to Rome when someone dropped it on my foot.'

One of my troopers was of hideous aspect with broken and blackened teeth. And I discovered why. We stopped at a roadside café for a drink and rather than wait for the man who brought the beer to produce a bottle opener, he struck the bottle forcibly against his bottom teeth and the beer foamed forth.

My next posting was to the Cameron Highlands to command an enlarged troop responsible for escorting food lorries up and down the hill. My troop sergeant, Sergeant Greetham, had won a Military Medal in North Africa during the War, and no one could have had finer support. The village or township of the Cameron Highlands was spread out around a golf course and two rather fine hotels, and at 5,000 feet the temperature was superb. From one end of the village a road wound its way down to the plain. At the other end there was a police post at a gap in the wire surrounding most of the settlement and the dirt road then meandered away across the plateau for thirty miles or so past various tea plantations managed by intrepid Europeans in almost permanent fear of their lives. Some had gone native and had Malay or Chinese girlfriends or wives. Most seemed to get their sustenance from gin or, in one case, cherry brandy.

One particularly demoralised planter invited us to stay for the night and he laid on a concert for our benefit. Some very beautiful girls danced for us – or rather they looked like very beautiful girls but at the end of the show turned out to be men. We were enjoying the entertainment when a volley of shots rang out and the place was plunged into darkness. The manager ordered one of the Malays to shin up a pole to see what was wrong with the lights, which were strung along the top of the wire surrounding the buildings. When he demurred the manager drew his pistol and the Malay went up the pole at great speed. I led a few soldiers out of the gate in the wire and prowled around for a while in the pitch dark, but not surprisingly did not come across a single bandit.

The journeys up and down the hill were very monotonous but we got a little innocent enjoyment at the half way mark where there was a Sakai camp in which both men and women were almost entirely naked. Down at the bottom was Kuala Kubu Bharu (or KKB), and there we sweated in steamy heat for a few hours before setting off back up the hill in late afternoon. As we climbed it got colder and colder and it usually began to rain, so we were glad of a hot bath by the time we got home.

Back again in Ipoh we were sent off every now and then to lay ambushes in the jungle in the hope of bagging a communist courier carrying dispatches from one bandit unit to another. We were never successful. With the jungle so thick and visibility so slight I thought that I was far more likely to hit a running terrorist with a blast from a shotgun than with a bullet from a rifle so I used to take out my twelve-bore. One night in the pitch dark I set an ambush, taking each man to the spot where I wanted him to lie, and at first light found myself looking down the muzzle of a bren gun. Sometimes, Borneo head hunters acted as guides for us and, through an interpreter, I asked one why we were so unsuccessful in our efforts to bag terrorists. The man answered that the terrorists could smell us a mile away, and indeed we did smell, having covered ourselves with all sorts of unguents designed to protect us from mosquitoes, leeches and other beastly things which inhabit the jungle.

I was determined to have at least one success over the terrorists and devised a brilliant plan. A track ran off into the jungle a few miles from Ipoh and I decided that if I could get my armoured car and APC (armoured personnel carrier) down the track for a few miles we could strike out from a secure base and perhaps score a notable victory.

Disaster soon followed. The APC slithered off the track and over-turned, the wireless would not work, nightfall was upon us and there was nothing for it but to sit tight until dawn. And then in the middle of the night some shots rang out. The only trouble was that it was impossible to see two feet in front of one's nose and extremely diffi-cult to know from which direction the shots had come. So we did precisely nothing. The next morning a party walked all the way to the main road and had to ring regimental HQ from a police station. We were then rescued in the most ignominious fashion – a number of surly soldiers having had to walk five miles with a very heavy winch in order to haul up the APC from where it had landed.

A few days later I went on another expedition and got completely lost. I reasoned that if we hit the railway line we had only to walk up it or down and we were bound to reach civilisation – so I asked my sergeant which direction was the railway line. Without any hesita-tion he pointed to the left. I asked the Corporal and he with equal confidence pointed to the right. I decided to go straight ahead and soon the line came in to view.

All good things come to an end. I sold my typewriter to pay my last mess bill and caught the train for Singapore. I made my way to the troop ship MV *Georgic* and offered my pistol to those on duty at an army post on the dock. They flatly refused to take it. I threatened to throw it in the dock and they said that if I did I would be court-martialled. I said I would take it on board ship with me and hand it in at Liverpool. I was told that that was prohibited. In desperation I hailed a taxi and asked the driver to take me to Changi, then British HQ on the island. Today a motorway runs from Changi Airport to the city centre. Then there was only a narrow country road and the journey seemed endless. But eventually I arrived at the Guard Room, handed in the pistol, got a signature for it and sped back to Singapore just in time to catch the ship.

Three weeks later we arrived in Liverpool. In the eighties I went as a minister to see a youth project at the mouth of the Mersey and there was not a ship to be seen, but in 1952 we were in a mass of shipping as we waited for the tide to turn. Eventually we entered the river and then began to come alongside, and on the quay I could see my parents and my sister Zoe. The next morning I disembarked and, after a quick word with the family, boarded a train bound for the Royal Armoured Corps headquarters, Bovington. I had 180 men under my charge, all due to leave the army, most with homes in the north of England and all fed up at not being allowed to go home at once. I sensed the danger and resolved to keep a very careful check on numbers. On leaving Crewe my 180 had shrunk to ninety-eight, Stafford left me with seventy. Before we arrived at Euston I gave my depleted band a strong lecture on the dire consequences which would follow if they did not board the train at Waterloo in three hours time, but at Waterloo my band of followers had dwindled to forty-three and when we got to Wool, the station for Bovington, there were only seventeen left.

CHAPTER FIVE

Starting at the Bar

My national service now at an end, it was time to join the barristers' chambers in Manchester where I was to be a pupil of James Warden Stansfield. Stansfield was the shyest man I have ever met. A table and chair were provided for me in his room and he threw a few sets of papers at me and asked me to read them. No further words were spoken till 1 p.m. when he asked me to accompany him to his club for lunch. He never said a word when we were walking there or during the course of lunch. After lunch we watched some people playing snooker as we drank coffee, again in silence. The afternoon was also spent in silence: and the following day I was told by the chambers' clerk, Randall, that Mr Stansfield had decided that I might be happier in a room with another pupil. From that time onwards I saw little of Stansfield and I cannot remember doing any work for him or receiving any advice from him. Luckily, however, the head of chambers was a very different type of man. John Addleshaw was enormously popular, not surprisingly as he was prepared to go to endless trouble to help the young people in chambers, advising them on their court cases, helping them to draft pleadings and write opinions. I suppose he could not have been very busy himself or he would not have had the time to help as he did. Work was not plentiful at the Bar in Manchester at the beginning of the fifties before legal aid became a growth industry; and the 300 guineas I earned in my first year, although not a record, was thought pretty good going.

The reason for my doing quite well was that I was the only barrister who lived in north-east Lancashire. Most Northern Circuiteers with chambers in Manchester lived in Cheshire. A few were scattered around Preston and Blackpool but there was no one near Burnley or Blackburn. My father's old firm lived up to its reputation for caution. One day the senior partner rang and said he had an important brief for chambers. My spirits soared but only for a moment; because he quickly added that it was a weighty matter which he was proposing to give to Stansfield. But plenty of other local solicitors gave me massive support and I scooped the pool at Burnley and Blackburn Quarter Sessions.

The Prosecuting Solicitor at Blackburn Quarter Sessions was a relative by marriage with a daughter called Ann. One day he rang up and said that I could have an extra brief provided I took his daughter to the Hunt Ball. I duly did so.

John Addleshaw had recently acquired a new pupil called Colin Muscroft. He came from Huddersfield but for some mysterious reason had sought a pupillage on our side of the Pennines. We thought he was quite a guy because his father was the manager of the Huddersfield Transport Undertaking and had his name on the side of every Huddersfield bus. Muscroft was given a voluminous set of papers by a solicitor friend and was asked to advise in a dispute arising out of a contract for the sale of a large quantity of cloth. Muscroft nursed and cosseted these papers like a mother might a newborn child. Each morning he undid the red tape, glanced at one of the 100 or so exhibits, sighed deeply and retied the tape. At eleven o'clock when coffee was served for those not lucky enough to be in court he walked round chambers with his baby seeking advice on the multifarious problems thrown up by the case; and advice, most of it contradictory, was always forthcoming

– advice in enormous quantities given from the depths of our ignorance. In the afternoon, after many lunchtime libations, Muscroft
would set to work on the papers but soon felt obliged to have a
nap after which it was time to catch the train back to Huddersfield.
In this leisurely fashion many weeks passed, but then Randall the
clerk began to relay disturbing news. The solicitors were asking
when the opinion would be ready.

On the scene at this stage came the great Neville Laski – a
very senior member of the bar, a Silk and the recorder of Burnley.
Muscroft was due to spend that night in Manchester attending
Bar Mess, and over the second decanter of port he told Laski that
he was rather over-burdened at that particular time by a complex
set of papers involving a cotton contract. Laski said that he had
spent much of his life at the Bar doing commercial cases and he
would call round at chambers at nine the following morning to
give his help. At nine prompt he arrived, picked up the papers,
undid the red ribbon, affected to peruse the instructions to counsel
and cried: 'Fetch a stenographer.' A shorthand typist appeared and
Laski proceeded to dictate a long opinion. The only trouble was
that when it was typed up and passed around chambers the unani-
mous view was that it was utter rubbish from start to finish. Poor
Muscroft's efforts had been in vain, the port had been drunk for
nothing and the hangover contracted to no benefit. He dolefully
replaced the ribbon round the papers, put them at the back of his
desk and went off for a drink.

Appearing before Laski at Burnley Quarter Sessions was a
sobering experience. Mr Foulds, the prosecuting solicitor, sat at the
table below Laski alongside the clerk and as each old lag appeared
in the dock Laski asked Foulds to read from a scrap book the
report in the *Burnley Express* of the man's last appearance, including, of course, the comments made by the recorder in passing
sentence:

In sentencing Smith to five years imprisonment the recorder Mr Neville Laski QC said: 'I am treating you with great leniency today but the time is drawing near when the public will have to be protected from your depredations, and if you ever darken these doors again you cannot expect the sort of extreme leniency you are receiving today. Condign punishment will be your lot.'

Nursing my first brief at Burnley Sessions I heard this exchange: 'John Smith you heard what I said when you last stood in that dock. You are a menace to society and you'll go to preventive detention for eight years.' 'But, Mr Laski, I've got cancer and I'll never live that long.' Laski: 'Well, do your best. Do your best.'

Everybody in our chambers lived in terror of being dispatched to the Court of Appeal, the Divisional Court or the Court of Criminal Appeal at a moment's notice having been handed what was known as a return from another set of chambers. This fate had actually befallen Kenneth Taylor in our chambers. He had been told at five in the evening that the following morning he was to appear in the Divisional Court against Henry Burton who was acknowledged to be the best advocate on the Northern Circuit. Ken nearly died of fright but survived the ordeal. Sadly, Henry Burton was killed a short time afterwards in the Harrow rail disaster.

In 1954 I tried my hand at acting, playing the parts of Captain Hardy in *Journey's End* and Algernon in *The Importance of Being Earnest*. The stage, the Bar and the political platform had all become part of my life and all scared me stiff.

It was in that same year that I joined a group of people bound for Luxembourg and Strasbourg to study the workings of the European Coal and Steel Community and the Council of Europe. One of the party was Mark Carlisle, who became a life-long friend. Another was Commander Courtenay who a few years later became an MP and then resigned after disclosing that the KGB had tried to blackmail him with photographs taken on a visit to Moscow. I am sure the visit to Strasbourg was most instructive but what sticks in my mind is the night when Mark Carlisle and I escaped from the ladies' seminary (the ladies were not in residence) where we were staying. We visited various night clubs, ran out of money at the last one, and had to wash up till four in the morning because we could not pay the bill. The brave Commander Courtenay discovered that we had jumped ship, guessed correctly that we were out on the town, visited sundry night clubs in his efforts to find us and eventually rescued us from the place where we were so usefully employed.

Shortly after this adventure I decided it would be no bad thing if I fought a hopeless seat in the coming general election. It would certainly put me in a stronger position to get a decent seat when later I felt I could afford to get into Parliament. I first had to get on the candidates' list and that meant a visit to Central Office in London for interview by the then vice-chairman of the Party, John Hare – later Lord Blakenham. I was ushered into his presence and he smiled brightly, told me to sit down and asked me whether I had been in the army. I said, 'Yes, the XII Lancers.' 'Oh!' he said, 'that's good enough for me. Thank you for coming. Of course you can be a candidate.' I felt rather cheated, having stuffed my head with information about the economy and three islands off the coast of China called Qemoy, Amoy and Matsu. It was as if I had taken my harp to a party and and no one had asked me to play.

Anyhow, in no time at all I became the prospective parliamentary candidate for the Farnworth Division of Lancashire, the sitting member being a most excellent former Mayor of Rochdale, Ernest Thornton. I became candidate in no time at all because no one else wanted the job. Not for the first time I wondered why on earth I had this compulsion to make my life a misery. I was still cripplingly shy and appallingly nervous when it came to public speaking. But

I was determined to fight an effective campaign and when the date of the general election was announced I took up residence in a pub in Walkden (pronounced Wogden) and began a full programme of daytime canvassing, factory visits and nightly public meetings. I owned a Ford Popular and on the first day I took it to a firm to have a loudspeaker fitted. When I returned I discovered that two holes had been drilled in the car roof and an enormous horn bolted on to it. I drove home at the weekend forgetting about this appendage. The horn hit the top of the garage, the back of the loudspeaker was driven through the Ford Popular's roof and my saloon was instantly transformed into a sort of coupé.

In the campaign Labour focused on the H-bomb, calling for disarmament under international control. Its other themes were rising prices (as a result of cuts in the food subsidies introduced in the War, sugar had gone up from 6d to 8d a pound and bacon from 2s/7d to 3s/6d), unemployment and the need to secure the future of the Lancashire cotton industry by control of imports from India. I talked of Britain's success on the world stage (we had played a key role in the Geneva Conference on Vietnam) and the way we had managed to dismantle war-time controls and get rid of rationing. People were finding it difficult to remember that as recently as 1951 the weekly rations were: butter – 3ozs; cheese – 1¼ ozs; sugar – 10 ozs; tea – 2 ozs; bacon – 3 ozs; sweets – 6½ ozs; and eggs – sometimes one, sometimes two. As for meat, until shortly before the 1951 election, the shopper was allowed to spend only eight pence a week, two pence of that having to go on corned beef.

My campaign began inauspiciously with a newspaper headline: 'HITCH AT TORY NOMINATION'. My inefficient agent had taken me to the town hall to pay my deposit and on his advice I had proffered a cheque for £150, but this the town clerk had quite properly refused to accept. There then came a day when along with other Lancashire candidates I was summoned to the Midland Hotel in Manchester to hear a pep talk from Prime Minister Anthony Eden, but none of us was impressed by him. He was asked about education and said it wasn't his subject, we questioned him about housing and were told to have a word with one of his aides ... and so it went on, with Eden revealing a complete lack of interest in, or knowledge of, anything but foreign affairs.

At the end of the morning of polling day I returned to the central committee room to get a progress report and on the locked door was a notice in the agent's handwriting 'gone for lunch', and the rest of the day I spent fearing that this and other examples of our inefficient organisation was going to lead to a humiliating result. In the event, however, the Labour majority came down with a bump and I came away from the count heartily glad the ordeal was over and reasonably content with the result.

In 1957 it was rumoured that I was to be the candidate at a by-election in Rochdale. Luckily I resisted the temptation to put my name forward – the result was a disaster. John Parkinson took terrible punishment from mill owners furious at the damage being done by foreign competition and he never stood for Parliament again.

At about the same time, however, I did miss a good chance. I was interviewed for Lancaster but lost to Humphry Berkeley, one of the oddest men ever to enter British politics. When an undergraduate he attended the Preparatory Schoolmasters Annual Conference masquerading as the headmaster of an obscure prep school, and in the various discussion sessions offered eccentric advice on how to run an educational establishment.

I used to do a lot of work at Lancaster Assizes. The court sat in the castle and on the steps going down from the dock to the cells below were branding irons and other instruments of torture. One hot summer afternoon, when I was defending one of six defendants in a long trial and had little to do, my eyes strayed to the jury box and I saw to my amazement that thirteen people were sitting in it. I sprang to my feet and began, 'My Lord.' 'Sit down, Mr Waddington,' said Mr Justice Paull. I sank back into my place, but after a moment or two my conscience pricked and I rose again. 'My Lord –' I began again. 'Mr Waddington, you are interrupting an important cross-examination. Will you please remain silent or I will report you to your Inn of Court.' Again I sat down; but it did not take me long to conclude that drastic measures were required. I leapt to my feet and before the judge had time to interrupt, I yelled 'My Lord, there are thirteen people sitting on this jury!' The judge looked at me with a face of fury but then began to count; and sure enough I was right. A little old lady had come to the Castle to watch the proceedings, had tucked herself in behind a file of people making their way across the court, had sat down where everyone else seemed to be sitting and then, when she realised her error, had lain low in the hope that she could escape at the end of the afternoon undetected. Needless to say the judge did not thank me for my public spiritedness.

At about this time I went to London to appear for someone in the Court of Appeal. I went to see him in the cells below the Lord Chief Justice's Court and on my way back took a wrong turning. I opened a door, stepped forward and found myself in the dock looking down on the Court of Criminal Appeal in session. I beat a hasty retreat. Later in the day I was half way through my submission that the sentence passed on the old lag I was representing was unduly severe when the Lord Chief Justice, Lord Parker of Waddington, interrupted me and asked whether I would be satisfied if the sentence was reduced to two years. 'No,' I said. 'Oh!' said the Lord Chief, with by now a note of tetchiness in his voice. 'What had you in mind?'

'Twelve months,' I said boldly. 'Very well,' said the great man, 'twelve months it is.'

There is some bleak moorland above Haslingden in east

Lancashire, and a moorland farmer was having an unhappy time. Someone was stealing his hens. So one night he decided to stay out late and give the intruder a nasty shock. Sometime after midnight a local villain, well known to the farmer and the local police, came prowling up the side of a dry stone wall close to the hen pen. The farmer stood up and shouted 'Come one step further and I'll blow your foot off.' The man stepped forward and the farmer fired his twelve bore and blew the man's foot off.

In due course the farmer appeared at Haslingden Magistrates' Court charged with wounding with intent. My job was to try to avoid his being committed to the Assizes on that serious charge where he might expect to receive a long prison sentence. And I was well pleased with myself when the magistrates accepted my submission that it was not a case of wounding with intent, agreed to deal with the case summarily on my client pleading to common assault and fined the farmer twenty-five pounds.

But that was not the end of the story. Soon the farmer was served with a writ and a claim for damages for assault, and my solicitor made clear that he held me entirely to blame for having advised the farmer to admit to assault. Some months passed and then the case came on for trial at the Assizes in Manchester. The plaintiff gave his evidence and I rose to cross-examine and to try and establish my plea of consent.

'The farmer said "Come a step further and I'll blow your foot off"?'
'Yes.'
'You knew that if you took a step further, he'd blow your foot off?'
'Yes.'
'So you asked for your foot to be blown off?'
'Yes.'
'You wanted your foot blown off?'
'Yes.'

The decision – judgment for the defendant with costs.

At five one evening I was told by my clerk that I had to run for the London train and appear in the High Court the next morning for plaintiffs claiming damages from the suppliers of a machine which was not performing as intended. On the train I feverishly examined the plans and had some difficulty in deciding which was the top of the plan and which the bottom. I did not sleep well that night. I did not sleep at all.

I arrived at the Royal Courts of Justice in good time, got robed and went and stood outside the court. Half an hour later a very flustered and unhappy member of the Bar (with a wig much whiter than mine) hove into view. 'How much will you take?' he said. I then made the biggest mistake of my professional life. Instead of asking for twice the sum suggested by my solicitors I asked for the very amount. 'Done,' said my opponent. 'Costs of course,' said I. 'Of course,' he said. And at half past ten I walked into court and asked Ashworth, J. for judgment by consent for £15,000 and costs. At 10.40 I was in the Strand hailing a taxi but wondering where my wife was likely to be. She had caught the train with me hoping for a few days' shopping and had set out that morning with a gleam in her eye. Harrods, I thought and 'Harrods!' I cried to the taxi driver, 'as fast as you can make it!' I rushed through the doors and there she was, caught red-handed at the very first counter. 'Come on, dear. If we rush we can get the twelve noon train to Manchester'; and we did rush and we did catch it. I was very popular with my clerk, less so with my wife.

But to talk of wives is to jump a long way ahead and to introduce my wife to this narrative I must go back to 1954 or 1955 when I met Hilary Green, daughter of the Alan Green for whom I had campaigned as an undergraduate. I took her out on a few occasions and then one night she asked me to stop the car on the way home because she had something important to tell me. She looked rather embarrassed so to help her I said: 'Don't worry. Let the best man win. Tony's a very nice chap and I am sure if you marry him he'll make you very happy.' She said: 'It's not Tony. It's Norman.'

When all this became known to the family there were many prophecies of doom, but Hilary would not be told and she duly married Norman, I being best man for no other reason than he didn't seem to have many friends. Then I had a stroke of luck. One of the bridesmaids was Hilary's younger sister Gilly. After the reception we went to a show and after the show to a night club – and with one or two ups and downs that was that.

CHAPTER SIX

Marriage and Nelson & Colne

G
illy was just about to go to Brighton College of Art, and half way through her first term there I went to see her. I had a peacock blue Morris Minor, easily recognisable at a considerable distance; and as I drove towards the front of the college still dressed in the black striped trousers I had been wearing in court that morning I saw Gilly run across the road and beckon me into a nearby side street. I assumed that she was trying to find me a convenient parking space and not the horrible truth that she was scared stiff that her bohemian college friends would see me in all my squareness. In spite of this somewhat inauspicious happening we soon became engaged. I have to confess that this was after Gilly had raised the subject of politics. 'I could not possibly marry a politician,' she said. 'One in the family, my father, is quite enough. I hope you are not thinking of standing again.' And I told her what I think I then honestly believed – that I had got politics out of my system.

A month or two later we paid a visit to St Helens which I imagine strengthened Gilly's views about politics. Mark Carlisle, who was to be my best man, was fighting a by-election there and we went to support him. In the morning we did a bit of desultory canvassing and in the afternoon Mark and his recently acquired fiancée, Sandra, and Gilly and I set off in a loudspeaker van to look for a crowd. There was nobody about when we got to the St Helens Rugby Club but we parked and awaited events. We heard a distant whistle and a few people began to appear. Mark addressed a few remarks in their general direction which one or two acknowledged with a genial shake of the fist or obscene gesture. Rather more people began to debouch on to the vast concrete area in the middle of which stood our minuscule van; and then the gates were opened and we were engulfed in a veritable tide of humanity. The girls leapt into the van, just in time for it to be picked up off the ground and shaken like a child's rattle. This was all done in great good humour while somewhere beside, or perhaps in part beneath, the vehicle Mark's voice could be heard battling against the uproar – 'Vote Conservative. Vote Carlisle for a better future.'

Gilly and I were married in Preston Parish Church on 20 December 1958. The venue was chosen for political reasons (Preston South being my father-in-law's seat). The date was chosen for legal reasons. A honeymoon over the Christmas holiday would lose me the least work. We went to Sicily and Rome and when we arrived at the Timeo Hotel in Taormina there was much tongue-clicking from the lady behind the desk who clearly thought I was a dirty old man who had run away with a child bride.

Back in Lancashire in January we found that the little house we had created out of the stables at the top of my parents-in-law's garden was not yet finished and when in February we did move in, it was freezing cold and we regretted having decided that central heating was a luxury we could not afford. What made matters even worse was that most of the curtains had not arrived – including the one designed to separate the living room from the dining room – and the bedroom was so cold that we woke up each morning with the top blanket soaking wet with condensation. But it did not seem to matter all that much; and I counted myself the luckiest man on earth.

Those were the days before rampant inflation hit Britain and we converted the stables and furnished them quite adequately with a gift of £5,000 from my father and a wedding present of £1,000 from Gilly's grandfather. I was earning quite a lot at the Bar and without any children and no school fees to pay we felt very well off. But I kept getting invitations to go before selection committees in the north-west and when, in 1959, Richard Fort was killed in a car accident and there was to be a by-election in Clitheroe, I was sorely tempted to go back into the fray. I realised, however, that it was expecting far too much of Gilly, and the temptation was resisted.

Looking back on our engagement it does seem to have taken place in the most unlikely circumstances for we were often rendered speechless when in each other's company. One night I took Gilly to a cocktail party at the judges' lodgings in Salford and we reached Besses o' th' Barn on the outskirts of Manchester before I summoned up the courage to say anything. In fact, one or two drinks turned it into rather a good evening. At the party the judge who was our host became alarmed at the speed at which the drink was disappearing and, at 7 p.m. when we were just beginning to enjoy ourselves, he hammered on the table and rudely declaimed, 'Gentlemen, all good things must come to an end.' We slunk out of the front door like whipped curs but got back our courage when at the top of the drive we spotted a member of the Manchester Constabulary standing to attention in a mobile sentry box. One shove and the box began to trundle down the drive, not at a great speed but fast enough to make it difficult for the officer to leave with dignity. So he remained upright and travelled to the bottom of the slope, cheered on by the bibulous spectators.

I am lucky to have some of Gilly's school reports from Moira House, Eastbourne – better known as MoHo. They reveal an interesting state of affairs and how well qualified she was for marriage. Autumn Term 1951: 'Seldom punctual for bed. Very untidy.

Thirty-five order marks against her name.' Spring 1952: 'Too often late for bed. Untidy.' Summer 1952: 'Most unpunctual downstairs. Better in bedroom.' Autumn 1952: 'Gillian breaks rules without compunction and goes her own way regardless.' Spring 1954: 'Persistently late for bed through playing. Is vague over time. Late for breakfast nine times.' Autumn 1956: 'Very pleasant upstairs but she does not take enough responsibility.'

If truth be told, Gilly was taking on an awful lot marrying when so young and marrying someone ten years older than herself. I think, looking back, that my insistence that we should marry before she had even completed her course at Brighton was quite unreasonable, but I can only say in my own defence that I was madly in love, that I knew a good thing when I saw it and I was simply not prepared to take the chance of waiting and her finding somebody else. I felt I could make her a good husband and I knew she would be a super wife, loyal and forgiving. For Gilly, marriage was an act of madness. In her journal she writes:

> I had already made up my mind on leaving school and viewing life's cornucopia of opportunities that politics in any form was quite out of the question. It came very nearly bottom of the list just before cleaning out the sewers or managing a mink farm.

I suppose we had our ups and downs like every married couple. Once, I threatened to go home to her mother. I knew I could not go home to mine. But we had some marvellous times and still do.

We had a miniature poodle called Sydney. One day Gilly went down the garden to have lunch with her mother, leaving the house unlocked. She returned home to find a masked burglar coming down the stairs. Sydney shot under the dining room table, teeth a-chattering. Gilly locked herself in the cloak room. After a conversation through the keyhole the burglar left and the constabulary were summoned. The sergeant went upstairs and when he came down again he offered to make my wife a cup of tea and began to explain that some burglars had very beastly habits and she had to prepare herself for the possibility that something very nasty might have happened to her dog. At first Gilly could not think what the man was talking about but, on going upstairs herself and seeing a pile of black curls on the white bedroom carpet, remembered that before going to lunch she had given Sydney his monthly trim. This was the evidence that had so impressed the officer and convinced him that he was in pursuit of a pervert.

While making a good living, I was not greatly enjoying life at the Bar. I seemed unable to lose a case and then forget all about it. Instead I always felt personally responsible if things did not go absolutely right. So when in 1960 my father-in-law suggested I should go off to America and see whether there was an opening for me in the Beloit Iron Works in Wisconsin. I leapt at the idea. Beloit manufactured paper-making machinery and had recently bought an interest in Walmsleys in Bury, a firm of which Gilly's grandfather had been chairman and managing director.

It was curious being in America at that time. Few there seemed to think world war and a nuclear holocaust could be avoided. Indeed, this dismal topic featured in almost every conversation and overshadowed my whole visit. Beloit as a town had nothing to commend it. It was built round a lake so polluted that anyone bathing in it would have been dead in minutes. I also saw an example of the dangers of keeping fit. The chairman of the company had a harness contraption rigged up in his private lavatory and, having performed his normal duties, used to haul himself up in the harness a few score times to strengthen his muscles. Shortly after I returned to England he was found dead in the loo.

The countryside round Beloit was flat and uninteresting but a thirty-mile drive took one to a fairly pretty lake from which, I was told, people thought nothing of commuting 100 miles to Chicago. One night we had dinner at a hotel called the Wagon Wheel. The manager said in jest: 'If a guest is given a room with a high number, he is advised to take a packed lunch for the journey.' And, indeed, it was about a mile from one end of the hotel to the other. The people in Beloit were immensely friendly and on my last night the lady with whom I was staying said: 'Gee David, I just love your accent. I'd like to hide you in my closet and bring you out whenever we had people in for dinner.' I came home sure that Beloit would not appeal to Gilly and resolved to settle down at the Bar.

In October 1960 James, our eldest boy, was born. My father lived long enough to see him but died of a heart attack on 17 March the following year. He was sixty-seven. In August 1962 Matthew arrived on the scene and soon turned out to be a bundle of trouble and the life and soul of the party.

We had a succession of girls to look after the children. One was a Danish girl called Kirsten, known as Puck to her family and friends. James went into Barclays Bank in Burnley and declared in a piping voice 'we have a new nanny and she is called "Fuck"'. The name proved particularly apt, and the house was besieged by boys from the village who had never had such luck.

In about 1963 Mark Carlisle was adopted for Runcorn to succeed Dennis Vosper, and again my thoughts turned to politics. They would probably have remained no more than thoughts had not the Nelson & Colne Association approached me and asked me to be their candidate for the 1964 election. After much doubt and indecision I accepted. I do not think Gilly was very enthusiastic, but she had probably by then come to realise that I had not got politics out of my system and there was no point in making a fuss when my efforts in an unwinnable Labour seat would surely come to nothing.

The Labour Member was Sydney Silverman and the name

Silverman was painted in enormous letters on the tallest mill chimney in Nelson town. Nelson itself was called 'little Moscow' by the locals and its town council, proudly pacifist, had before the War refused to allow the East Lancashire Regiment to march through the town.

A succession of ambitious Conservatives had fought the constituency over the years, none with much success. Harmar Nicholls was the candidate in 1945, Alan Green – my father-in-law to be – in 1950, Elaine Kellett-Bowman in 1955. In 1945 Harmar Nicholls was in the army, as were the two others invited for interview but fog in the Channel led to only Harmar turning up on the night. Glamorous in service dress he was duly selected and was then so intoxicated by his success that when he met the press outside the room he announced that he was going to challenge Sydney Silverman to an open debate. The Tories were horrified because they knew Silverman's reputation as a skilled and canny debater but there was no turning back. The Imperial Ballroom, Carr Road, was an enormous establishment with a tin roof, later used for big band concerts, and on the day appointed for the great contest it was packed. A vicar had been asked to take the chair and said that each candidate was to have exactly twenty minutes to state his case. He then took off his watch and placed it on the table in front of him. The debate then proceeded and to no one's surprise Harmar Nicholls had a very painful time. But at the end of the evening the vicar looked down and was horrified to discover that his watch had gone, stolen apparently by someone in the front row of the audience. This was good news for the Tories for the following day the headline in the *Nelson Leader* was not about Harmar's humiliation. It read: 'ELECTION MEETING DRAMA. VICAR'S WATCH STOLEN.'

To come across Sydney Silverman in a motor car was an unnerving experience. He was so short in the body that he could not see over the steering wheel of his Jaguar and oncoming motorists were confronted with what appeared to be a driverless vehicle. He was also a wily creature. There was a church service to herald the opening of the 1964 campaign. The vicar told me that I was to read the Old Testament lesson and Sydney the New, but he did not reveal that Sydney had insisted on choosing his own lesson. I read over the one that I had been given and was somewhat disappointed to discover that it was little more than a long genealogical table, beginning 'Abraham begat Isaac; and Isaac begat Jacob' and thereafter down through the generations. But the day came, the service began and after singing a psalm I went up to the lectern and read the lesson with all the verve I could command, returning to my pew well satisfied. We then sang another psalm and it was Sydney's turn. 'Revelations Chapter 21' he said and then, with a voice quivering with emotion, 'I saw a new Heaven and a new Earth...' When *he* was finished, I suspected that *I* was finished and that the campaign was lost before it had even begun. Sydney, however, had forgotten that Revelations Chapter 21 is part of the funeral service and some may think it poetic justice that a few years later he was under the sod and I was MP for Nelson & Colne.

But back to 1964, and in a debate organised by the local churches, Sydney revealed how short could be his temper. He stormed off the platform because he disliked the way I answered a question about race relations. I pointed out the obvious – that we were hardly likely to have good race relations if we did not have firm immigration control – but it was not an answer to Sydney's liking.

In my election address I said that Labour's slogan 'Thirteen Wasted Years' was patently untrue. In thirteen years of Conservative government the living standards of the British people had improved more than in the previous half-century. I did not claim that the government had bestowed all those benefits. I did say that what had been achieved could only have been achieved in a free enterprise system where individual effort, initiative and savings were encouraged, and that was the sort of system we would maintain.

It all seemed very reasonable but I knew that I and all fighting under the Conservative banner were in difficulties – thirteen years was a long time and 'Time for a Change' was an attractive slogan for the unthinking. At the time I did not think it helped that the Tories were led by Alec Douglas-Home who looked like a figure from the past and did not appear a match for the nimble, quick-witted Wilson with all his talk of the 'white heat of the technological revolution'. I later came to see that Alec had done a fine job in almost impossible circumstances. For years the BBC in particular had seized every opportunity to portray the Conservative government and the Conservative Party as not just old-fashioned but degenerate and probably corrupt. In David Frost's programme *That Was the Week That Was* individual MPs in Conservative marginals were picked upon as idle, incompetent, or both, with none of the evidence of wrongdoing – cash for questions and the like – which fuelled the 'sleaze' campaign against the Tories in the 1990s. So to have run Wilson so close was quite a triumph for Alec Douglas-Home. And, with a fall in the Labour majority to 2,644, I was quite pleased with my own result.

Mark Carlisle was now in the House as member for Runcorn and I could not help feeling that, if I had arranged things better, I could have been in the House myself. But my restlessness and determination to get back into the fray clouded my judgement and I closed my mind to the fact that despite his thin majority Harold was in a very strong position. He could go back to the country at a moment of his own choosing claiming that he needed a bigger majority to carry out Labour's programme.

It was in this state of mind that I fell to the blandishments of Conservative Central Office and got myself adopted as prospective candidate for Heywood & Royton. It was a weary place, according to Gilly 'curled around Rochdale like a sooty feather boa', and next to it was grim Saddleworth Moor where at about that time Brady and Hindley were burying their victims. Until 1964 the constituency had been represented in Parliament by Tony Leavey (Conservative) but had then been won for Labour by Joel Barnett, who later became a Labour minister and in 1983 a peer. Joel's 1964 majority was beguilingly small – 800 – but nobody told me before I threw my cap in the ring that a vast new overspill estate had just been completed at Darnhill – eight tower blocks which Joel later referred to as 'his eight pillars of wisdom'.

It was with great enthusiasm that I started working the constituency. I was described in the *Daily Express* as passionately provincial and quoted in the local paper as saying: 'If you ask me for one reason why the Tories did worse here in the north-west than anywhere else, it was because we had too many MPs who dissociated themselves from the region as soon as they became MPs. They went to live in London.'

The Conservative agent was a very elderly gentleman called Jim Somerville who had been in the job for longer than anybody could remember. The constituency Association provided him with a car, and one night I was coming out of a pub where I had been garnering votes and saw that Jim, having removed the back seat from the car, had packed it with sheep.

Meanwhile, Gilly had fallen back on the maxim 'when in doubt have a baby'. No one, however, had reminded her that it might be two, and it came as quite a shock to learn that twins were on the way. When the twins were born Jenny had dislocated hips and, on the advice of John Charnley, who pioneered artificial hips for elderly people, she was put in plaster from neck to toe. She had tremendous spirit and at children's parties used to propel herself across the room by deft use of her powerful ankles. Alistair, her twin brother, with thumb in mouth, rode on her back as if astride an armoured warhorse. When in 1966 the general election campaign began, Gilly and I moved into a hotel outside Rochdale, taking Jenny with us but leaving Alistair with my parents-in-law. Late at night we lay in our beds with Jenny in a cot between us, trying without much success to rock her to sleep.

It was a nightmare fortnight. There was little response on the doorstep to my plea that Harold Wilson was only having an election because he knew it was now or never, that there was bad news round the corner and Wilson wanted a bigger majority under his belt before the bad news broke. I listed Labour's broken promises, principally their 1964 pledge that they would not need to increase the general level of taxation. That pledge looked pretty sick in 1966 after swingeing increases in income tax and hikes in the taxes on petrol, cigarettes and beer. So did their pledge to halt the rise in the cost of living, for costs had risen steeply and mortgage rates were at their highest level ever.

In spite of many difficulties I managed to whip my supporters up into a frenzy of excitement and we had a magnificent rally on the last night when I shouted myself hoarse. But to no avail. The jovial Joel was returned to Westminster on April Fools' Day 1966 with his majority greatly increased. And Harold Wilson set out to make complete fools of us all and bring down on Britain a financial crisis of massive proportions.

In 1968 Enoch Powell made his 'rivers of blood' speech. Shortly afterward the Clitheroe Association asked him to speak at Padiham and as a former candidate I was invited along. There were queues of people trying to get into the hall and a sizable demonstration outside by banner-carrying Pakistanis. The atmosphere inside was electric and everyone waited with eager anticipation for the inflammatory rhetoric associated with the name of Powell. But he rose to his feet to deliver a dry as dust speech on the future of the ports industry which left people groaning with boredom. I do not know whether he did it as a prank or thought Padiham was on the seaside. But it taught the audience a good lesson.

Late in 1967 Juby Lancaster, MP for South Fylde, announced his decision not to stand at the next general election and I was invited to put my name in for the seat. One of the front runners was Alan Green who had lost Preston South in 1964 and had failed to regain it in 1966, but he was quite happy for me to put my name forward as well in case the Association wanted a younger man. At about the same time Nelson & Colne were in the process of adopting a candidate for a by-election following the death of Sydney Silverman, and Association chairman Derek Crabtree asked me to put my name forward. I had to tell him that I was awaiting interview at South Fylde and could not do so.

At Easter 1968 we had arranged to take the children to Swanage for a short holiday, and on the day we were leaving home I received a letter from Richard Sharples, then vice-chairman of the Conservative Party, asking me to ring him as a matter of urgency. I did so from a call box on the journey south and he asked me to withdraw my name from South Fylde so that I could accept the invitation from Nelson & Colne. I told him I was not prepared to do so but asked him to get Nelson & Colne to postpone their selection for a week, i.e. until after the meeting at South Fylde. He said he could not possibly do so and the upshot was that Nelson & Colne selected a man called Penfold with bizarre consequences. I then attended the selection at South Fylde and together with Elaine Kellett-Bowman was eliminated, leaving Alan Green and Edward Gardner to fight it out in the final. No doubt I was very obstinate but at the time I thought it was right to stick to my guns.

Derek Crabtree and the other Officers at Nelson & Colne were now landed with Penfold who, not being a local man, would not have been their first choice, and they soon began to seek a way out and pestered me with phone calls asking me to challenge Penfold even at that late stage. I could not see how I could possibly do so, but I was left in no doubt that on the night set for Penfold's formal adoption there was going to be trouble.

The night came and I was on the drawing room floor mending the vacuum when the telephone rang. It was Phil Somers, the treasurer of the Association. Would I come to the Nelson Club as quickly as possible? There had been a spot of bother. The general meeting of the Association had refused to adopt Penfold and wanted to adopt me. It sounded very strange and if I had had any sense I would have said so and stayed at home. But I got in my car and ten minutes later was parking outside the club. Phil Somers ran down the street towards me with a happy grin on is face which for the moment allayed my fears. In the secretary's office I found a disconsolate Penfold and also Jean, the widow of John Crabtree who had for many years been a much respected Association chairman. Jean warned me that there would be big trouble if I went into the meeting but Phil Somers and Derek Crabtree, who by then had joined us, said they were in a terrible spot because of the rejection of Penfold. The by-election was almost on them, there simply was not time to start the selection procedure all over again, and they begged me to go in to the meeting and accept the candidature. So into the room I went and onto the platform. There was an uncanny stillness, a frosty, icy calm as Derek Crabtree asked me if I would be the candidate and I replied: 'Yes.' The motion that I should be adopted was then put to the vote and carried by a show of hands: but I could see from the disapproving and angry faces of some in the audience that there was a substantial minority who did not like what had happened and probably thought that there had been a carefully engineered conspiracy with me a co-conspirator.

There was work to be done and I have never worked harder in

my life. I rang up my clerk to tell him that I could not be in court for the next week and I set about visiting every single person who I was given to understand might have disapproved of my adoption, and eventually I persuaded each and everyone of them that there had been no jiggery pokery on my part and that I would be a worthy candidate in the by-election.

CHAPTER SEVEN

Becoming an MP

Preparations for the by-election had to be made speedily and I set to work with a will. In the midst of it all I got a telephone call from a Paul Watson who said he was making a number of 'year in the life' films. He had recently completed a year in the life of a race horse and now wanted to do a year in the life of an MP. He had decided that I was going to win the by-election so wanted to follow me round before, during and after the campaign and throughout the coming year. I saw no harm in the idea but it turned out to be a gruelling experience. It caused great merriment among our friends when we started turning up at cocktail parties with a camera crew in tow. When eventually the film was shown on television Barney, our fell pony (true name Hades Hill Jupiter) was the star, tearing across the moors with Gilly on top. When Gilly was not on horseback she was seen and heard philosophising in a very plummy voice about the ills of the world and the beauty of Lancashire while driving a car at breakneck speed round twisting country lanes.

My opponents in the by-election were Betty Boothroyd, Labour, later to become famous as a truly great Speaker of the House of Commons; a Liberal, David Chadwick; and an Independent, Brian Tattersall. Tattersall stood for tougher immigration control and the restoration of hanging. Capital punishment was much in the news with Sydney Silverman having introduced a Private Members'

Bill leading to its abolition, and Ian Brady and Myra Hindley having recently been tried for the Moors murders. I felt abolition had been a mistake but I did not make much of the issue. There were plenty of other things to talk about, particularly the dismal performance of the Labour government.

An array of important people came to support me including Alec Douglas-Home (whose public meeting attracted 1,000 people), Quintin Hogg and Selwyn Lloyd. Betty Boothroyd was supported by Barbara Castle, Anthony Wedgwood Benn (as he still called himself), Emanuel Shinwell and George Brown. None of their meetings were well attended and Betty herself made greater play of a telegram of support from Annie Walker of the Rover's Return in *Coronation Street*. Selwyn Lloyd stayed with us at Whins House. When he came down to breakfast we asked him whether he had slept well. He said: 'Yes, until about seven o'clock when I had two visitors in my bed. Once I had got Alistair to take his wet trousers off we became good friends.'

Gilly worked unceasingly – attending meetings every evening and canvassing all day. We campaigned in beautiful weather and ran from door to door so that we would cover every street. I made much of the fact that I was the local man, I complained that Nelson & Colne had been neglected and its industry allowed to decline while the government lavished vast subsidies on Merseyside.

The government had at about this time encouraged Courtaulds to set up in Skelmersdale. Courtaulds were naive enough to believe that outside the traditional textile areas they would be able to introduce efficient, new, labour-saving working practices. In fact, it was only a matter of months after the establishment of the factory that troublemakers moved in from Merseyside and after that it was downhill all the way. It turned out to be a major disaster for Courtaulds and a major disaster for north-east Lancashire which could well have used the new investment. All this was just around

the corner when the by-election took place, but all my most pessi-
mistic prognostications were borne out by events.

A week before we polled there was a by-election in Oldham,
and that safe Labour seat fell to the Tories. I began to relax. It
seemed inconceivable that I could fail to win Nelson & Colne
after that result and so it happened. At about 1 a.m. on 28 June
the acting returning officer announced that I had won with a
majority of 3,522. There had been an 11.4% swing from Labour
to Conservative which, if reflected countrywide, would have given
the Conservatives a massive 250 seat majority. The votes cast for
each candidate were:

Boothroyd (Labour) 12,944
Chadwick (Liberal) 3,016
Tattersall (English Nationalist) 1,255
Waddington (Conservative) 16,466

The next day was an anticlimax – a call from a newspaper at 8 a.m.
asking for my comments and after that virtually the whole day with
Paul Watson's camera crew. But I did receive a call from the Chief
Whip, Willie Whitelaw, to check that I would be reporting to his
office at 2 p.m. the following Tuesday before taking my seat.

On the Monday, Gilly and I plus Matthew and James set off for
London and stayed overnight in my father-in-law's flat in Whitehall
Court. The camera crew said that they wanted film of my getting
into a taxi at Whitehall Court and getting out at the Palace of
Westminster and that it would be impossible, for obvious reasons,
for one crew to do both shots. Could we therefore be filmed getting
into a cab on the Monday? 'Yes,' we said, but unfortunately when
we hailed a taxi on the Tuesday it was a red one and the completed
film showed that the cab we had got in to had turned red on the
short journey down Whitehall.

Matthew, then aged six, announced that he liked London and was going to stay until his teeth fell out. But his patience was exhausted long before the moment came for me to approach the Table flanked by Willie Whitelaw and Mark Carlisle. I then handed the returning officer's writ to the clerk and took the oath to the loud baaing sound which is customary on such occasions. The whole thing went without a hitch, but only just. Minutes before I was due in the chamber I woke up to the fact that I had lost the writ, and a feverish hunt ensued. Eventually it was discovered in one of the many lavatories in the Palace. The experience led to a slight alteration in my perception of the Labour Party. How easy it would have been for some malicious fellow to have flushed the writ away, leaving me embarrassed and seatless!

After taking the oath I shook hands with Mr Speaker King and then went to meet the Leader of the Opposition. Ted Heath had become leader three years before, it being thought that he was a great debater who would knock spots off Harold Wilson. But in office he never showed himself able to knock spots off anything or anybody. As an elder statesman he learned to make a good authoritative contribution from the front bench below the gangway but he had few debating skills and his stodginess of approach made him a sure loser in any tussle with the wily Wilson.

I had only been in the House for two days when I received a telephone call from the clerk of my Manchester chambers asking me if later in the week I was prepared to sit as a deputy County Court judge somewhere in London. This would allow my colleague Bob Hardy, who had contracted with the Lord Chancellor's Department, to sit as a judge on that day, to take over a brief of mine, a libel action in Leeds. At the eleventh hour someone pointed out that if I were to sit, my career as an MP would come to an abrupt end because as a result of the House of Commons Disqualification Act I would have disqualified myself from membership of the House, thereby precipitating another by-election. I was then begged by Bob to go and explain to the lady in the Lord Chancellor's Department why he could not sit and why I had turned out to be an inappropriate replacement. I set off and, after journeying along many corridors and ascending and descending many staircases, I eventually found a little old lady sitting alone in a tiny office at the bottom of a gloomy stairwell somewhere in the bowels of the House of Lords. I apologised for troubling her and she said: 'I can assure you it is no trouble. In fact I am delighted to see you. I have been in this office for thirty-five years and you are the first person who has ever visited me.'

The next day I was in the chamber at 2.30 p.m. for prayers, and thereafter I always tried to attend prayers once or twice a week. I am addicted to the Book of Common Prayer and cannot understand why modern churchmen think it clever to substitute the banal for the beautiful. It is an insult to ordinary people to say they cannot understand the language of the early seventeenth century; and, if teachers cannot be bothered to explain to children how the meaning of words sometimes changes over the years, they are not fit to be teachers. Daily prayers in the House are a constant reminder that Christianity has helped to shape virtually every facet of British life from democracy to law, to morality, literature, art and education. At her coronation the Queen pledged herself to maintain the laws of God and as Supreme Governor of the Church of England she symbolises the important place the church has in our constitution. Nowadays it sometimes seems that we cannot even trust Her Majesty's judges to protect the Christian traditions on which this country is founded, and that makes it even more important that Parliament should do so. Daily prayers should remind all of that task.

MPs are enormously privileged to work in the Palace of Westminster – a building of rare beauty – but in 1968 one heard little recognition of this and there were constant complaints about working conditions. In 1979 when things had greatly improved some Members were still complaining. A new Labour Member in 1979 actually told me that as a post office worker grade 'x' he was entitled to 'y' cubic feet of space, and it was outrageous that in the House of Commons he was having to share a room with five other Members. He did not get any sympathy from me. When I got into Parliament I was so grateful to be there that I would willingly have worked in a boot cupboard. But I did not rate a boot cupboard and I dictated my correspondence, as did most other Members, sitting on a bench downstairs on what was called the interview floor. Now in the same area are hundreds of filing cabinets stuffed full of the useless correspondence generated by over-generous secretarial allowances. In 1968 we did not have offices and we did not have lavish secretarial allowances, but we still managed to do our work to the satisfaction of our constituents. Offices have, in fact, brought with them many problems as well as costing the taxpayer a lot of money. They have helped to empty the smoking room which used to be a splendid place to get to know colleagues and discuss events. When some new offices for Members came along in the early eighties, an Ulster Unionist Member told me that now his best friend and one of the chief sources of smoking room gossip spent all his time upstairs in his room canoodling with his secretary. He was unconvinced that this made Parliament a more efficient place or his friend a better Member.

Anyhow, I was grateful to have got into Parliament. I found life very congenial and I wasn't the only one or there would not have been a queue of people wanting to get in and another queue of people trying to get back in after being thrown out.

I made a pot-boiling maiden speech before the summer recess just to get it out of the way and then settled down to making a minor nuisance of myself. I must be the only person who benefited personally from the Russian invasion of Czechoslovakia in August 1968, for that led to what I considered a very happy event – the recall of Parliament in the long recess.

Soon I was put on the standing committee of the Post Office Bill, the measure which turned the Post Office from a government department into a public corporation. Our side argued strongly for the telecommunications part of the business to be separated from the postal part, an approach adopted in the early 1980s Telecommunications Act.

The following year I was on the committee of the Ports Bill – an even duller measure, but I was beginning to learn the art of time wasting with a purpose, the purpose being to delay the progress of government business and keep some government supporters engaged upstairs on the committee floor and hopefully out of worse mischief.

But the whips did not really wish to keep me fully engaged in the Palace of Westminster. My job was to hold Nelson & Colne at the coming general election and if that meant missing divisions to attend events in the constituency, so be it. Gilly and I set out to involve ourselves in as many activities in the constituency as possible, to take an interest in everything that was going on, in the hope that people would feel we were doing a good job and would be prepared to vote for us even if they did not think much of the Tory Party or Mr Heath.

During the 1960s there had been a steady increase in the number of Pakistanis living in the constituency, and each year more of them were finding their way on to the electoral register. I made great efforts to get to know them and show an interest in their concerns. Once I was asked to support an application to bring a young man into the country to marry a constituent's daughter. The boy arrived and we were invited to the nuptials which took place in the Silverman Hall. The father greeted us at the door with: 'All my English friends I want to go upstairs. All the Pakistanis I ask to go downstairs.' 'Why,' I said, 'do you want all the English upstairs and all the Pakistanis downstairs?' 'Upstairs champagne,' he said, 'downstairs orange juice.'

A few weeks later I was visiting the Salvation Army hostel when the bride popped her nose round the door and asked me to come out and speak to her. I asked her what was wrong. She replied: 'He is no man. You got him into England so please get him out.'

Nelson and Colne were two very different places. Nelson grew out of a village when cotton weaving came to the valley towards the end of the nineteenth century. Colne was a place of some antiquity with a fine old parish church, and those who lived there considered themselves a cut above those who lived two miles down the road. The town had a rousing song, much in use at mayor-making. It went like this:

> Who's he that with triumphant voice
> So loudly sings in praise
> Of his dear native hills and vales,
> His home, his early days.
>
> More loud by far than he, I'll sing,
> In praise speak higher still,
> Of native home most dear to me,
> Old Colne upon the hill.
>
> (Chorus)
> Bonnie Colne, Bonnie Colne,
> Bonnie Colne, let come what will,
> Thou'lt ever be most dear to me,
> Bonnie Colne upon the hill.'

While still a pretty new MP I had a brush with General Gowon, the ruler of Nigeria – then engaged in a bloody war against secessionist Biafra. I was sufficiently naive to write a personal letter to the General enclosing a letter from a constituent complaining about the many atrocities perpetrated in the war; and, to my astonishment, received a personal letter back from the General in which he berated me in most intemperate language for daring to interfere with the domestic affairs of Nigeria. The General cannot have had much to do with his time.

I also had an interesting encounter with Robert Maxwell which perhaps sheds some light on that extraordinary character. He was chairman of the catering committee in the House of Commons and already showing signs of megalomania. In those days I was writing a regular column for my local newspaper and, running out of anything to say, I put in a few lines about the poor food in the House of Commons. I had no reason to believe that the great Maxwell was an avid reader of the *Nelson Leader* and I was surprised when a few days later I received a letter from him in which he complained at my lack of courtesy in not telling him of my concerns about the food in the Palace of Westminster before rushing to the press.

One of the truly memorable occasions during the run-up to the 1970 general election was Bernadette Devlin's arrival in Parliament after she had won Mid Ulster in a by-election. On 22 April 1969, and within an hour of taking her seat, she made her maiden speech and, although it was full of monstrous nonsense, the fluency, command of language and complete self-possession of this 21-year-old left everyone spellbound. The Reverend Ian Paisley then made his contribution and a wit remarked that it was the only speech delivered on the floor of the House of Commons which could be heard distinctly on the floor of the House of Lords.

In 1968 the government had introduced the Parliament (No. 2) Bill which would have allowed existing hereditary peers, but not their successors, the right to attend the House of Lords but not to vote, and would have created a House of voting peers based exclusively on patronage. Left wingers in the Labour Party joined forces with right wingers in the Tory Party led by Enoch Powell to defeat the measure, both factions believing that the scheme, supported by both front benches, would weaken still further the very few constitutional checks on abuse of power by the Executive.

It was a splendid opportunity for a new Member. I supported the rebels and gloried in the discomfiture of the government. Eventually the government abandoned the measure, using as an excuse the need to introduce urgent legislation to penalise unofficial strikers and bring some semblance of order into the ever more chaotic industrial relations scene. Eventually this measure was also abandoned, largely as a result of Jim Callaghan's decision to side with the TUC against Barbara Castle's modest attempt at reform. Callaghan was later alleged to have stated that the key to success for a Labour government was to find out what the trade unions wanted and give it to them; and certainly he practised in the late 1960s what he later preached.

In January 1969 I went on a trip to North Africa sponsored by the Ariel Foundation. My travelling companions were Keith Speed, Peter Archer and David Marquand. Algiers was shabby. The flowers which used to decorate the centre of the city were no more. The government was building an enormous steel mill with Russian money but had no idea as to who would want the steel when they had made it. Tunisia, with a far more successful economy, was dull – apart from our meeting with President Bourguiba who showed us numerous photographs of people he said were friends shot by the French in the fight for freedom. We were impressed with Libya which had suddenly become enormously rich following the discovery of oil, but we did not fully appreciate how the reforms aimed at bringing the country into the twentieth century were also releasing other forces. It had been decided to move Parliament to the green hills of Cyrenaica, King Idris's homeland. The parliamentarians were to sleep in long barrack rooms on army-style beds. We arrived on a Saturday; the parliamentarians were coming on Monday to start their labours on Tuesday and already at the foot of each bed were laid out two neatly folded blankets, a mess tin with knife, fork and spoon and a chunk of bread for their first breakfast.

We travelled across the border into Egypt and as we approached Cairo there were bunkers along the side of the road housing Russian MIG jets. We visited some of the fifteen ships trapped in the Great Bitter Lake since the Six-Day War, and we went up to Aswan and saw the dam being built.

I cannot pretend that all parliamentary trips are educational but this one certainly was; and it certainly broadens one's mind getting to know Members on the other side of the House.

In January 1970 I joined the board of J. B. Broadley Ltd, makers of leather cloths and coated fabrics in Rossendale Valley. This was at the invitation of Michael Jackson, who died a few years later after the firm was taken over by Ozalid. He was a good man and a very good businessman, and I am very grateful for the opportunity I had to learn at his feet. I also went on the board of Wolstenholme Bronze Powders Ltd. – later renamed Wolstenholme Rink Ltd. – a firm of which John Wolstenhome (goalie for Bury football club as well as a businessman and Gilly's grandfather) was co-founder. I think all this broadened my experience and made me a rather better MP than I would otherwise have been.

In 1969 James went away to school, to Aysgarth in North Yorkshire. The poor boy hated going and for many months before leaving home used to get into our bed in the early morning and beg to be allowed to stay with us. Once he said: 'If you let me stay, I'll do all the housework and the cooking.' We felt dreadful, particularly when I myself had been so homesick, but we also felt we had to grit our teeth and do it for his sake. If he had stayed at home he would have been the only one of his friends not going away to school. The awful day came when we motored over to Aysgarth and left him there but the next day the headmaster, Simon Reynolds, telephoned to say he had settled in well. However, James's own letters did not bear this out, and for the first few years he suffered greatly. Matthew went to Aysgarth a year-and-a-half later and, although in constant trouble, loved school right from the start. While Matthew thrived, James lamented and after nearly two years at school wrote:

> I hope you are well; I'm not. I hate it here and besides last night I could not get to sleep until half past one and woke up at five to six. Please, please do something about it. I won't say anything about this in my Sunday letter because I don't want a master to see it. Please again do something and please send a nice parcel. From JAMES.

Matthew on the other hand wrote:

> On Wednesday we had great fun because it was a power cut. On Tuesday we saw the film *Demetrius and the Gladiators*. It was a good film because it showed gladiators fighting and other spectacular things. The Emperor in the end got killed and I think it served him right. He was a stupid person.

In the early summer of 1970 Harold Wilson called a general election. He did so after the Labour government had got up to a monstrous piece of trickery. The Parliamentary Boundary Commission had reported and by law the government had to present to Parliament for approval the order implementing its proposals for changes to constituency boundaries. The report was not to Labour's liking so, while complying with the law by presenting to Parliament the order, they then whipped the Parliamentary Party to vote the order down. As a result, the election was to be fought on the old boundaries giving Labour an advantage they did not deserve.

Gilly became ill with glandular fever and was unable to take part in much of the campaign. It went well enough from my point of view although, according to the polls, we did not seem to be making much headway nationally. But on the last morning a more encouraging poll was published and in Nelson & Colne we felt we would be all right. We were – just. The result was:

D. Waddington (Conservative) 19,881
E. D. Hoyle (Labour) 18,471
Conservative majority 1,410

The Party was back in office with a perfectly adequate majority of thirty-one seats.

CHAPTER EIGHT

Heath's Government: Defeat

What set the tone for the new parliament was the fact that the Labour Party had expected to win and felt that it had been cheated of the victory it had deserved. Usually in British politics a party which loses an election after a period in office is pretty demoralised. Its members accept that they would not have lost had they not made mistakes but that their defeat does at least give them the opportunity for new thinking. This was not the mood of the Labour Party in 1970. It did not see the need for new thinking, and it was going to make sure that Ted Heath had no honeymoon. Sometimes its attacks seemed pretty trivial. I remember in particular the synthetic anger when in the summer of 1970 the Minister for Posts, Chris Chataway, found a new chairman for the Post Office. And Labour supported every bit of industrial unrest in the country, hoping that strike after strike would show the country that the Conservatives could not govern.

The government suffered from some real ill luck. It was certainly a terrible blow when only just over a month after the election Iain Macleod, the new Chancellor of the Exchequer, died; and then came events which scuppered the government's promise not to feather-bed industry and aid lame ducks. It was bad enough when Upper Clyde Shipbuilders ran into difficulties and had to be rescued, but the Rolls-Royce affair was even more damaging.

Rolls-Royce found itself in financial difficulties after entering into an unwise fixed price contract for the provision of the RB 211 engine for the Lockheed TriStar, and the government had to nationalise the aerospace division of the company. It was not only a major crisis: it made us a laughing stock, with John Davies as Secretary of State for Industry quite unable to make a convincing case for what was being done. Then came the Leila Khaled affair and the government, which had been elected to pursue a tough law-and-order policy, cut a sorry figure when the hijacker of an El Al plane was allowed to go free in exchange, it seemed, for the release of the passengers of another plane hijacked by Arab terrorists in Jordan.

In the general election campaign Ted Heath had sought a mandate to negotiate terms for Britain's entry into the EEC and first Tony Barber then Geoffrey Rippon were given the job of negotiating. In July 1971 a White Paper was published setting out the terms agreed, and there then followed a most brilliant exercise in business management and whipping by Francis Pym. He persuaded the Prime Minister that in the six-day debate on the principle of entry the Conservative Party should have a free vote. Without a whip it was likely that more Conservatives would vote against the motion approving entry than would do so if there was a whip, but he believed, and he was proved right, that if the Tories were not whipped, far more pro-Europeans in the Labour ranks would vote for the motion. The motion was carried by 356 votes to 244 with thirty-nine Conservatives voting against the motion and two abstaining, and sixty-nine Labour members voting for the motion and twenty abstaining. Getting a second reading for the Bill proved far more difficult and it is doubtful whether it could have been done had the Prime Minister not made the division a vote of confidence, saying that if the vote went against the government he and the whole Cabinet would resign. The closing stages of the debate were a nerve-wracking business. With the Prime Minister declaring that if the vote went against the Bill 'this Parliament cannot sensibly continue', a second reading was obtained by just 309 votes to 301.

In October the Conservative Party Conference had voted decisively for EEC entry. I was unhappy because of what seemed to me the betrayal of the Commonwealth, and New Zealand in particular, through our having to adopt the common agricultural policy; but I could see the importance of trade with Europe for British industry and although the Commission's supranational ambitions were already evident, I thought we and other countries would together tame the beast. I certainly did not think that we would finish up with the undemocratic mess which is today's EU.

I DAVID CHARLES WADDINGTON do declare that well and truly I will serve the Queen as one of Her Counsel learned in the Law and truly counsel the Queen in Her matters, when I shall be called, and duly and truly minister the Queen's matters and sue the Queen's process after the course of the Law, and after my cunning For any matter against the Queen where the Queen is party save in so far as I may be therein allowed or licensed I will take no wages or fee of any man I will duly in convenient time speed such matters as any person shall have to do in the Law against the Queen as I may lawfully do, without long delay, tracing or tarrying the Party of his lawful process in that that to me belongeth. I will be attendant to the Queen's matters when I be called thereto.

QC's Oath

At the beginning of the parliament, Attorney-General Peter Rawlinson had asked me to be his Parliamentary Private Secretary, and I accepted. There is nothing very glamorous in being a PPS, but it was considered the first step on the ladder. I also decided to apply for silk (to become a Queen's Counsel) because travelling back to Manchester night after night after voting in the House and then, after a hard day in court, getting back to London for another vote was proving a great strain.

My application was successful, and the declaration which one then had to make was truly extraordinary; reading it was a challenge because of the absence of punctuation marks.

I had not been well since Christmas 1970 but soon after all this I began to feel really ill. I went to hospital, where it was at first thought I had a brain tumour, but then after a series of tests encephalitis was diagnosed. This then led to epileptic fits. On one occasion I passed out in the House of Commons and came to in Westminster Hospital. On another occasion I passed out in the Lyons snack bar on Bridge Street and again woke up in hospital, this time with a large cut on my forehead. It was an incident which had an odd sequel. Years later I received a letter from a man who said that he was disgusted at my discourtesy in never having written to him to thank him for coming to my rescue when I had been taken ill in Westminster. He had ruined his shirt in doing so and wanted £5 for a new one. I, of course, had no idea who had looked after me and certainly had no knowledge of a shirt ruined by my blood. But I had no reason to doubt his word and he got his money.

One Friday morning when I arrived back in Manchester off the night sleeper I discovered that my car had been stolen from the car park. I walked to the bus station, caught a bus to Accrington and then another one to Whalley, getting off at a call box on the way from where I intended to phone Gilly. But having got in the box I could not remember our number and when I started looking in the phone book I could not remember what my name looked like in print. I walked to a shop and I asked the surprised man to look up my telephone number for me and ring my home, which he duly did and Gilly came to the rescue. All this was followed by another spell in hospital, but eventually things came right, and the only lesson to be learned is: don't get encephalitis. It tends to lead to tasteless jokes about swollen headedness, but I found it a very unpleasant and terrifying condition. I must not, however, forget that it was at that bleak time that a very marvellous thing happened. Our youngest child Victoria was born.

Back at Westminster I resigned as PPS, but tried to get back into my parliamentary work. It was a depressing time. I was one of a bunch of backbenchers who had been enrolled to travel the country and explain the Industrial Relations Bill. This was a measure of inordinate length and complexity which sought in numerous clauses to distinguish between fair industrial practices which would attract legal immunities, and unfair practices which would not.

It is easy now with hindsight to see that this was entirely the wrong approach. There was no need to put the trade union movement into a legal straitjacket. All that was required was to remove their anachronistic privileges which was what eventually happened in the eighties. But at the time we could at least argue that, unlike the Labour government, we had not set out with the aim of fining strikers. This Bill, unlike the Labour one, was not about criminal penalties but civil remedies for those harmed by unfair action. What we wanted was to strengthen the arm of responsible trade unionists against the wildcats and set in place better procedures for dealing with disputes. And for all its complications, the Bill did give the trade unionist rights he had never had before such as longer periods of notice and compensation for unfair dismissal.

Clearly something had to be done to deal with growing industrial anarchy and the violence being used in pursuit of so-called industrial disputes. During the 1972 building workers' strike, coaches were hired to transport so-called 'flying pickets' to various building sites with the object of stopping work going on there. When some of the pickets eventually appeared to stand their trial at Shrewsbury Crown Court they were described as having swarmed onto a site 'like a frenzied horde of Apache Indians, chanting "Kill, kill, kill, capitalist bastards"; this is not a strike, it's a revolution.' The trial judge, Mr Justice Mais, described it as 'a terrifying display of force, with violence to persons and property putting people working on the sites and local residents in fear'. I gave short shrift to a trades council delegation urging me to raise in Parliament the plight of the men who had been sentenced.

But when the Industrial Relations Bill became law it soon began to cause trouble. The National Industrial Relations Court (NIRC) issued warrants for the arrest of three dockers who it was alleged had wilfully disobeyed a court order to stop blacking a container depot in east London. A shutdown of the docks was threatened and the Official Solicitor went to the Court of Appeal and got the order set aside.

But what really caused morale on our side of the House to reach rock bottom was the government's decision to introduce a price and incomes policy, thereby contradicting almost everything said by the Party at the general election. And, of course, it was this policy which led eventually to the miners' strike and the government's downfall.

Along with all my colleagues I argued that we could not give in to the miners' claim. Firstly, we would be saying there was no future in moderation and that extremism paid. Secondly, we would have moved one stage nearer the catastrophic inflation Germany experienced in the 1920s. Soon people would be bringing their money home in wheelbarrows and the pound note worth little more than waste paper. Like my colleagues, I pointed out that many trade union leaders had said that the communists were using the miners' dispute for political ends and suggested that Wilson knew this and should come out and say so. After all, he himself, when Prime Minister, had recognised that 'a tightly knit group of politically motivated men' were behind the seamen's strike in 1966. He had also talked in those days of 'one man's pay increase being another man's price increase'. But when I went off to do a live television debate in Rawtenstall with Eric Heffer and Cyril Smith, I was not very successful in selling these arguments and had a rough ride. I could, however, take some pleasure in the fact that I annoyed Eric Heffer so much that when the show was over but with the cameras still on us he took a swing at me. That is the sort of thing which makes good television.

Meanwhile Gilly was beavering away in the constituency. She was a Samaritan and had also launched a project to help the homeless. We were soon proud owners of a house in Padiham for battered wives which was almost always occupied by someone in urgent need. Once, in breach of all the rules, she went on her own to see one of her Samaritan customers. She was in such a hurry to get to his rescue that she left her car in the street unlocked and with its headlights on. The police came along and concluded that she had been kidnapped. They knocked on the door of a nearby house and were rather aggressive with the occupant who seemed to think they were accusing him of secreting the MP's wife on his premises. He protested that it was the last thing he would do. He was Len Dole, the Labour agent.

When the House of Commons met in January 1974 the whips were busy canvassing opinion as to whether we should go to the country on a 'Who rules Britain – the miners or Parliament?' ticket. I felt then, and still feel, that we would have won if we had gone there and then, but while we stood ready for the off, no one fired the starting gun. Instead, the press was full of charge and counter-charge as to what the offer for the miners meant and with rumours that the government and the National Coal Board were at logger-heads. By the time Parliament was dissolved the advantage had passed to the Opposition who used the simple slogan: 'We'll get Britain back to work'.

It was a difficult campaign in Nelson & Colne, but I was reason-ably confident that I would squeeze home because of all the spade work we had put in over the years. I did – by 179 votes. In the country Labour failed to get an overall majority but won the largest number of seats and after Ted failed in his attempt to form a coali-tion with the Liberals, Wilson accepted the Queen's commission to form a government.

Sadly, my father-in-law Alan Green lost in Preston South and never got back in the House. It was the end of a very disappointing political career which started with such promise, but was a perfect example of how dedication and loyalty to a particular area can be a person's downfall.

Looking at the press cuttings I seem to have spent much of the February 1974 campaign attacking the Liberals. What infuriated me was that at a time of national crisis the only things they talked about were the local railway line and the need to change the elec-toral system to secure the return to Parliament of more Liberals to talk about the local railway line.

When I look back on the Heath years my recollection may be coloured to some extent by the poor health from which I suffered for much of that parliament and my poor spirits at that time. But they were very gloomy years – years when sometimes the country seemed on the verge of anarchy with the leaders of the TUC quite unconcerned about the welfare of the nation and prepared to play politics at every turn. The Tory leadership looked pitifully weak. We had lost a really big figure in Iain MacLeod within a few weeks of the 1970 election. Enoch Powell was never in the government because of his 'rivers of blood' speech, Reggie Maudling had soon to resign because of the Poulson affair; and although we had a fine Foreign Secretary in Alec Douglas-Home, the Home Secretary and the Chancellor never looked right in their respective jobs. Robert Carr and Tony Barber were both men of intellect and courage but neither of them looked strong and fully in control of events. Tony Barber in particular was frail physically and had a reedy voice which is a great disadvantage in politics. Ted prided himself on taking us into the EEC but the people accepted rather than applauded the decision, being persuaded it would be good for British trade. But as the years went by it became more and more apparent that what we had signed up to was something very different from a common market and power was being drained away from our own Parliament and handed to an unelected bureaucracy in Brussels; as a result public support for the EEC steadily fell. In the Tory Party there was the beginning of a deep divide between those who believed that having joined the club we had no option but to go along with the majority, and those who felt that sooner or later we would have to leave if we wanted to remain a sovereign nation.

Ted Heath was a complex character and the following reminiscence may surprise many. In the autumn of 1973 he came to speak in Nelson & Colne. A rally was to be held in the Imperial Ballroom in Nelson, with all the local MPs and Conservative candidates from round about. Ted was to fly to Manchester but at lunchtime we were told that Manchester Airport was closed because of fog and he was flying to Weedon (Leeds/Bradford) instead. His arrival would be delayed by about an hour. I suggested that we should procure an organist and I would lead the singing of popular songs. The suggestion that I should sing was greeted with derision and rightly so, but someone else was enlisted to carry out the same task. As the moment for Ted's arrival drew near I went and stood out in the road and eventually the car drew up and out got Ted and Douglas

Hurd who was not then a Member of Parliament but Ted's political secretary. After Ted had made his speech I was called upon to give a vote of thanks, and we were just about to leave the platform when a little lady in the front row stood up and in a quavering voice said: 'I say three cheers for Mr Heath. Hip, hip, hooray! Hip, hip, hooray! Hip, hip, hooray!' She then gave us the first line of 'For he's a jolly good fellow' and we all joined in. The song over, we moved next door where the nobs were to gather for a private drink with the Prime Minister. And as we stood waiting for the reception to begin, Ted, to my astonishment, took a handkerchief from his pocket, dabbed his eyes and said: 'No one has ever sung "For he's a jolly good fellow" for me before.' He was genuinely touched by the reception he received that night and the one he got the following day when he went to a football match at Burnley's Turf Moor.

Early on in the 1970–74 parliament I was one of about twenty backbenchers invited to dinner at No. 10, and when I arrived I found that I was to sit on Ted's left and Jill Knight on his right. I begged Tim Kitson, Ted's PPS, to bestow the honour of sitting next to Ted on another but there was nothing doing: and I was quite relieved when, after we had sat down, Jill Knight decided to do the talking. This phase of the dinner, however, ended abruptly with Ted deciding that he had had enough of woman talk. In a gesture of calculated rudeness he turned his back on Jill, lifted his eyes to the ceiling as if in supplication and invited me to say something.

On another occasion I arrived at Downing Street for one of the usual summer receptions and, as Gilly and I climbed the stairs, we were dismayed to see that no one was following immediately behind. The consequence was appalling. We were stuck with Ted. 'Good evening, Prime Minister.' 'Good evening.' 'It was a good afternoon in the House, Prime Minister.' 'Yes.' 'Lovely weather we're having, Prime Minister.' 'Yes.' I was beginning to wonder whether 'Yes' was the only word left in his vocabulary. I was in despair. I had to do something drastic. 'When are you next going sailing, Prime Minister?' I had struck oil. 'Next month and I am taking *Morning Cloud*.' Then he spoiled it all. There was obviously no room for a woman in a conversation about sailing, so he turned to Gilly and with an imperious wave in the direction of the dining room said: 'You'll find the Gainsboroughs next door.'

Once, at a conference in Blackpool, a group of us from Nelson & Colne were having a jolly time at a reception in the Winter Gardens when Ted bore down on us and froze my normally garrulous supporters into total silence. The hush was only broken when Bernard Rothwell, chairman of my Association, said: 'Don't you sometimes feel, Ted, you'd rather be watching Th'orse of Year Show?' And Ted laughed.

I am sure that Ted was a very worthy man, but I never ceased to be astonished by his lack of elementary political skills. In the 1966 election the Conservative manifesto was entitled 'Action not Words'. I do not know whether Ted chose the title himself, but he certainly must have approved it, and it provided a vivid example of his failure to understand that politics is not just about doing the right thing. It is about using words to win minds and persuade people of the rightness of what is being done in their name. 'Action not words' in the world of politics is a recipe for disaster and Ted's short period as Prime Minister duly ended in disaster.

He then revealed a very petty streak in his frustration at being replaced as Leader of the Opposition by Margaret Thatcher. The bitterness he could not suppress spoiled him as a man, and Alec Douglas-Home got it entirely right when he said: 'It's such a waste. I always liked him very much. He's capable of great kindness and sensitivity too. He mucked it all up. You must not allow yourself to have a vendetta, particularly with a woman.'

Anyhow, Wilson was back in office where he busied himself giving the trade union bosses, who were the ones who had really beaten Ted, all they wanted. Parliament met and Michael Foot, the Secretary of State for Employment, introduced his first Trade Unions and Labour Relations Bill which repealed the Industrial Relations Act except the part which had increased the rights of trade unionists by giving them compensation for unfair dismissal and the right to longer periods of notice.

I was on the committee on the Bill along with a new member who was obviously a master of the intricacies of labour law and a rising star, Leon Brittan. In the chamber I had a difficult time. Whenever I rose to my feet at Prime Minister's Question Time the PM referred to me as 'the honourable member soon to finish his time in this place'. I had the smallest majority in the House and no one expected me to survive the next general election which, thanks to Labour's tiny majority, could not be long delayed. The expected election came in October 1974. Each evening we finished up canvassing in the dark and I remember how sinister looked the hordes of complete strangers being bussed into the constituency by Douglas Hoyle, the Labour candidate. Members of his union, ASTMAS, were all dressed alike in black leather jackets. They did not do it to frighten, but frightening they certainly looked.

During our time at Nelson & Colne we had become friendly with a number of very unusual people, some of whom would not normally have been expected to socialise with Tories. Wilf Banks, a life-long socialist with a little goatee beard which he had grown out of sympathy with Sydney Silverman – who had sported a similar appendage – had become a real chum. So had Stan Iveson, the national chairman of the Independent Labour Party. He had spent so much time chatting to Gilly during the February count that there were a lot of tongues wagging in Nelson and eventually poor Stan felt moved to write to the papers. His attempt to stem the rumours only made him the butt of more jokes, his letter in the *Nelson Leader* being captioned in bold type: 'They are just good friends'.

Things finally came to a head on the night of the October count. Just when my political future hung in the balance, Stan had a heart attack: and while not a single member of the Labour Party lifted a finger to help, the wife of the Tory candidate proceeded to give him the kiss of life. And, so effective was it that Stan recovered and went on to live for many more years.

When the result was declared I was out by 669 votes. Douglas Hoyle, who is now in the Lords and has become quite a pal of mine, held the seat until 1979 when he was defeated by John Lee. John lost the new seat of Pendle in 1992 and then went off and consoled himself by joining the Liberals. He is now also in the Lords.

Meanwhile, in the country Harold Wilson just achieved an over-all majority – by three seats. By 1976 that majority had disappeared as a result of by-election defeats, but the government managed to soldier on, bolstered for a year by the Lib–Lab pact. Then, on 28 March 1979, it lost a vote of confidence by one vote.

CHAPTER NINE

Out of Parliament
and Then Back

At first after my defeat I felt rather sorry for myself, but the feeling did not last long. First thing on the Friday morning after polling day Elspeth Stuart Mills (now Elspeth Pennant Williams) rang up and suggested we went on a walk round Malham Tarn, and half way round I realised that, far from feeling sad, I felt as if a large block of concrete had been lifted off my cranium and I was a free man again. My health also soon recovered.

My secretary, Jean Davy, who had been staying with us for the closing stages of the campaign, spent hours on the telephone trying to get herself another job and eventually she was successful. I, on the other hand, was jobless and had to decide whether I was going to practise in London with all the added expense of accommodation down there, or whether I was going to stay in the north. Doing that of course meant putting into reverse all the plans of the last few years and trying to lure back some of my old clients in Manchester.

I felt that for years I had been lucky to enjoy job satisfaction. Of course there had been peaks and troughs and at times the troughs had seemed pretty deep; but the peaks had more than compensated for them. It was even exhilarating to stand on the edge of the precipice knowing there were plenty of people standing behind ready to deliver a hefty shove to speed one's passage back to the bottom; and I would not have missed it for the world. I thought my defeat was the end of the road for me and any sadness was tinged with deep thankfulness for a wonderful experience and the great privilege of having served as an MP.

I got a nice letter from Ted Heath. I have been very critical of him and it would be quite wrong if I did not make plain that he was most gracious and kind to me after my defeat.

In January 1975, at the annual general meeting of the Nelson & Colne Conservative Association, I announced that I did not wish to be readopted as their candidate. And there can be little doubt that at that time I did feel that my career in politics was at an end, because in the same month I also declined an invitation to go for interview at Skipton.

On 26 April 1975 my mother died. She suffered a lot of pain towards the end and it was a merciful release. But her death was another sad happening after a difficult year. She was a lovely person who throughout her life never thought of herself but lived for her family. A few months before the end she wrote to us all:

My dear children,
 Thank you all a thousand times for all you have done for me in my life – I am sorry about my being tiresome in the last few years.
 All my love to you,
 Mummy.
 Could fill a book but can't write much.

At the end of 1974 a case of murder at the Habib Bank Rochdale brought a little light relief. A father and son were in a café opposite the bank and when the manager came out of the front door the son got up from his seat, ran across the street and thrust a dagger into the back of the manager's neck. Both father and son were charged with murder, the Crown alleging that immediately before the son had set off across the street the father had shouted in Urdu: 'Kill him.' My equipment for the defence included an Urdu dictionary, with the aid of which I managed to persuade the incompetent interpreter that the words uttered could have meant 'kill him', 'to hell with him' or 'fuck him'. The jury acquitted and the man's family gave me the dictionary as a memento.

But one case in which I was involved was a tragedy for the accused and caused me much worry and unhappiness. Stefan Kiszko faced trial at Leeds Crown Court for the murder of an eleven-year-old girl called Lesley Molseed: and I was briefed for the defence with Philip Clegg (later His Honour Judge Clegg) as my junior. Peter Taylor (later Lord Chief Justice) appeared for Crown. The jury returned a verdict of murder and our appeal to the Court of Appeal was dismissed.

Many years later, after I had become Home Secretary, solicitors acting for Kiszko wrote to the Home Office alleging a miscarriage of justice, and the matter was referred to the section in the Home Office which in those days looked into such cases. I gave instructions that when they had looked in to the matter the case should not come to me but to one of the ministers of state. However, the section submitted its report after I had left the Home Office and it was my successor, Kenneth Baker, who decided that the case should be referred back to the Court of Appeal because of new evidence casting doubt on the correctness of the conviction.

In February 1991 the case came up for hearing with Stephen Sedley (later Lord Justice Justice Sedley) acting for Kiszko and he had an astonishing story to tell. Medical evidence, he said, demonstrated that sperm found on the girl's clothing could not have come from Kiszko so he could not have been the killer. Furthermore, evidence to this effect had been available at the time of trial but had not been disclosed to either the defence or the prosecution. The conviction was set aside and Kiszko, after sixteen years in prison, was a free man.

The following Sunday a leader appeared in the *Sunday Times* alleging quite falsely that in the trial I had run a defence without Kiszko's authority. In making this assertion the leader writer was apparently relying on the fact that at an earlier hearing before the Court of Appeal Stephen Sedley had said there was a suggestion that I had acted without authority, but the leader writer failed to mention that at the full hearing when the conviction was overturned Sedley had told the court in plain terms that he was completely satisfied that advice had been given to Kiszko and his authority properly obtained.

The following day I issued a statement to the Press Association in these terms:

> The *Sunday Times* yesterday reported as if it were a fact the allegation made at the hearing in the Court of Appeal in December that Mr Kiszko's defence team put forward an alternative plea of manslaughter at his trial without his authority.
>
> As the leader of that team at the time I must make it quite clear that there is no truth in that allegation which was not pursued at the resumed hearing before the Court of Appeal last week.
>
> The last thing I wish to do now is to say anything which might cloud the happiness which last week's Court of Appeal decision will have brought to Mr Kiszko and his family after their appalling ordeal and so I will say no more than that his defence at the trial was properly conducted in accordance with our advice and his instructions on the basis of the information available to us at the time.
>
> Had any of us then known of the forensic evidence which persuaded the Court of Appeal that Mr Kiszko could not have committed the crime, the matter would have taken a very different course.

That should have been an end of the matter, but the upshot was that for years I received obscene, insulting and threatening letters from people influenced by what *The Times* and other papers had said. It was frequently alleged, among other things, that I had used my position as Secretary of State to delay the referral of the case to the Court of Appeal. None of my tormenters seemed prepared to accept the truth – that the whole appalling tragedy would not have happened had it been revealed to the Crown, let alone the defence, that there was evidence that Mr Kiszko could not have produced the sperm found on the dead girl.

In about 1977 Jenny went away to school. It was her own wish. She was not getting on very well at Westholme in Blackburn and she felt that with all her brothers away she must be missing something. When, however, she arrived at Queen Margaret's in York she found the work very hard and at first was pretty miserable. In one letter home she described what happened when on one occasion she did pass an exam:

I had my last exam today. It was phisics [sic]. Well you know the pass mark is forty and if you get anything over it is really good. Well, I got fifty-two and I passed. It was so nice because they said the results and it went like this. 'Yvonne Dicson 38 – fail, Alison Leslie 53 – pass, Jennifer 52 – pass. When the teacher told me what I got and said I had passed they all cheered and shouted Huyror [sic].

In 1978 I attended a Northern Circuit dinner in London and found myself sitting next to Mr Justice Kilner Brown who was then the presiding judge on the circuit. He said that he had been asked to find out whether I was trying to get back into the House of Commons or whether I had given up my political ambitions and wanted to go on the circuit bench. I said that at last I felt I had got politics out of my system and I had given up all ideas of going back into the Commons. Three weeks later I was at home when the telephone rang and I learned that David Walder, our own well-liked member for Clitheroe, had died of a heart attack. I knew at once, in spite of all I had said to Kilner Brown, that fate was calling. I simply could not pass up the chance of inheriting a safe seat in Parliament – and not just a safe seat but the seat where I lived and had my roots. I had to throw my cap in the ring, but I also knew that I could not possibly leave matters to take their course and just wait and see how I got on in the constituency selection process. For all I knew the Lord Chancellor might write any day asking me to take an appointment. Worse, he might pick up the papers one morning and read that the person who had been saying he had given up politics and wanted to go on the bench was being considered for selection as the Conservative candidate for Clitheroe. I would never be able to look the man in the face again. So I wrote to Kilner Brown saying that I would well understand if he thought I had taken leave of my senses but I really had meant what I had said when I had spoken to him a few weeks earlier. I did not, however, mean it any longer and I was going to take my chance at Clitheroe. I knew I was burning my boats. It was the gamble of a lifetime but one I had to take, and it made the following months altogether too exciting.

Eventually there came the day when I went to the Crest Hotel in Preston for the first round of interviews and took with me Victoria our cheeky younger daughter, then aged seven. I sat waiting for my interview along with three other would-be candidates and after a little while noticed that Victoria was missing. I set off to find her, opened the door of what turned out to be the room in which the interviews were being conducted and there she was sitting on the knee of the Association chairman. When I came back and laughingly related the story to my fellow interviewees, one said that it was clear he was wasting his time and he was going home.

But all was not over. I was through to the last four but at least one of the other three was a powerful contender, Jock Bruce-Gardyne. Jock had one thing against him. Some years before, he had inherited a safe Scottish seat but over the years he had seen it transformed first into a marginal seat and then, in October 1974, into a gain for the SNP. Anyhow, the Tories in Clitheroe decided that I was the better bet and duly selected me. Jock went off to be selected for Knutsford and an even bigger Tory majority.

A deliciously cruel story went the rounds. One of Jock's former constituents in South Angus happened to ask a member of the press visiting that part of Scotland: 'What has happened to Master Jock?' and got the reply, 'He's been selected for Knutsford with a 20,000 majority.' 'Oh!' said the Scotsman, 'it'll nay be enough for Master Jock.' Sadly the matter was never put to the test for Jock, having given distinguished service as a Treasury minister, contracted cancer and had to leave the Commons and ministerial office. He faced his misfortune with enormous courage and after a short time in the Lords died when still a comparatively young man. His death was a grievous loss to Parliament.

The Clitheroe by-election took place in the depths of winter – the 'winter of discontent'. So there was no shortage of speech material for a Conservative candidate. It was a time when words were spoken which shamed us as a nation. Bill Dunn (an ambulance driver) was quoted as saying, 'If it (industrial action) means lives lost, that's how it should be.' NUPE steward Stephen Eaton did not want to actually kill cancer patients but he seemed to think that delaying their treatment was quite okay. 'The only effect we are having on the treatment of cancer patients,' he said, 'is perhaps to slow it down.' Trade unionism seemed to have become a sick joke.

Margaret Thatcher came up to speak. I think she was the first Tory Leader of the Opposition who deigned to attend by-elections and she certainly entered into the spirit of mine.

Margaret arrived early one morning and our first port of call was Perseverance Mill, Padiham. The mill workers, male and female, wore 'Vote Labour' badges and when Margaret tried to engage a female cloth-looker in conversation she got nowhere, with the lady refusing to look up and answer her questions. Margaret would not give up. She did not move away as I might have done and look for a more comfortable customer. She stood her ground and made it plain that she was not for leaving until she got a reply, and eventually by sheer persistence she wrung out of the woman not only a reply but a smile. In these somewhat icy conditions we emerged into a mill yard packed with surly weavers; but our spirits soon revived for there across the road, hanging out of the upstairs windows of Progress Mills (our family firm) were smiling faces. Shouts of 'Vote Maggie' from a few were soon taken up by the rest, and the Labour supporters at Perseverance, while not put to flight, were put to shame. The difference between the two receptions was almost certainly due to the fact that Progress Mills was very much a family affair run almost single-handedly by my cousin John, where union wages were paid but the union itself had a minimal presence. I felt pretty smug about the whole business because I had told Margaret's office that the right place to visit was Progress and that Perseverance should be left well alone. The know-alls in London, however, said that it was quite wrong for the Leader of the Opposition to visit a nineteenth-century-looking place like Progress. She had to be supporting the best of modern industry. Anyhow, Margaret thought that here was a lifeline to be grasped and linking her arm with mine she set off across the road, dashed through the front door of Progress and into the waiting arms of the workers. We never looked back. From that moment onwards her visit to the constituency was a triumphal progress. The streets of Great Harwood were so packed that our cavalcade ground to a halt. There were bigger and even more enthusiastic crowds in the town of Clitheroe and in Longridge.

It was a very cold day and we repaired to the Punch Bowl at Hurst Green for lunch with the chairman of the Association, James Rawson, sitting on Margaret Thatcher's left. To my surprise he opened the conversation by suggesting it was about time we went for proportional representation. I thought the Leader of the Opposition would choke on her shrimp cocktail. 'Well,' she said, 'I suppose that is an excellent idea – if (and then a pause and a sniff) you don't want the Conservative Party to ever win another election.' James looked glumly at his plate and except for purposes of consumption did not open his mouth again. We then set off for Longridge and I was so carried away by the occasion that my hand found its way on to my leader's knee. Anyone who has found himself in that predicament knows that it is very much easier to get into that sort of mess than it is to get out of it. A quick withdrawal only serves to draw attention to the earlier act of folly, and a stealthy withdrawal only prolongs the time in which one's misdemeanour may be discovered. But all turned out all right. The Leader of the Opposition did not appear to know what was troubling me, and on our arrival at the Conservative Club she was ready with another spirited oration with which to complete her tour.

CHAPTER TEN

On the Ministerial Ladder

Polling Day came and I was back in the House with a major-ity of 12,500 over Labour. When the result was announced I moved the customary vote of thanks to the returning officer, pointing out that the same swing throughout Lancashire in a general election would mean Labour seat after Labour seat falling to the Tories and our becoming the government. I got a cool recep-tion which the President of my Association said was due to 'our not liking politics in Clitheroe'.

Taking my seat a second time was a bit of an anti-climax, and when on the Thursday I went to the weekly meeting of the 1922 Committee to be welcomed back little seemed to have changed, with Edward du Cann still chairman. It was said of Edward that when a young member asked him the time he put an affectionate arm round his shoulder and said: 'What time would you like it to be, dear boy?' And his somewhat oleaginous manner was not to everyone's taste; but over the years he worked hard for the Party and had for a time been Party Chairman.

The next few weeks only served to remind me how boring could be the life of a backbencher, but I did not have to endure it for long; for on 28 March came the 'no confidence' vote which brought about the fall of the Labour government.

That night the catering staff in the House of Commons were on strike and the dining room and tea room were closed. In those days there was an open-fronted coffee bar on Bridge Street and there, on the evening of 28 March, MPs and other vagrants stood eating bacon sandwiches and sipping hot drinks from chipped mugs while waiting for the ten o'clock division. When it came and the government lost, Jim Callaghan rose to say that he would recommend to the Queen that Parliament be dissolved; and shortly thereafter I was back home preparing for yet another election.

It was an election which set me something of a problem. So hard had we worked during the by-election only a few weeks before that we had hardly left a door un-knocked. I decided, therefore, to ignore the towns and villages and visit the isolated farms. I had a splendid reception from people who assured me that a visit from a politician was like a visit from outer space. In the event I was back with a majority of 11,579, the Conservatives had a majority of forty-four seats, and Britain had her first female Prime Minister.

On the day the new Parliament met I was sitting in the dining room when I was told that the Chief Whip wanted to see me. I went along to Michael Jopling's room and he asked me if I would like to be a whip; *not*, he stressed, a junior whip but a Lord Commissioner of the Treasury with the chance of promotion into a department sometime in the future. I fell for the story and joined the Office.

The next night I was again in the House of Commons dining room when the Prime Minister, who was at the next table, called over to me: 'What's that new member doing in the dining room without his jacket on? Go and have a word with him.' And I got up and gave Tony Marlow appropriate advice. The new Prime Minister also made it very plain that she did not like ministers on the front bench putting their feet up on the Table, even though it was an old custom of the House. 'You would not treat the furniture in your own home like that.' But tradition proved a lot stronger than her objections and this was one battle the PM lost.

The Whips Office was then, I think, of a very high standard. We had a lot of fun but took our responsibilities very seriously. 'Parties,' said Enoch Powell 'need whips as civilisation needs sewerage.' And we carried out our sometimes unpopular duties with the relish of well-paid sanitary inspectors. In the top office next to that of the Chief Whip sat Michael's deputy, John Stradling Thomas, Spencer Le Marchant, Tony Berry, Carol Mather, John MacGregor, James Douglas-Hamilton, Peter Morrison (the pairing whip) and myself. Downstairs in another office were the junior whips, Tony Newton, Bob Boscawen and Peter Brooke.

Spencer, with the grand title of Comptroller of Her Majesty's Household, gave us racing tips, sometimes putting money on horses for us and only confessing what he had done when he handed over the winnings. Tony Berry was Vice-Chamberlain of Her Majesty's Household and as such had on Mondays, Tuesdays, Wednesdays and Thursdays to send to the Queen a telegram of not less than 300 and no more than 750 words telling her of the goings-on in the House. Another of his duties was to stay behind at Buckingham Palace during the State Opening of Parliament as a hostage for the Queen's safe return.

James Douglas-Hamilton (then Lord James Douglas-Hamilton and now in the House of Lords as Lord Selkirk of Douglas) was a worrier. One Monday morning he reported that a friend of his who was a candidate for a Scottish seat had got himself into terrible trouble with his prospective constituents. Excessive zeal had led him to attend funerals to which he had not been invited.

James was a man of impeccable manners and when, later, he was translated to the Scottish Office those same good manners got him in to trouble. The driver of his official car was a rather elderly lady and the other drivers in the department complained that whenever his car stopped on arriving at its destination James, instead of waiting for the driver to open the door for him, jumped out and opened the door for the driver. They thought this was not in accordance with precedent and should be discouraged. Back in the Whips Office and when not writing a book about his uncle, a spitfire pilot, James drove himself and us insane with his tales of woe about the Scottish Conservatives backbench committee. Albert McQuarrie MP complained that the election for the officers of this committee of ten members had not been conducted properly. He knew this because before the election he had canvassed all the other nine members and each one had promised him their vote for chairman. How, therefore, could he not have been elected? The ballot papers were recounted with new scrutineers. There was only one vote for McQuarrie – presumably his own.

Bob Boscawen had during the War suffered terrible injuries which he bore with great fortitude, and he was a great companion. He and Carol Mather who, like Bob, had won an MC in France in 1944 and had been on Monty's staff, were the old soldiers who did their best to keep the rest of the office and junior MPs in order and properly dressed. On one occasion Carol reprimanded Tristan Garel-Jones for wearing a particularly bilious long, green Loden overcoat. 'The last time I saw anyone wearing a coat like that,' he said, 'I shot him.'

Michael Jopling, the Chief, took himself very seriously, and with good reason. A new government formed from a party which has been out of office for some years has a lot of tricks to learn, and a lot of things can go wrong when it comes to the management of business in the House. New ministers did not always turn up in the chamber at the right time and when they did turn up did not realise that what they said was not of the slightest importance. What was important was that they should keep talking until close to but not a second later than ten o'clock. Whips in their turn had to be ready to move the closure when the minister did sit down to prevent the business being talked out, or a member of the Opposition getting the last word. One awful night in the summer of 1980 a minister was not in the chamber when his business was reached. Spencer Le Marchant, the whip on duty, jumped up and down at the dispatch box bawling 'I beg to move' while the Opposition yelled 'Resign' and Michael Foot asked the Speaker to adjourn the House. Eventually Jim Prior, who had been in the corridor behind the Speaker's Chair, rushed into the chamber and began to make a speech in place of his missing junior minister. Unfortunately, he picked the wrong speech on the wrong subject and uproar continued unabated.

There was another occasion when things went very wrong. I reported to the Chief that there was much muttering in the Smoking Room about some business on the Order Paper. There were rumours of a rebellion and the possibility of a government defeat. 'Don't worry,' said Michael, 'Get all those people into the chamber to hear the minister winding up'; and at half past nine I flushed the mutterers out of the Smoking Room and pushed them into the chamber. They listened to the minister's winding-up speech and then, to a man, marched into the lobby and voted against the government. The next morning there was an emergency meeting in the Whips Office. A new edict was issued: 'Do all you can to keep our backbenchers out of the chamber. When a minister is replying to a debate encourage no one to listen.' Perhaps the strict enforcement of this command accounts for the many years of Conservative government which followed.

During the 1979–80 session I was the whip attached to the Department of the Environment and as such was responsible for the Housing Bill of that year. Monica Ferman wrote of the committee stage of the Bill in the *New Statesman* of 21 November 1980:

Kaufman led the eight Opposition members of the committee against John Stanley's eleven Conservatives. Plaid Cymru had one member – Dafydd Elis-Thomas, who saw fit to vote with Labour on all issues except one.

Kaufman was of course the wit and jester of the committee. He flirted outrageously with the chairman. On 14 February he opened proceedings by wishing Miss Fookes 'a happy St Valentine's Day from all your bashful admirers'. A few sittings later, when an amendment was described as 'a Trojan horse in the Bill' he winked, and she dimpled delightfully as he turned to the Chair and asked 'but who is Helen of Troy?'

David Waddington, the government whip, seldom spoke except in Greek, spending more time searching for his supporters in the corridors just before a vote was taken in a division. He usually returned with an Hon. Member – such as John Major – only slightly mauled.

One day the Chief said that as a great privilege the whips had been invited to go along to No. 10 for tea – a golden opportunity for us as business managers to tell the Prime Minister how we felt things were going on the political front. We trooped in to the drawing room and for a while there was desultory conversation. Suddenly, Tony Newton (who after a very distinguished career went to the Lords as Lord Newton of Braintree and, sadly, died in March 2012) had a rush of blood to the head. 'Prime Minister,' he said, 'my wife is a school teacher and you have no idea what is happening in our schools these days. My wife says that in the mid-morning break the pupils are copulating in the bushes.' You could have heard a pin drop. It is the only time I can remember the PM being rendered speechless. Afterwards we made poor Tony's life a misery, constantly questioning what had made him commit this act of political suicide and assure a dramatic end to his career when it had barely begun. In fact of course, Tony went on to great things and we will never know whether the Prime Minister misheard what he said or was greatly impressed by his frank exposition of a matter of great social significance.

Spencer Le Marchant and I were early risers, always in the office by about 8.30 a.m. He used to spend his time ringing the stock-broking firm in which he was a partner. I used to see my secretary and get on with the constituency correspondence. One morning I rang my secretary and she said she was very busy and could not possibly come to do my work. Spencer overheard and passed me a note – 'sack her' it said. 'Can't,' I scribbled back, 'who am I going to get to replace her?' 'Keep her on the line' whispered Spencer and started dialling furiously. 'Got one!' he cried. 'Well, Mrs -----,' I said, 'I think the time has come for us to part.' Half an hour later, thanks to Spencer, a secretary with impeccable credentials stood at my desk and many of my problems were solved.

In September 1980 I went on a Commonwealth Parliamentary Association (CPA) visit to Malawi – my travelling companions being David Ennals, Bill Whitlock, John Wilkinson and James Kilfedder. David Ennals was well-meaning but sometimes some-thing of an embarrassment. President Banda was much given to dancing with the ladies of the country at great rallies staged so that they could demonstrate their love for him. Once, in the middle of the bush we came up behind a lorry in the back of which were forty or so women. We were told that they were on their way back from National Day where they had been dancing for the President. 'Signal to the lorry driver to stop,' said Ennals, 'I want to dance with them.' And in the middle of nowhere forty or so exhausted women were asked to disembark so that D. Ennals MP could caper and cavort around them, doing what he imagined was a Banda-like leap, skip, hop and glide, with fly-whisk raised to heaven.

The Malawian MP who was looking after us said that in his view mice were far more tasty than sausage when they were fried with their fur burnt off. Custom had it, he said, that you start with the tail and finish with the head. Perhaps he was pulling our legs. In Blantyre a poster in a school classroom explained the nutritional value of and best way to cook caterpillars and ants. At one village David Ennals asked the headman if he had to go far to get his water. He replied: 'No, I've got eight wives'; and he looked very well on it. So, in fairness, did the wives.

Later in the trip we visited a hospital out in the wilds and a woman needed a blood transfusion. John Wilkinson very courageously offered to provide blood but, much to our amusement, half an hour after doing so he fainted.

I decided that it would be a great pity not to visit Rhodesia in the dying moments of UDI. There were no direct flights from Malawi because of sanctions, so I flew via Johannesburg. As the plane approached Salisbury Airport the cabin staff insisted on the blinds being drawn because, they said, of the risk of a missile attack, and when we entered Meikles Hotel other guests were leaving their rifles with the hall porter.

By the end of 1980 I was the whip for the Department of Trade and Industry, Keith Joseph being Secretary of State, and each morning had to attend the minister's meeting. Keith's right-hand man was Viscount Trenchard who, I imagine, was recruited to the government because of his expertise in the City, but who had the quaintest ideas as to how to perform as a minister. Keith himself had some odd habits. On taking the chair at a morning meeting he would cry 'Agenda!' which was the cue for everyone to shout out what he wanted to have discussed that morning. Every morning Tom Trenchard shouted out 'Private sector!' and every morning Keith responded in a pained voice, 'Not the private sector again.' Michael Marshall, the junior minister, had a room with a leaky roof and on entering one had to avoid tripping over one of the many buckets on the floor.

In January 1981 I was sitting in the Whips Office when Michael Jopling phoned from No. 10 and asked me to get round as soon as possible. When I got there he was standing outside the PM's room with his face wreathed in smiles. 'I reckon I've done pretty well for the office. Three of you are to be promoted – Peter Morrison, John MacGregor and you; you because I have persuaded the PM that it is necessary to have a lawyer in the Department of Employment to look after trade union reform and they are losing their lawyer as a result of Paddy Mayhew going off to the Home Office. Leon Brittan whom he is replacing is to be Chief Secretary.'

Jim Prior had been Secretary of State for Employment since the general election and had been much criticised for his so-called softly softly approach to the trade unions. Reform of industrial relations law was urgently required but Jim had taken the view that there would be big trouble with the unions if reform came in other than small doses. The result had been a very tame first Trade Union Bill, which made some small inroads in to the closed shop and outlawed some more blatant types of secondary action i.e. industrial action against employers not directly involved in an industrial dispute.

None of this was to the liking of Margaret Thatcher and when I went to see her on my appointment she made it clear that she wanted a metaphorical bomb put under Jim. The horrors of the closed shop were much in the public eye at that time because of the case of the Sandwell dinner ladies who had been sacked by the Sandwell local authority for refusing to join a union; and the Prime Minister was determined to see that abuse of union power of this or, for that matter, any other sort was stopped.

Jim was a delight to work with and very well liked by his officials. They, however, seemed to think that the Department of Employment's role was to see that the interests of the trade union movement were properly represented in government. That, to put it mildly, was not how the Prime Minister saw things, and I had come back into Parliament heartily fed up with the irresponsibility of the trade unions and their pretensions to be almost a partner in government. In my view, the Conservative government was there to bring about radical reform in the field of industrial relations, to get rid of, not condone, abuse of power by the trade union barons and to look after the interests of ordinary working people.

Jim knew he had to prepare for the next step in trade union reform, but he was not inclined to say how big he thought that step should be and was in no great haste to make the next move. One thing in particular was absolutely clear. He had shut his mind entirely to the most obvious way forward which was to remove from trade unions the immunity from actions for damages for the wrongs of their servants or agents which they had won in 1911.

Peter Morrison and I had joined the DE on the same day and being the most junior of all the departmental ministers had to share a driver named Trevor; and I, like he, lived south of the river. That meant that Trevor called for me first in the morning, and then went on to collect Peter from Cambridge Street. Usually, however, Trevor was late, putting forward as an excuse the fact that the hamster had got out.

I was the minister responsible for health and safety, and one of my first tasks was to try and sort out a problem concerning an ICI site in western Scotland. There was a dock at which explosives were loaded and unloaded, and someone had woken up to the fact that the local authority had built an enormous sports complex, dance hall and recreation centre across the water from the dock. Surely, if there was a massive explosion on the dock at a time when the centre was full many lives would be lost. An expert on safety worked out what was called the societal risk, not the risk of one person being killed but the chances of a lot of people being killed, and he advised that the risk was unacceptable. A careful measurement had been made of the distance from the dock to the sports complex, a careful survey had been carried out of the quantities of explosives being handled and a meticulous note had been taken of the number of people frequenting the local authority's establishment at times when the dock was being used. After that, the whole lot were multiplied together and divided by the square root of the town clerk, and the answer was that something had to be done. Up to Scotland I went and talked over the problem with the local authority, then with ICI and then with the HSE (Health and Safety Executive) experts, but no reasonable solution to the problem could be found. But a solution was found. The man who had measured the distance from the dock to the sports hall was asked to get out his measure again and have another go. Off he went and soon returned triumphant. The sports hall was 200 yards further away than he had originally thought and the experts, having made another of their elaborate calculations, delivered their verdict: 'On the new evidence now available there is no need to do anything'. Business could continue as usual; and I could return to London to claim that another knotty problem had been resolved.

In September 1981 there came a major reshuffle. In the summer Mark Carlisle had told me that he felt his job was at risk. I was sad for him but it was difficult not to smile at the story he told to justify his pessimism. 'I was asked to go to No. 10 for breakfast,' he said. 'When I got there the PM told me that Keith Joseph would be joining us shortly. I did not like the sound of that because I knew Keith wanted my job. But worse was to follow. I sat at the table where there was a nice bowl of strawberries and was about to tuck in when the PM shouted: 'No, Mark! Those are for Keith. There are prunes for you on the sideboard.' 'I knew then,' said Mark, 'that the game was up.'

In another important change in the reshuffle Jim Prior was moved to Northern Ireland, and Norman Tebbit descended on the DE in fighting form. He gave instructions that a special alarm system should be placed in his office because some demonstrators had in the last weeks of Jim's reign managed to get past the security at the front doors and all the way up to the ministerial floor. A few days passed and Norman realised that, in spite of his orders, nothing had been done. He summoned the man responsible who had the temerity to say that he had decided that the matter of the alarm was not a top priority. Norman's rage not only terrified the delinquent official, who left shaking like a leaf, but the message that the new Secretary of State was not a man to be trifled with spread through the department like wildfire.

Norman's time at the DE showed how one man with determination can change the ethos of a whole organisation. What he did in a remarkably short space of time was change the DE from being the apologist of the trade union movement to being its scourge. His mischievous humour at first horrified officials; his blistering attacks on the TUC, the union leaders and all those concerned to look after the one-legged, black lesbian rather than Mr and Mrs Ordinary English caused consternation. But in time officials began to enter in to the spirit of things and even share in a bit of the mischief. We began to work up a really radical new Employment Bill and told the parliamentary draughtsmen that it was going to be called The Extension of the Rights of Employees Bill to emphasise how the rights of ordinary people which had been invaded by the trade unions were now to be restored to them. Devising such a controversial title was quite a good ploy because Whitehall spent so much time thinking of arguments against the proposed name of the Bill they had little energy left to attack the substance. And plenty of substance we were determined there should be, principally the virtual abolition of the closed shop and the removal of nearly all the legal immunities the trade unions had attracted over the years.

Norman and I both quoted with relish the report of the 1903 Royal Commission set up after the Taff Vale judgment. For, with Sidney Webb one of its members, it had strongly urged that trade unions should be liable like everyone else for wrongful acts.

There is no rule of law so elementary, so universal or so indispensable as the rule that a wrongdoer should be made to redress his wrong. If trade unions were exempt from this liability they would be the only exception, and it would then be right that that exemption should be removed.

This fundamental principle was first accepted and then rejected by the Liberal government of 1906. It was high time, in spite of the extension of the immunities by Labour governments in 1965 and 1976, that the principle was reaffirmed.

We were introducing the Bill at just the right time. Unemployment and industrial change had reduced the membership of and weakened the trade unions. The public were fed up with their behaviour and there was no way the Labour Opposition could make the status quo look respectable.

One cause célèbre about this time caused me much embarrassment and Norman much mirth. For years an absurd body created by the DE had been used to help enforce the work permit system. It was called VOCA which I think stood for the Vocal and Orchestral Concert Association. Before I arrived at the DE I had imagined that the work permit system was there to help enforce immigration control and to prevent foreigners coming in to the country and pinching British people's jobs. Not on your life. The DE considered that the work permit system was there to protect vested interests from competition and, in this instance, to ensure that British people were not able to listen to foreign orchestras.

I was told that VOCA had for long ruled that foreign orchestras should not be allowed to give more than five concerts on a visit and I was therefore advised that the Los Angeles Philharmonic Orchestra, which had contracted to give seven performances, was out of order. The necessary work permits could not be issued. I was told that if the permits were issued lasting damage might be done to the BBC Symphony Orchestra and indeed music in Britain would die, and the country would become a cultural desert. In short, civilisation as we knew it would come to an end and posterity would hold the new Parliamentary Under-Secretary of State for the Department of Employment entirely responsible. Could I really take such a burden on my inadequate shoulders? Clearly not. The work permit applications must be refused.

But I had not reckoned with Mr Jasper Parrot (not Carrot), an impresario who was, I suppose, the agent for the Los Angeles Philharmonic Orchestra and responsible for arranging the tour. Neither had I reckoned with Mr Parrot's energetic and persistent MP, Sir Brandon Rhys-Williams.

Brandon and J. Parrot came to see me. I listened patiently but, sticking to my departmental brief, refused to budge. Brandon promptly applied for an adjournment debate and I still refused to budge; and afterwards he and Parrot accosted me in the Central Lobby and complained bitterly about my intransigence.

They demanded to see Norman Tebbit who, having other things on his mind, told them to jump out of the window, or words to that effect. It was not the reply they had expected, and that very evening Brandon, still suffering from the lash of Norman's tongue, went up to the Prime Minister in the division lobby and in loud and querulous tones complained about (a) the decision and (b) the way he had been treated by Norman. Looked at from Brandon's point of view there was good news and there was bad news. The bad news was that a whip quickly reported to Norman that Brandon had been sneaking to the PM at which Norman strode across to Brandon, picked him up by the back of his jacket and shook him with some vigour. The good news for Brandon was that his remarks made a great impression on the Prime Minister – so great indeed that the next day she phoned Norman, gave him an enormous rocket and told him that his civil servants and his under-secretary must have been quite mad to refuse the work permits and the decision had to be reversed forthwith. Norman, hooting with laughter, told his private secretary that his mistress's orders had to be obeyed, but he did not utter a word of complaint to me, or about me to anyone else.

He deserved a present. I bought a large stuffed parrot and numerous coloured hat pins which I proceeded to stick in the bird. I then presented it to Norman who suspended it on a piece of string above his desk where it remained for many months to come. Visitors, high and low, always asked him to explain the parrot which he did with great gusto and in terms which would not have amused its namesake. To this day I do not know whether the pins worked.

On a Friday towards the end of 1981 there was a debate on unemployment on an Opposition motion. Many thought I was crazy to volunteer to reply on behalf of the government, and the Opposition was very cross having expected the government to put up someone from either the Treasury or the Department of Industry. But I did myself a good turn. My speech went down very well and earned me a nice compliment from Jack Weatherill who was in the chair. I wound up in the debate on the second reading of the Employment Bill which contained the Tebbit proposals for reform of trade union law, including the virtual abolition of the closed shop. I was flattered when Cross-Bencher of the *Sunday Express* wrote, 'Many Tory MPs rate it one of the most aggressive and intelligent winding up speeches in years'. A friend quipped, 'If you don't look out you're going to get yourself promoted and then you'll be in a real mess.'

At Christmas 1981 I noticed that Norman was about to go home with not one but two dispatch boxes. I commiserated with him for having so much work to do over the holiday. He looked rather sheepish and opened up the boxes one of which contained a melon and the other smoked salmon.

At about this time I was asked to take part, with Angus Ogilvy and one or two other nobs, in a rather swell event in the City of London. Young people had been invited to show their skill in arts and crafts; and their achievements were laid out for inspection in the Mansion House. This is a cautionary tale and explains why MPs and ministers get pretty angry when told by the press that they are living it rich while poor journalists have to sustain themselves on little but baked beans and beer. We all looked at the entrants and what they had produced, and we dished out the awards. Then it was our turn, and we stepped forward to receive a little thank you for our efforts. Angus Ogilvy was presented with a pretty little silver dish, the next in line a rather fine painting, the third some brass candlesticks. I had not come expecting anything, but I cannot deny that by now my appetite was whetted. I was full of expectations but far too well brought up to show disappointment when I was handed a well-turned bread board.

When I think of 1982 I think of the Falklands, not of my own work in the Department. On the day after the Argentine invasion I, along with a number of other junior ministers, went to the PM's room in the House of Commons to hear the Prime Minister talk about what had happened and what was to be done; and then on the Saturday the House met for an emergency debate. It was a disaster, with a dreadful speech from John Nott. I travelled back to London on Monday convinced somebody's head was going to have to roll and, in the event, Peter Carrington, one of the most capable members of the Cabinet and one of the most honourable of men, resigned; as did Humphrey Atkins, the foreign affairs spokesman in the Commons and Richard Luce. John Nott went when the war was over.

The behaviour of the BBC during the Falklands War was appalling. In the country there was a great upsurge of patriotism and pride in the way our forces had responded when called upon to repel aggression, but the BBC and its employees seemed to find such emotions quite incomprehensible. In reply to criticisms that the BBC never referred to 'our' forces during the war and seemed to show no particular emotional commitment to them, Mr Richard (later Sir Richard) Francis, managing director, BBC Radio, said the BBC carefully distinguished between 'Argentine' and 'British' forces, but 'we [the BBC] have no task force in the South Atlantic; and the BBC has no role to boost the morale of British troops or rally the British people around the flag. The widow of Portsmouth is no different from the widow of Buenos Aires.'

The BBC may have thought it smart and trendy to be uninvolved in the war; but they were entirely out of step with the British people, as were also all too many churchmen. There was no doubt about the pride of the servicemen who attended the service in St Paul's on Monday 26 July 1982 – pride in a job well done. They had come, I am sure, to thank God for giving us victory, but those responsible for arranging the service could not bear to talk in those terms and had devised a wishy-washy theme of thanksgiving for the cessation of hostilities. When the Church does not reflect the pride and joy of ordinary men and women at a job well done in a righteous cause it cannot be surprised if congregations walk out of the doors.

I got back to London on the first Monday of the New Year and there was a message from Downing Street asking me to ring the Prime Minister. I rang to find that I was to be Minister of State at the Home Office with responsibility for immigration matters, in place of Tim Raison.

CHAPTER ELEVEN

Entering the Home Office

On 7 January 1983 *The Guardian* reported:

> Into Mr Raison's hot spot comes a minister who has travelled fast
> since joining the government. David Waddington is a barrister
> and businessman who found no difficulty in facing out Labour
> indignation at the rising unemployment figures when he served
> under Mr Tebbit at Employment. A tough and combative parlia-
> mentary operator he has clearly been given a flattering promotion.

It was kind of *The Guardian* to write in those terms, but I
was arriving at the Home Office faced with a problem for
which there was no solution. In December there had been a
Tory backbench rebellion when new immigration rules, making it
easier for foreign wives to gain admission to the country, had been
thrown out by the House of Commons. The obvious course was to
table new rules tightening up the admission criteria, but this had
been made more or less impossible by a ruling of the European
Court of Human Rights extending the right of a man to bring into
the country a foreign wife. So there were difficulties ahead, but I
was not fully aware of them when the next morning I arrived at the
Home Office in good cheer and ready for action. The correct postal
address of the building was 1 Petty France but Willie Whitelaw, the
Secretary of State, had soon spotted that to call it that would make

us all a laughing stock so it was decided to pretend that it was round the corner and to call it 50 Queen Anne's Gate. And there at the door of 50 Queen Anne's Gate I was greeted by Sir Brian Cubbon, the Permanent Secretary, and taken up to see the Secretary of State. Willie, sprawled on a sofa and in an expansive mood, told me what my job was and told me to get on with it.

The next day, at the routine morning meeting, I met my fellow ministers – Paddy Mayhew, the other Minister of State, Rodney Elton, under-secretary in the Lords, and David Mellor, a new under-secretary in the Commons. My place at the table was directly opposite Willie but the view was somewhat obstructed by two ornamental brass prison gates and a clutch of truncheons.

My private secretary and assistant private secretary were both hard workers dealing with the enormous number of immigration cases finding their way to my office. So many indeed were there that the files had to be wheeled in on hospital-style trollies, hundreds at a time. Cases found their way to the minister's office as a result of what were known as MPs' representations. Broadly speaking, the minister was not troubled with a case unless an MP had come on the scene at the request of one of his constituents. If an MP had become interested, the case was not dealt with by an official but looked into by the minister personally who then had to write to the MP telling him of his ruling.

A typical case arose in this way. A Pakistani living in Bradford would sponsor a visit to England by some friend or relative. When the friend or relative arrived at Heathrow the Immigration Service had to decide whether he or she was a genuine visitor intending to return home after a short stay in Britain or a would-be immigrant determined to get into Britain and stay in Britain. If the immigration officer, having questioned the person about his or her background and intentions, determined he or she was not a genuine visitor he would refuse entry. The relative would then go to his or her MP and the MP would ring up Heathrow or the Home Office and demand that the person should not be removed back to Pakistan until the MP had made representations on the person's behalf. The representations were considered by officials who drafted a letter of response for signature by the minister. The minister considered the case and either signed the letter which had been offered up to him or rejected official advice and drafted a different response. All this took many weeks if not months. Sometimes the MP would not take 'no' for an answer and either demanded a meeting so that he could argue the case in person or bombarded the minister with letters raising new points and daring the minister to remove the passenger before he had answered all these points in minute detail.

This meant that a person who was clearly not entitled to enter the country was often able to stay for months, and many tried to use the time they had won to make themselves irremovable. Marriage was one obvious method. Another was to get a job and then get a body like the Joint Council for the Welfare of Immigrants (JCWI) to argue that in a matter of months he had made himself entirely indispensable either to the British economy or the race relations industry or both.

There were then all the cases in which people, having been given permission to enter as visitors or having been refused entry as visitors but granted temporary admission, disappeared into the undergrowth. Years later a man would be picked up by the police and then you could be sure it would be argued on his behalf that although he had cheated and lied to get into the country, and had then, by disappearing, cost the taxpayer a mountain of money, he should be allowed to make his home here.

There was then the problem of husbands and wives. Should men settled here be able to import wives? Should wives settled here be able to import husbands? In principle, yes. I would consider it an appalling interference with my daughter's rights if she was prevented from coming back to England to live here with her Australian husband. But she was born here. She is British. Should someone who is not British have the same rights? And surely, whatever the answer to that question, a person settled here should not be able to use marriage as a mere device to get someone into the country.

We were constantly told that we had to respect the institution of the arranged marriage. If a man wanted to bring a woman into the country for marriage he should be allowed to do so, even if he had never clapped eyes on her, even if he had been paid a substantial sum of money to marry her and thus facilitate her entry. But when it came to an application by an Indian or Pakistani girl in England to bring in an Indian or Pakistani boy and we argued that the custom of the arranged marriage required the woman to go and live in the man's home not the man to travel half way across the world to come and live with the woman, a completely different set of arguments were paraded. How could the woman, having lived in England for some years, be expected to face the rigours of the Indian climate?

The self-proclaimed experts on these matters, and there were many, insisted that we were grappling with a non-problem. The number of people in Britain whose origins lay in the Indian subcontinent was already very large. In a few years' time boys and girls who had grown up in Britain would not be looking overseas for partners. They would be marrying those who had been brought up in the same way as themselves. Illiterate peasants from the Punjab would not suit them. All this completely ignored the appallingly low living standards which most people in the Indian subcontinent endured. For them, winning the right to live in Britain was like winning the football pools, and those who had been lucky enough to get to Britain were expected to give their relations back in the subcontinent the chance to enjoy some of the same riches. The custom of the arranged marriage was a ready tool ready to help them carry out this family obligation.

There were also rather more sinister reasons why the father of an Indian or Pakistani girl in Britain might prefer her to marry someone from the subcontinent. The boy would be likely to make a far more docile son-in-law than a boy brought up in Britain, and certainly would not expect the same sort of wage. Indeed, if he caused any trouble, if he became too demanding, he could be told that if he did not watch out the Home Office could be enlisted to speed his passage home.

And so, as the years went by, we did not see fewer people entering the country as husbands and wives, as fiancés and fiancées. We saw more and more; and by the time I left the Home Office there was not the slightest evidence of the flow abating.

But back to the immediate problem with which, at the beginning of 1983, Willie and I were faced. The immigration rules which had been thrown out by the House had tried to comply with the ruling of the European Court of Human Rights without allowing completely free entry for spouses and fiancés, but at the general election the Conservative Party had promised to toughen up immigration control not weaken it and, in saying that a man could import a wife or fiancée provided his primary purpose in marrying or contracting to marry the girl was not to obtain entry into the country for her, the rules marked a weakening of the control. And, said the Tory backbenchers, if we cannot do what Parliament wants to do because of a bunch of unworldly lawyers in the European Court of Human Rights, we are in a real mess and the government had better try and get us out of it. Much the same arguments against equally unworldly decisions of the Court are advanced today.

Willie and I went to see the executive of the 1922 Committee where there was much hand-wringing but no suggestions as to how to sort out the mess; and eventually with heavy hearts we decided we had no option but to table another set of rules broadly similar to those that had been rejected. All we could do as a sop was make a change in the burden of proof and require an applicant to prove that the primary purpose of the marriage was not to obtain entry rather than make the immigration officer show that it was. By offering this very small concession we managed to persuade a reluctant House to let the new rules through.

There was one type of case which a minister always dealt with, even if no MP had shown an interest in the matter. Every case of a person claiming the right to stay in Britain because of fear of persecution in the country from which he had come deserved, and got, the most careful consideration.

Back in 1983 there was a Refugee Council which took an interest in the welfare of those who sought asylum, but there was no formal procedure to ensure that individual cases were brought to the attention of the council. Often, therefore, the only investigation into a claim for asylum was carried out by a refugee section at the headquarters of the Immigration Service in Lunar House, Croydon.

Before my arrival in the Home Office a man called Papasoiu had travelled to Britain from the Continent and had walked into a police station in the East End, presumably to ask for help. He could not speak a word of English and at first the police, who called in numerous interpreters to assist, did not even know the man's nationality. Eventually, however, someone recognised him as a Romanian and when questioned by a Romanian interpreter Mr Papasoiu said that he had been imprisoned in Romania for trying to leave the country without permission and on his release had made a second and successful attempt at escape. Naturally he was frightened of going back and wanted to stay in Britain as a refugee. He did not explain why he had chosen Britain as his place of refuge or how he had found his way to Britain.

At subsequent interviews the story was enlarged and enlarged, and eventually Mr Papasoiu was saying that he had been imprisoned not once but three times and each time had been imprisoned for three years, making nine years in all. Enquiries were made through our post in Bucharest and the Home Office was told that it was most improbable that Mr Papasoiu had been treated as he suggested. On the basis of this information, and because Mr Papasoiu, with his changes of story, could hardly be thought a reliable witness, the application for asylum was turned down.

This was the state of play when I came on the scene. The application for asylum had been rejected but no arrangements had been made for Papasoiu's removal; and in due course I was asked by officials whether appropriate arrangements should be put in hand. No one suggested to me that the refusal of asylum did not necessarily mean that he should be removed. Still less did anyone suggest that the case should go forward to the Secretary of State for him to decide whether and, if so, when removal should take place. As far as I could see the buck stopped with me. And I accepted the advice given me by officials that there was no chance of any other country accepting Mr Papasoiu and the only place to which he could be returned was Romania, the place from which he had said that he had come.

I do not know how it came to the notice of Bernard Braine (then MP for Essex SE) that Papasoiu was about to be removed, but on the very day on which removal had been planned Bernard rang me up and asked me to reverse the decision. I said that in the absence of new evidence I did not think I could. He was not pleased and delivered a broadside on the BBC. The case was then taken up by others and soon there developed a press campaign of vilification and abuse the likes of which I had never before experienced, and have never experienced since. In the *Sunday Express* Michael Toner virtually accused me of being a murderer. Every word spoken by Papasoiu was accepted as gospel truth, every rebuttal by the Home Office was summarily dismissed. Toner's choice phrases included:

> Papasoiu was bundled into an aircraft bound for Bucharest. And now is in gaol there, helpless in the power of a regime he loathes and fears. Without hope. He has been trying to get here (to Britain) for fourteen years. He made three attempts to get out of his native Romania before he finally succeeded. For those attempts and for his defiance of communist discipline he has served a total of nine years in Romanian gaols. It is idle now to speculate what persuaded David Waddington and his advisers to commit this wicked act. It is too late now for Mr Papasoiu. He is finished. We shall deserve to share in the shame which he (Waddington) has brought upon the whole country.

Gradually the truth emerged, much no doubt to Mr Toner's displeasure. The Romanians would not allow Papasoiu to enter the country and in due course he arrived in Austria where, it turned out, he was wanted for crimes committed on a previous visit.

When next the British people saw Papasoiu he was on television yelling from a window at his Austrian refugee camp that he wanted to marry the girl who, while he had been in England, had been teaching him English. The English girl promptly announced that she had already rejected his advances. Then came the news which proved that the Home Office had been right all along. It was discovered that, far from being in prison in Romania, Mr Papasoiu had spent the previous ten years wandering around Europe, much of the time in Italy.

For nearly a month Gilly and I suffered appalling abuse from Toner and others, but when the Home Office was entirely vindicated only the *Daily Mail* wrote anything which could, by the greatest stretch of imagination, be termed an apology. From Toner himself there was a deafening silence.

The whole episode taught me many lessons. I learned of the reluctance of the British press ever to admit they are wrong. I learned that it is not enough for a minister to make the right decision. He has got to take a great deal of time dressing up that decision in the right language so that the dumbest of journalists will understand why it had to be taken and the most astute lawyer cannot say that it has been taken without proper consideration of all the facts and without following the proper procedures. It also taught me that the first job of a Minister of State is to take the shot and shell which might otherwise rain on his Secretary of State. I certainly performed that task admirably.

Following the Papasoiu case it was decided to remove the distinction between asylum and refugee status – a distinction not recognised by anyone outside the Home Office. Far more important, it was decided that in any future case where an individual was claiming asylum but was unrepresented by lawyers, the Refugee Council would be told, so that it could make representations on the individual's behalf. The decision turned out to have wide and not altogether satisfactory implications because when the flow of people seeking asylum later increased dramatically, long delays in processing applications were aggravated by delays on the part of the council.

Soon the 1983 election was upon us, the first in which I was given a fairly big speaking role outside my own constituency. It is easy to say now that the Falklands War and the reviving economy made success certain; but the advantage could all have been thrown away in a bad campaign. But thanks to Cecil Parkinson, the campaign was as slick and professional as any I have known. I only spent five days in Ribble Valley; the rest of the time I spent travelling round the country. Perhaps keeping out of the way accounted for my substantial majority. The result in Ribble Valley (which had been created in the wake of boundary changes earlier in the year, but with Clitheroe town still its centre) was:

Carr (SDP/Alliance) 10,632
Saville (Labour) 6,214
Waddington (Conservative) 29,223
Conservative majority 18,591

The government had increased its overall majority to 144. I went down to London as soon as it was clear that the government was safely back in office. I busied myself spring-cleaning the pantry in our house in Courtenay Street while I waited for a call from No. 10. Nothing happened and eventually I rang what I hoped was still my private office and asked the chap who I hoped was still my secretary to try and find out what was going on. A few minutes later I learned what I should have known all along. If ministers were staying put they would not hear anything. I was advised to come into the Home Office at once to see the new Secretary of State, Leon Brittan.

Leon was sitting on the same sofa as the one from which Willie had greeted me. He looked quite overcome and kept saying 'I can't believe it.' Neither could several others, who told me that they thought promotion from Chief Secretary to Home Secretary far too big a step. Goodness knows what the same people thought when not all that long afterwards someone was promoted from Chief Whip to Home Secretary.

In September 1983 Gilly and I went on a visit to India, Pakistan and Bangladesh. Our travelling companions were Hayden Phillips, the under-secretary in the Home Office responsible for immigration and later Permanent Secretary in the Lord Chancellor's Department, and Jim Acton, my Private Secretary. The purpose of the trip was to see how immigration control operated in the subcontinent where all applications to come to Britain for settlement were processed. Visitor visas had not yet been introduced, but even so there was a considerable burden of work at our posts.

Arriving in Karachi we visited our small post there and then flew up to Islamabad. Pakistan was out of the Commonwealth at the time so our host was the Ambassador, Sir Oliver Forster. Anthony Goodenough, later a High Commissioner, first in Ghana and then in Canada, and after retirement a neighbour of ours in Somerset, was Head of Chancery. We went up to Murree, a hill station, and on to Nathi Gali where there was a pretty little church, locked but, as one could see through the windows, in perfect condition. On the way down we stopped in a square in the centre of garrison town called Abbottabad (the place where Bin Laden met his death). When Jim was not looking I strode across the road and into a shop. Minutes later Hayden realised I had gone, turned on Jim and grasping him by the collar shouted: 'You've lost the minister!' A frantic search followed which ended in an army surplus store where I was inspecting the ties on display. I picked the best-looking one which turned out to be the tie of the Pakistan Army Junior Catering Corps.

In those days there was an English-language newspaper in Pakistan called *The Leader*. One letter in the correspondence columns read thus: 'On behalf of the Punjab Town Residents Association I seek the cooperation of your esteemed daily and request you to kindly highlight our grievances through your bold columns. The main problems of the residents are enumerated seriatim below.' There then followed a catalogue of misfortunes of monstrous proportions.

In the same edition there was a headline 'TRAIN SEAT SELLERS' GANG ATTACK RAILWAY WORKER':

An organised gang engaged in selling seats in passenger trains is operating at the Caritt Railway Station. The members of the gang board the train in the washing yard and occupy most of the seats. When the train comes on to the platform the passengers find all the seats occupied. The gang's agents at the platform then strike deals with the needy passengers and sell seats at fantastic rates. Yesterday when the members of the gang tried to board a passenger train in the washing yard, shunting porter Mazhar Sultan tried to prevent them. At this the gang members attacked Mazhar.

In Islamabad there was the second largest British Embassy in the world. This was largely because of the number of immigration officers and Foreign Office staff there to process applications by people hoping to come and live in Britain.

A member of the embassy staff was in trouble. He had been in the habit of visiting a local restaurant, always taking with him his own pot of tea. The owner of the establishment had accepted that he was a young man of eccentric tastes who liked only one particular blend of tea which was not obtainable in Islamabad. Unfortunately, a zealous priest interested in the strict enforcement of the laws prohibiting the consumption of alcohol began to take a close interest in the young man's behaviour and one night he brought to the restaurant a policeman who insisted on inspecting the contents of the teapot. It contained whisky. The whole incident received much publicity in the Pakistani press and became known as 'The Teapot Scandal'.

On the morning of our last day in Pakistan we set off for Mirpur in Azad Kashmir, the area from which very many people had come to settle in Britain. In Mirpur I was ushered into a suffocatingly hot schoolroom where I met many of the elders and people who were reckoned to have immigration problems. Throughout my discussions I was constantly interrupted by an argumentative individual squatting on his haunches at the back of the throng. Shortly after returning to England I went to address a meeting in Rochdale. The hall was packed with Pakistanis and I began my address by explaining my responsibilities in the Home Office and telling them that I had only recently got back from Pakistan where I had gone to study immigration problems. As I spoke my eyes roamed round the room, and to my amazement I saw sitting in the front row the very man who had plagued me in Mirpur. 'What the devil are you doing here?' I said. 'The last time I saw you you were making a thorough nuisance of yourself in Mirpur.' He was astonished to be recognised and the rest of the audience thought it a colossal joke that I had already encountered in their homeland a well-known local barrack-room lawyer and loud mouth. They gave me a very easy time for the rest of the evening, with members of the audience constantly pointing at the pest in the front row and giggling.

One girl I saw in Mirpur said that she had only recently arrived from England, having come to meet her fiancé for the first time. 'What do you think of him?' I said. In a broad Lancashire accent she replied, 'He's bloody smashing.'

In another interview I asked a young boy why, if he really wanted to marry the girl to whom he said he was engaged, he was not prepared to have her live with him in Pakistan. To my surprise he did not say that the girl did not want to leave England. His answer was that he could not stand the weather in Pakistan.

After Mirpur we were taken to see a dam which had recently been completed and then to a village and a school where we were supposed to be meeting a group of people described to me as local lawyers. I was escorted up onto a platform where a table was laid for lunch for ourselves and one or two nobs. We were, as usual, running behind time and I said that I had to get down into the body of the hall at once and mix with the lawyers. That was my undoing. Mix I did, and every now and then a tasty morsel was popped into my mouth. Sat down on a sofa flanked by two voluble lawyers I allowed a pink custardy substance flecked with flies to be placed in my hands, and unthinkingly I dispatched it in the normal fashion.

In the afternoon we flew to Lahore and then on to Delhi. I was already beginning to feel distinctly odd, but the High Commissioner Robert Wade-Gery and Sally, his wife, had arranged a working supper and somehow or other I had to stay on my feet.

We were due to fly to Agra the following morning but by bedtime it was obvious that I would be in no fit state to make the journey. Sally Wade-Gery produced sundry multi-coloured pills and I fell in to a deep sleep. Gilly went to Agra, I slept on and at about noon I woke to the telephone ringing and the Wade-Gerys inviting me to join them for lunch. I did not feel at all bad. The onset of illness in India can be dramatically quick, but often so is the recovery, and I was very grateful to Sally for her pills.

After a busy day or two in Delhi we were entitled to a mid-tour rest. We flew up to Srinagar and spent two days on a houseboat on the Dal Lake. There were quite a few houseboats, each of them, I was told, separately owned. Rather confusingly, however, every one of the owners was called Mr Butt. Abdul, the assistant of our Mr Butt, said: 'May the blessings of Almighty Allah be upon you and you'll have a helluva good time.' We then went up to a hill station called Pahalgam, 8,000 feet up in the Himalayas. As we arrived, in a torrential downpour, five or six young boys on ponies tore down the main street towards us. The shops flanking the street had quite impressive fronts but were built as if for a film set with no backs. We booked into our hotel and then in the afternoon we hired a taxi to take us further into the mountains, but when we reached the police post at the end of the town our driver refused to take us because, he said, of the danger of landslides. At the police post alongside the policeman in his box were two scruffy individuals with two scruffy ponies. Gilly, who had earlier expressed a wish to go for a ride but had seen no ponies for hire in the town, asked the two men if we could have a ride on their ponies and eventually, after an initial show of reluctance and when, with assistance from our driver, a price had been agreed, the ponies were handed into our care.

We set off past the police post and the road wound its way up the mountain side via a series of hairpin bends. Soon, however, the ponies had the common sense to realise that a great deal of effort would be saved if they, as it were, ironed out the bends, and, having adopted this course they soon reached the summit. Going up was not too easy for the riders. Coming down was terrifying.

We returned to our hotel and were told that a rare treat was in store for us. We could watch *Gone with the Wind* on television. Gilly was delighted. I was nervous. On every previous occasion on which she had watched *Gone with the Wind* she had become pregnant. But I took the risk, and competing with the spectacle on the screen were Pahalgam's golden eagles as they swooped down past our bedroom window to forage in the hotel's rubbish bins.

We travelled on to Dhaka in Bangladesh. A day or two later we were due to fly up to Sylhet, but at the airport we were told that there was some delay because of the weather and we were two hours late for our planned meeting with Sylhet politicians. The fried eggs cooked for the nine o'clock meeting were waiting for us at eleven and we ate them with a smile. Sylhet is set in splendid countryside with tea gardens spread over the surrounding hills, and it was an important place for us to visit because it was from this part of Bangladesh that very large numbers of people had come to settle in Britain. The region which borders on Assam is a long way from the sea, but for decades men from there had travelled down to ports such as Chittagong and then spent their lives as seamen. This meant that long before air travel and mass immigration the citizens of Sylhet knew a fair amount about the outside world, some of them even having relatives who, having found their way as seamen to British ports, had decided to stay there. So we were there to see our immigration staff up there at work and learn how they investigated doubtful claims to settle in Britain.

Immigration staff from Dhaka wanted to investigate the case of a woman who was claiming the right to join her father in Britain and we set off across the paddy fields to the village where she lived to try and find out whether she was the daughter of the English resident and, if she was, whether she was a child or an adult and, if an adult, whether she was still single. At the house we were offered various strange drinks which our guides advised us to refuse; and a young boy then shot up a tree and presented us with coconuts which did us all a world of good. We then set off back to Sylhet, the officers armed with copious notes which, together with statements from the man in Britain, they would study before ruling on the case.

The soil of Bangladesh is very fertile but the rural population is vast and struggles to live above starvation level. The spur to emigrate is therefore obvious, and when we were there every conceivable subterfuge was being used to obtain entry into Britain. Large numbers of demonstrably false applications were refused, but when an application was refused a new application was at once lodged and this meant that the backlog of applications was growing longer and longer. Every effort, therefore, had to be made to root out fraudulent claims in the hope that it might discourage similar fraudulent claims from others.

I had to make it plain to the press that there was no prospect of our already large staff in Dhaka engaged on the processing of applications being increased even further. It was all very well talking about people having to wait in a queue before their applications to enter Britain were dealt with. We were overwhelmed with cases – a large proportion of which were fraudulent. A typical case was one where a man applied on behalf of someone he claimed to be his son. The son was asked how many brothers and sisters he had and said 'two'. The man claiming to be the father replied in similar terms but was then confronted with his tax return in which he had set out the names of six children. The man admitted that he had indeed claimed for six children but said he had done so incorrectly and only in order to get a bigger tax allowance. Customers of this type were quite indignant when their immigration applications were turned down, not appearing to realise that having shown themselves to be untruthful in one respect they could hardly complain if people were reluctant to take what they said in another matter at its face value.

CHAPTER TWELVE

More Home
Office Tribulations

S hortly after arriving home I received a notice that as a Minister of State I was entitled to a quarter of buck from the Royal Parks. The buck could be delivered anywhere in the London area but not to Lancashire, so I asked for it to be left at the Home Office so that I could take it home with me on the train at the weekend. On the Friday I gave it to my driver Pearl to put in the car and we set off for Euston. We had not gone far when Pearl began to complain about the smell. She could not see why she should be expected to transport rotting carcasses as well as ministers.

By this time we were travelling under the bridge at Embankment tube station and, having had enough of the complaints, I told Pearl to stop. I jumped out of the car and, hoping no one was watching, stuffed the haunch of venison into a litter bin attached to a lamp post. We then drove away at top speed. No doubt the parcel was later spotted by a patrolling policeman and its contents reported as a dismembered human corpse.

In October 1983 came the Party Conference at Blackpool. A motion had been tabled by the Billericay Conservative Association urging the government to 'end all further permanent immigration from the new commonwealth and Pakistan, to increase financial and material provision for voluntary repatriation and resettlement, and to repeal all race relations legislation so that all United Kingdom citizens are equal before the law'. It was what was called a balloted motion, chosen for debate by the constituency representatives. I was the minister who had to answer on behalf of the government, and clearly it was not going to be an easy occasion with most of those present wanting tougher immigration control.

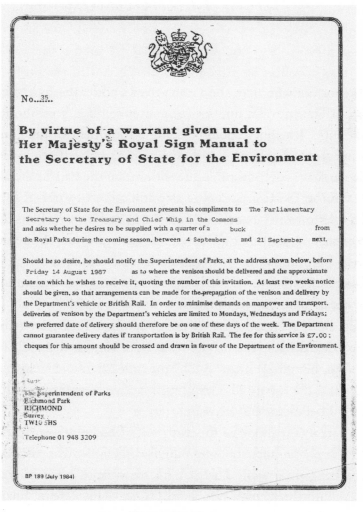

No...35.

By virtue of a warrant given under Her Majesty's Royal Sign Manual to the Secretary of State for the Environment

The Secretary of State for the Environment presents his compliments to   The Parliamentary Secretary to the Treasury and Chief Whip in the Commons and asks whether he desires to be supplied with a quarter of a   buck   from the Royal Parks during the coming season, between 4 September   and 21 September   next.

Should he so desire, he should notify the Superintendent of Parks, at the address shown below, before   Friday 14 August 1987   as to where the venison should be delivered and the approximate date on which he wishes to receive it, quoting the number of this invitation. At least two weeks notice should be given, so that arrangements can be made for the preparation of the venison and delivery by the Department's vehicle or British Rail. In order to minimise demands on manpower and transport, deliveries of venison by the Department's vehicles are limited to Mondays, Wednesdays and Fridays; the preferred date of delivery should therefore be on one of these days of the week. The Department cannot guarantee delivery dates if transportation is by British Rail. The fee for this service is £7.00 ; cheques for this amount should be crossed and drawn in favour of the Department of the Environment.

The Superintendent of Parks
Richmond Park
RICHMOND
Surrey
TW10 5HS

Telephone 01 948 3209

BP 189 (July 1984)

Venison Entitlement

The debate was opened by Harvey Proctor, MP for Billericay, and there were loud cheers when he said: 'Enough is enough. The provisions of the Immigration Act enabling people to return home should be publicised and improved and generous resettlement grants should be provided. Race relations could be improved at a stroke by the abolition of the Commission for Racial Equality.' Paul Nischal, the only Asian to speak in the debate, was shouted down and the mood in the hall was unpleasant. After the first few moments, however, my speech was well received. 'We are indeed all equal before the law,' I said. 'We don't need a motion from Billericay to tell us so. The government is not in the business of telling people who have their homes here, who even have become British Citizens, "You are unwelcome here. Here's some money. Clear off."' I claimed credit for the government's tightening of immigration control, saying that net immigration from the West Indies had ceased, but an end to all immigration had never been the policy of the Conservative Party and *could* never be the policy of any government in a free society. I finished by saying that if the conference decided that all legislation underpinning the principle of non-discrimination on grounds of race should be wiped off the statute book it would be sending a message that we no longer believed in a fair and just society.

The *Daily Telegraph* reported on 14 October: 'Far Right routed in heated race debate. The far right had been confident that it would embarrass the government. But by the time Mr David Waddington wound up the debate to a standing ovation, the mood was firmly against Mr Proctor and his supporters.'

Whatever the mood of the conference I had obviously annoyed some people because for weeks afterwards Gilly, who had stayed up in Lancashire while I went back to work in London, had to put up with threatening phone calls. One night a man called and demanded that I should support the compulsory repatriation of immigrants. 'If your husband won't agree,' he said 'we'll send the boys round to break his legs.' Gilly replied with spirit, 'I hope you do send the boys round. I'll enjoy breaking *their* legs.' The calls ceased.

One interesting incident that autumn proved that when it came to scheming, the Home Office had much to learn from the Foreign Office. In train was a large programme to move civil servants out of London to the provinces. At about the same time the Foreign Office, supported by some committee looking into the efficiency of government, suggested that the Home Office should take away from the Foreign Office responsibility for the Passport Office. Not much wrong with that except that when, after the handover, most of the Passport Office was moved out of London, the Foreign Office, by some sleight of hand, treated the movement as fulfilling *their* obligation to disperse.

Difficult cases still came across my desk with monotonous regularity. If I had been determined on a quiet life, I could have given way every time an MP had argued that somebody or other should be allowed to stay in Britain. I would have been the darling of *The Guardian* newspaper. But I never had that ambition, so I struggled on, trying to deal with cases on their merits, with the press always making a fuss if someone was turned down and always remaining entirely silent if someone's claim was allowed.

One troublesome case was that of a lady called Afia Begum who, while living in Bangladesh, had agreed to marry a fellow Bangladeshi living in England. Unfortunately, a short time later the man she was to marry died in a fire in London, and Afia was told the sad truth that the visa she had obtained to enter Britain as a fiancée was no longer valid. It seemed rather a harsh ruling until one was brought face to face with the fact that this had been an arranged marriage between total strangers and while she still had a mother, father, brothers and sisters in Bangladesh she had no friends or relatives in Britain to come to. But she thought that, by getting the visa, she had won the prize of a better life in Britain and, determined to try and hang on to the prize, she boarded a plane to London. On her arrival the Immigration Service refused her entry but granted her temporary admission so that she could sort out her affairs with the relatives of the deceased fiancé. That was the signal for the launch of a vociferous campaign on Afia Begum's behalf, demanding that, although she was neither a bride nor a fiancée, she be given permanent settlement.

Some of the tactics used by the campaigners were embarrassing and disruptive. Sometimes they were quite amusing. One night I went to a public meeting in Bradford to explain government policy but after each sentence of my speech a line of pretty girls in the middle of a block of seats half way down the hall shot to their feet, each with a placard bearing a letter of Afia Begum's name. Before anyone could do anything about them they sat down again only to rise once more at my next utterance.

Afia Begum then disappeared and a body which said it was fighting on her behalf announced that they were protecting her. She was somewhere in London and they would not surrender her until the Home Office announced she could stay the country. After a great deal of time and effort had been expended she was eventually found and returned to her own family in Bangladesh.

Another Bangladeshi called Mohammed Idrish came to England sponsored by the British Council and began to study for a technical qualification much needed in his own country. After a few months he abandoned his studies and thereby lost his right to stay in Britain. But he then quickly married a girl in the hope that he could stay as a husband. There could be no doubt that that was his motive because he left the girl within three weeks of the ceremony and disappeared. When found a year or so later he said he was doing important voluntary work for the immigrant community and in spite of having cheated the British Council and his own country, not to mention the lady whom he had married, the immigration appeal tribunal gave him leave to remain. I dread to think what sort of message that sent out to others minded to cheat and lie their way into Britain.

At about this time we took Victoria to Buckingham Palace where she was presented to the Queen. The Queen asked her what she would like to do for a career. Victoria replied that she would like to be a journalist. The Queen commented, 'I hope you won't be one of the grumpy ones.'

When I first arrived in the Home Office I was told I was to be in charge of a Data Protection Bill which was in the legislative programme for that year. There had to be a Bill to bring us in compliance with a 1981 Council of Europe convention on data protection, but the whole concept was still in its infancy and many thought that all we needed to do was follow other European countries and have a short Bill which did no more than put a statutory duty on those holding data to look after it properly. The Home Office, however, had other thoughts. Every company processing or storing personal data would have to register with a new 'registrar for data protection', and specific duties placed on the shoulders of those who held data. When the Bill became law I was packed off to Canada with my secretary, Liz Johnstone, to explain to the Canadians what we had been up to and address a conference on data protection in Toronto. I did not think much of Toronto or the conference but enjoyed a visit to the Niagara Falls.

Very much more important than the Data Protection Act was the Interception of Communications Bill which I helped Leon Brittan to take through the House at about the same time. It put telephone tapping authorised by the Secretary of State on a statutory basis and outlawed telephone interceptions not so authorised; and it was to be the model for later legislation putting the security service on a similar statutory basis. Gerald Kaufman was the shadow Home Secretary and I will long remember the skilful way in which Leon handled him and disarmed Labour opposition to the Bill. 'One day, Gerald,' said Leon, 'you will be occupying the chair in which I am now sitting and bearing the heavy responsibilities I am now bearing; responsibility for the very safety of the nation.' As Leon spoke you could see Gerald settling back more comfortably into his seat and dreaming he was across the way in Leon's.

In October 1984 Gilly and I set off for the Party Conference at Brighton and installed ourselves in the Grand Hotel. Our room was at the back of the second floor. On the Thursday night we went to bed as usual and just after 2.40 a.m. I was awoken by a loud bang. Gilly sat up in bed and said 'They've done it. They've bombed the conference centre.' 'Nonsense,' I said, but I went into the bathroom and stood on a chair to look through the window on to the stair well separating the back of the hotel from the front. At that moment there was an enormous crash which I took to be a second explosion but which was in fact part of the building collapsing, and we then hurried out of the room and, along with many others, made for the fire escape. Down in the street and walking along the side of the hotel we could see nothing amiss but when we turned the corner onto the promenade we saw the gaping hole in the front of the building.

We knew roughly where our friends John and Roberta Wakeham's bedroom was (or rather where it had been) and feared the worst. There were a number of very shaken people on the promenade including Walter Clegg (the MP for North Fylde) who had suffered minor injuries. Graham Bright, who was then my PPS, came along and said he had a room in a hotel down the road and we could spend the rest of the night there. So to his hotel we went and at about eight o'clock we set about ringing the children.

Meanwhile, the Prime Minister, having got out of the hotel, had

had about an hour-and-a-half's rest at Lewes Police College before going on the radio to say that the conference was continuing with its business. When it met, John Gummer, Party Chairman, was told that someone had phoned saying there was a bomb in the hall. It was probably a hoax and if it wasn't there was no hope of clearing the building before the bomb went off, so John sat tight and kept the news to himself.

When the morning session ended Gilly and I were asked to go behind the platform to see the Prime Minister. I am not sure why but I suppose it was because we were friends of John and Roberta Wakeham and it was thought we might be able to help in some way. The Prime Minister turned to me and said: 'Three bishops came to see me this morning wanting to pray for me, and they had me down on my knees.' She then added crossly: 'As if I had nothing better to do!' She said that the thought of having to go on to the stage and make her speech was just more than she could bear, but Gordon Reece*, sitting on the arm of her chair, said 'You know you can do it. When you go onto that platform the whole world will be cheering you on and willing you to make the greatest speech of your life.' Willie Whitelaw was there with Celia his wife. There was much talk about who was going to identify Roberta's body. Celia said 'Willie is absolutely hopeless at that sort of thing. He can't possibly go.' So I drew the short straw and it was agreed that I should go with Bob Boscawen. But that was after Margaret's speech which was, as we all expected, a tour de force.

I then went up to the hospital and into intensive care. Margaret Tebbit was lying on her back, looking in terrible shape, but she was conscious and said 'What about the parrot?' obviously recalling

---

* Sir Gordon Reece, adviser to Margaret Thatcher 1975–9, Director of Publicity, Conservative Central Office 1978–80, and public affairs consultant.

Norman's and my private joke at Mr Jasper Parrott's expense. John Wakeham was further across the room. He was in terrible pain. I did not know whether to tell him about Roberta but he seemed to know she was dead. I went up to see Norman Tebbit who was in another ward upstairs. We had earlier seen him lifted out of the debris left by the blast and you could see then the pain he was enduring. In hospital he told me there was a gap in his side with room for a small suitcase, but he was determined to get down to see Margaret in intensive care as soon as he could persuade the doctors to let him out of bed, and he was down with her the next morning. I then stayed up at the hospital in case John Wakeham wanted anything, but it was not long before the Whips Office moved in in strength, and my services were no longer required.

I then soon learned that Tony Berry (MP for Enfield Southgate), who I had known from Oxford days and had then been a colleague in the Whips Office, was among the dead. He had been a good friend. Also among those murdered was the Chairman of the North West Area, Eric Taylor, with whom Gilly and I had been having a drink the night before. His funeral was a glorious celebration of patriotism with a brass band belting out 'Land of Hope and Glory'. Eric would have loved it.

In 1985 the Zola Budd case hit the headlines. Leon Brittan was still Home Secretary and he asked me to see whether there were any difficulties in the way of Zola Budd obtaining British Citizenship so that she could run for Britain in the Olympic Games. Her father, having applied for and obtained a British passport in South Africa on the basis of his father's birth in Britain, travelled here with Zola. She was then still under the age of eighteen; and as the daughter of a British citizen could expect to be registered as such herself. But an almighty row broke out when she got her British citizenship, it being alleged among other things that she, a white South African, had been put to the top of the queue while millions of black people were waiting patiently for their own applications to enter Britain to be dealt with. The argument was completely fallacious, those advancing it deliberately confusing the right to British citizenship with the right of a foreigner to come to Britain for settlement. To the best of my knowledge, there was at that time no queue of people waiting abroad for their applications for British citizenship to be processed. What the critics were really arguing was that the Home Office should have sat on Zola Budd's papers long enough to make sure that she missed the Olympics and then, when she had missed the games, should have produced the passport she was entitled to all along.

What happened thereafter was really quite appalling. Racial bigots set about making Zola Budd's life a misery and eventually destroyed her running career. I wrote at the time: 'Perhaps the churches will take a little time off from encouraging illegal immigrants to defy the law and will instead preach the simple message that being born white in South Africa is not a mortal sin. Still less should being white disqualify a person from international athletics.'

Nobody would have thought from the ill-informed criticism and press attention focused on cases like Zola Budd that most of my time was spent going round the country speaking to and getting on well with ethnic minority groups. But in November 1985 I was invited to speak at Manchester University and there I did not receive the polite and friendly reception I was used to. The Union was packed with people out to make trouble and as I tried to speak above the uproar I was jeered and spat at by a foul-looking young man who placed himself immediately in front of me. Eventually a rush of people invaded the platform, and the police moved in and carried me away to safety. The case had an amusing sequel. The Council of Manchester University appointed a disciplinary committee to look into the incident, but the committee got nowhere. A young black man volunteered that he was the fellow who came on to the platform and hit me, but I knew one thing beyond a shadow of doubt. There was not a black man in sight. So his attempt at martyrdom failed miserably and the inquiry ground to a halt.

Bill Molloy, Labour MP for Ealing North and later a member of the Lords, wrote me a note which I treasure. It read, 'David, I hope the hand of the thug that aimed a punch at you rots and drops off.' But the best letter I got was from a Mr Angus Macnaughton (of Ascot) who wrote:

> While deploring the behaviour of the students of Manchester University ... I was surprised to see you quoted in the press as saying that 'they acted like pigs'. Pigs are peaceable, orderly creatures, much abused by men. They do not deserve this pejorative description. In fact, in all the animal creation, only man is capable of the excesses with which we are so familiar today.

In a leader entitled 'Blind Eye?' the *London Evening Standard* was very censorious:

> Television viewers could see it plainly enough. Spit was running down his face. His jacket was soaked with beer. At least one of the punches thrown at him, and a hefty one, appeared to land on its target. This was not some war criminal being paraded in front of his victims. It was the Minister of State at the Home Office, Mr David Waddington, attempting to deliver a speech on immigration at Manchester University. Mr Waddington was neither foolish nor optimistic in expecting his opinions to be heard in what is supposed to be a forum for opinions. Manchester University is not a lunatic asylum for the criminally insane. But what happened there last week was far uglier and more violent than a normal student demonstration.

People who witnessed this vicious hooliganism on their television would have every reason to suppose that the university authorities would by now have taken firm measures, hauled the most repulsive troublemakers up and expelled them. However, the authorities would appear to have been somewhere else that night and seen nothing, to judge by their response. This has been to give the students' union executive sixteen days to prepare a report on the incident, which will be scrutinised by the University council on 26 November. If this report is 'not satisfactory' the question of withholding some part of the Union's £573,000 grant 'is bound to arise'.

This reaction is timid and inadequate; it is also off-target. To fine the Union some £30,000, as happened at Warwick University in 1983, won't worry the thugs. It will simply penalise the great majority of student union members who took no part in the viciousness. To put the onus on the union to identify the troublemakers is a pathetic evasion of responsibility.

It is the reputation of Manchester University itself which has been sullied; it is up to the university authorities to punish the minister's assailants.

So absorbed was I with my own ministerial responsibilities, I did not feel deeply involved in the events surrounding the miners' strike. But I do know that the successful outcome was largely due to Margaret Thatcher. The traditional Home Office line was that we did not have a national police force and while one force could ask for help from a neighbouring force, there could be no question of the government directing another force, or forces, to help one which was under pressure. When, therefore, in 1972 the West Midlands police could not prevent the mob blockading the Saltley Coke Works, no reinforcements were sent to Birmingham to relieve the situation. That led to the chief constable giving up the struggle and the coke works having to shut down.

In 1984, however, Margaret Thatcher was Prime Minister and *she* was not going to allow a shameful outcome like that. Day after day newspapers had had on their front pages pictures of miners fighting with police as the police tried to make it possible for other miners to get to work, and the Prime Minister made it plain that a way had to be found for other forces to help the police in Yorkshire. A few days later I came back to London from Lancashire by the A1, and as I travelled south streams of police vehicles were travelling north to the Yorkshire coalfield to do their duty on the Monday morning. A political strike doing great damage to the country was on the way to being defeated.

A little later Leon Brittan was removed from the Home Office and Douglas Hurd was brought back from Northern Ireland to take his place. Douglas Hurd had to deal with some riots, but for a time my end of the shop was relatively quiet. Then, with the whole system of immigration control bogged down because MPs were showering my office with repeated representations whenever we made a move to remove from the country a person who had no possible right to be here, I exploded at Question Time and said it was about time 'abuse' of the system stopped. Later in the afternoon I was summoned to Douglas's office and Douglas, with a rather pained expression on his face, said that he did not mind my stirring things up as long as I had some idea what I wanted to get out of it all. I said I wanted a set of rules governing representations by MPs in immigration cases and he sent me off to work them up.

In the House of Commons Douglas was not as robust as I would have wished, being careful not to use the indelicate word 'abuse' to describe what had been going on. He said that all I had been trying to do was call attention to some 'misuse' of the system; but I had no real reason to complain. I had got my way and in an astonishingly short period of time produced a booklet setting out 'guidance for MPs in immigration cases'. This guidance has, with

ABOVE LEFT My father, on the left of his brother George, the school bully.
ABOVE RIGHT Pa, glad to be in uniform again as a member of the Home Guard in 1940.
BELOW My parents' wedding at Habersham Church, Lancs.

ABOVE In between my sisters (L to R: Ann, Mary, Zoe and Nancy).

LEFT Receiving the Stick from Field Marshal Sir William Slim.

ABOVE Campaigning in Peterborough, 1948.
BELOW Our wedding – Preston, 20 December 1958.

LEFT Arriving at Westminster to take my seat in June 1968.

BELOW The family with Clitheroe castle in the background – taken during the Clitheroe by-election, February 1979.

ABOVE The family on holiday in Devon, 1978 (L to R: James, Matthew, Victoria, Alistair, Gilly, Jennifer and I).

BELOW Basil with Victoria, me and Gilly.

Victorious at the Ribble Valley count in 1983.

BELOW One of the final photographs of Margaret Thatcher with her Cabinet (I'm front row, third from left).

RIGHT *Private Eye*'s satirical take on the Strangeways riots (signed by my office).

ABOVE Bermuda's Government House in all its glory, looking rather intimidating on our arrival.

MIDDLE With HM The Queen on her visit to St George's, Bermuda in 1994.

BELOW Gilly and I in the carriage going to the Opening of Parliament, Bermuda 1996.

various amendments and refinements, stood the test of time and it has greatly improved the efficiency of the system without taking away from MPs their right to make representations.

But we had to take further steps if our immigration staff in Britain were not to be overwhelmed. Everyone knew that it was people from just a few particular countries who were putting most of the pressure on the immigration system. Many from these countries came for settlement, having obtained entry clearance at a British post abroad to do so. Many more came pretending to be visitors but intending to stay permanently if they possibly could. Surely those saying they wanted to visit should obtain visas abroad just like those saying they wanted to come for settlement. That way their credentials would be checked before they set out on their journey and they would not suffer long delays waiting to be examined at Heathrow. It would be better for the bona fide traveller and take an enormous weight of work off the Immigration Service. It was all common sense, but the fact that something is plain common sense does not mean that it will not cause a row in Parliament; and the introduction of visas for the Indian sub-continent, Nigeria and Ghana caused another great fuss. The most spurious arguments were mounted against the policy. It had to be racist: otherwise why weren't Americans being required to obtain visas? As if tens of thousands of Americans had the same economic motive for wishing to come to Britain as people in countries with pitifully low living standards.

Bill Deedes put the matter well in the *Daily Telegraph* on 3 September 1986:

> Labour spokesmen who berate this (the introduction of visas) as discriminatory and racist really must clear their minds. Do they favour unrestricted immigration? If not, they have to accept that, amid this enormous traffic (5,550,000 people coming on visits

each year), sifting the lawful from the unlawful entries to this country can no longer be satisfactorily done off desks at Heathrow. Opposition spokesmen crying 'racist' have two questions to answer. Do you accept restricted immigration? If so, where is cheating most effectively checked – there, or here?

Gradually the storm subsided and the policy helped enormously to lessen the pressures on immigration control.

The other measure that helped enormously, but again was very controversial, was the Carriers' Liability Bill which provided that if an airline, for example, brought someone to Britain without the proper documents the airline suffered a penalty. No one seriously imagined that many of those arriving in Britain and claiming refugee status were in fact refugees and our system of control was being overwhelmed as a result of people arriving without any valid claim. The Act worked wonders, but Lord King (then chairman of British Airways) and others complained bitterly, saying that it was a diabolical liberty to require BA employees to look at passports and see that people had the proper documentation before setting out on their journey. We were, however, surely right to assume that BA employees could read and it was hardly surprising that, with the help of the Immigration Service, they soon got used to the new requirements.

Sometimes my duties in the field of immigration control brought me close to despair. I see that on 18 September 1985 I wrote in the *Clitheroe Advertiser*: 'My immigration job is impossible. Everyone demands firm immigration control, but a sizeable slice of the population screams blue murder whenever an attempt is made to enforce it.' At that particular time I was in trouble over a two-year-old Pakistani boy who had been refused entry to the country. The child's mother and father were fit and well, living in Pakistan with the little boy's sister, but had, so it was alleged, agreed to hand over the boy to the father's brother in England. Britain at that time did not (and for all I know may still not) recognise adoptions in Pakistan because proceedings in that country were not considered to provide sufficient safeguards for the interests of the children concerned. That did not stop a group of churchmen writing to *The Guardian* complaining about my 'separating' the child from its 'parents' by refusing the child entry into Britain. The Home Office had the last laugh because at the eleventh hour the true parents refused to hand over the child to the brother, but I cannot remember the Church of England Board of Responsibility conceding that it might have been in error.

On one occasion a delegation from the Church of England Board came to the Home Office to talk of their concerns and their leader claimed that he knew of a case of a lady from the Caribbean who, having had a child in Britain, was not being allowed to stay here. The child, however, could not go back with her to the Caribbean because, being born British, he had no right to live there. Hayden Phillips said: 'Which country in the Caribbean does she come from?' Back came the reply 'Jamaica'. 'That's funny,' said Hayden Phillips, still batting away as under-secretary responsible for immigration, 'The last time I heard that story the woman came from Barbados. Have you ever met the woman?' 'No.' 'Do you know her name?' 'No.' And, of course, we never did discover any such woman.

In 1986 I became a bencher of Gray's Inn and on being called paid 'caution money' of £1,000. To this day I do not know what the money is for. To pay for broken glass or bent silverwear in the event of the bencher running amok? Also in 1986 rumours began to circulate that I was to be deputy chairman of the Conservative Party. I do not know where they started and so far as I know they never had any foundation.

In the autumn of 1986 Gilly and I went to Hong Kong to see the Vietnamese refugee camps. I also had to meet a number of people, particularly leaders of the Indian community in Hong Kong, about the Hong Kong Nationality Order which I had recently helped take through the House of Commons. This provided that those who ceased to be British Dependent Territories citizens on the Chinese takeover in 1997 would have the right to acquire British National (overseas) status; but there was genuine concern among those who were not ethnically Chinese and had, therefore, no expectation of acquiring Chinese citizenship, that they might be left stateless. Members of the Indian community pointed to the fact that when the East African Asians were expelled from Kenya and Uganda the Indian government made clear that those expelled were Britain's responsibility not India's, and these Indians in Hong Kong wanted to know what would happen to them if at some time in the future they were forced to leave what had become their homeland. I pointed out that there was no question of their finding themselves stateless, that they were being offered a form of British nationality and under the Joint Declaration they were guaranteed the right of abode in Hong Kong. I was, however, authorised to give an undertaking that we would look sympathetically at the case of any British national who, in spite of the Joint Declaration, came under pressure to leave.

On our arrival at one of the refugee camps a guard of honour of scouts and guides was formed to greet us. The movement had been introduced by one of the refugee organisations and had proved immensely popular among the Vietnamese. The scout and guide movements had every reason to be proud of what was being done in their name.

At the end of 1986 I got a letter from the Prime Minister in these terms:

I have it in mind on the occasion of the forthcoming list of New Year honours to submit your name to the Queen with a recommendation that she may be graciously pleased to approve that you be sworn of Her Majesty's most honourable Privy Council. I should be glad to know if this would be agreeable to you. I shall take no steps until I have your reply.

I replied without delay and on 1 January 1987 became a 'Rt Hon.' I received a very nice letter from Willie Whitelaw, appreciated because he knew better than most the difficulties of the job I had been trying to do. On 10 February I reported at the Privy Council Office to be rehearsed by Mr (later Sir Geoffrey) de Deney, Clerk of the Privy Council, in the art of kneeling and kissing the Queen's hand and was then whisked off to Buckingham Palace for the ceremony. In the words of the official announcement: 'This day David Charles Waddington Esquire, was, by Her Majesty's Command, sworn of Her Majesty's Most Honourable Privy Council, and took his place at the Board accordingly.' The oath of a privy councillor as administered by the clerk may seem archaic but it is modern and crystal clear compared with the oath, now abandoned, which I took when I became a QC.*

A nice cartoon appeared in *The Times* on Friday 6 February 1987 arising out of demands in Parliament for a relaxation of the licensing laws. I was portrayed as Nelson putting a bottle of brown ale to my blind eye. I had forgotten about my involvement in all this until I went through my papers, so I don't think it can have loomed large in my workload. We were not, however, ducking the issue as the cartoon tended to suggest. Indeed, not very long afterwards a reform measure went through the House.

What greatly increased my workload at this time was the decision to introduce legislation to deregulate Sunday trading on the lines of the Auld Report. Eventually, the Bill was lost on second

---

* The oath I took on becoming QC is on page 84.

reading, but that was not my fault. It was decided that Douglas Hurd should open the debate because it was a Home Office measure and the winding-up should be left to Kenneth Clarke, then the DTI minister in the Commons, because of the provisions in the Bill concerning the rights of employees. Douglas's opening was a disaster. When answering an intervention he gave the impression that there would be no Party whip during the committee stage. I whispered to the Chief Whip (John Wakeham): 'did you know anything about that?' 'Certainly not,' he said. The measure was done for before we had hardly got started because the backbenchers could see what we could see – that if the Bill ever got into committee, without a whip it would never get out. As a result, our side decided that there was no point in prolonging the agony and threw out the Bill there and then.

My role prior to the debacle had been to keep in touch with all the interest groups, speak in the country and on television in favour of deregulation and try and keep the Party on side. I, like most Conservative MPs, had to put up with a lot of aggravation. I found the opponents of reform incredibly sanctimonious. One woman in Clitheroe told me at great length that she was able to organise her life in a way which avoided the need to go shopping on Sundays and she was surprised I could not organise mine. She looked at me pityingly when I said I often arrived back in London at nine o'clock or later on a Sunday evening and I did not think I was doing anything very wrong when I called at a shop in Tottenham Court Road and bought myself a loaf of bread and a sausage roll. The churches organised a meeting in Clitheroe and the vicar in charge told me that I was there to hear the views of ordinary people on the issue. The audience did not seem to me to be particularly ordinary. For a start it did not seem to include all those ordinary people in Clitheroe who bought a Sunday paper, who went to the car wash or to fill up with petrol on a Sunday, who took the family out for a ride in the car on a Sunday and stopped at a café or pub for lunch. But I listened patiently, comforted by the fact that the vicar had said that there would be no vote at the end. Unfortunately for me, in the closing minutes he suffered a rush of blood to the head, forgot his promise and decided to have a vote after all. The result was astonishing, beating all political records. Against Sunday trading 492: for Sunday trading 4: with four abstentions. Another Waddington record!

Towards the end of my time as Minister of State there was a great fuss over our attempts to remove sixty-four Tamils who arrived with bogus credentials and then claimed asylum. There was also the notorious case of Viraj Mendis who, having come to England as a student and then abandoned his studies, had married in an attempt to stay in the country. The marriage only lasted a couple of months but when steps were taken to return him to Sri Lanka he claimed he was a communist and Tamil supporter. He would therefore be persecuted if sent home. Eventually he was given 'sanctuary' in a church in Manchester and a campaign started on his behalf.

One day a crowd of demonstrators descended on Clitheroe and started baying outside the Conservative offices where I was holding my surgery. Gilly went out into the street and, without saying who she was, advised them to march round the town to rally support. She then tacked herself on to the back of the procession, singing lustily with the rest: 'Viraj Mendis is a warrior. David Waddington is a bastard'. The people of Clitheroe had a really good day.

At New Year 1987 we were kept awake by a series of phone calls about Viraj Mendis – some threatening, some obscene. When the phone rang for the umpteenth time, Gilly leaned across the bed, grabbed the receiver out of my hand and shouted: 'We know where you are. My job is to keep you talking until the police come and get you.' A rather pained voice replied: 'Madam, I am the police. The *Daily Mirror* has just rung the police in Manchester to say that they have received a message from an anonymous caller saying that a bomb has been placed in your house and that you have three minutes to get out of the place. Well, you had three minutes but this call has taken so long, there's probably now only thirty seconds.' Gilly jumped out of bed. I said 'What's going on?' She said 'I'll tell you in the garden.'

One night in the middle of January we were in Denny Street when a mob assembled outside the front door and started bawling abuse about the Mendis case. I rang the police and a very senior officer with a lot of braid on his shoulders read out a long statement saying they had to disperse. One of the mob stepped forward and without a flicker of a smile said: 'But our train for Manchester does not leave for another hour. Can't we carry on shouting for just a few more minutes?' 'Certainly not,' said the officer, at which the mob muttered and grumbled off down the road, and we went to bed in peace.

After I had moved on to be Chief Whip, Viraj Mendis was eventually removed to Sri Lanka where our embassy monitored his progress. He went back to live with his well-to-do parents, showed no interest in the Tamils and was himself of no interest to the Sri Lankan authorities. Mr Stewart, who was British High Commissioner in Sri Lanka from 1984–7, wrote to the *Daily Telegraph*:

> I was intimately involved in the affair from the time that Mr Mendis first claimed that he would be in danger if he returned to his own country. Having now retired from the diplomatic service I have no particular axe to grind, but I would like to set the record straight. Mr Mendis first claimed that he would be arrested on return because he was a well-known supporter of the Tamil cause. In 1985 and 1986 none of the Tamil activists with whom I spoke had ever heard of him. Nor, although I and my staff monitored

the British papers to gauge the extent of support in Britain for the Tamil separatist cause, had we encountered any mention of his name.

When Mr Mendis made his claim, I made discreet inquiries with the Sri Lankan authorities to see whether he was wanted by them for any offence. I did this before there had been any publicity about him in the country. Neither the police nor the security authorities had any record of him. In fact, when publicity about his case became widespread, it took the authorities some weeks to identify Mr Mendis as there was no record of him in any of their files.

When David Waddington, then a Home Office minister, visited Sri Lanka in 1987 he obtained from the President and from the Secretary of Internal Security, in my presence, categorical assurances that Mr Mendis was not wanted for any offences in Sri Lanka and that no action of any sort would be taken against him if he returned.

He now claims that if he returns he will be in danger from one of the chauvinist Sinhalese groups. He has no stature in any of the political or terrorist groups either of the left or of the right; of the Tamil or of the Sinhalese sides. Neither the government nor the various terrorist groups have any interest in Mr Mendis or in his continued existence in or out of Sri Lanka.

The truth is that Mr Mendis and his supporters have erected a cause célèbre here in Britain about nothing at all. He has succeeded in over-staying his leave to be here for some ten or more years. Mr Mendis is a young man who has managed to enlist sympathy here about his importance in his native country where no one seems to have any malign, or indeed any, interest at all in him.

On 19 February 1987 a piece in the *Daily Telegraph*, headed 'WHY DR NO CAN'T BE MR NICE GUY', by Nicholas Comfort, summed up pretty well the difficulties of the job I had been doing for over four years:

> There are two ministerial posts even the most ambitious MP hopes to avoid: under-secretary at the DHSS dealing with social security cases, and minister of state at the Home Office responsible for immigration. The second job is the worse, as the blunt Lancastrian QC is now discovering.
>
> Given that his job has always been regarded as one of the classic 'no-win' positions in government, Waddington is now trusted to ride out storms like the current furore over his attempt to deport sixty-four Tamils who arrived with bogus credentials and claimed asylum.
>
> His handling of the introduction of visas from India, Sri Lanka, Bangladesh, Nigeria and Ghana last year, and his whittling away of MPs' right to defer expulsions while they look into the facts has infuriated the Opposition but left few scars. He even got away last month with announcing that police and immigration officers had detained twenty-six suspected illegal immigrants from West Africa who were working for contract cleaners at two Home Office buildings.
>
> And there is a strongly Dickensian aspect to him as he meets Labour anger at a new visa scheme or the deportation of Tamils with cries of 'humbug'. Much of the job is psychology, telling the serious appeal from the hard luck story or detecting when the Opposition's apparent fury is really just ritual. In the Commons Waddington has, for this government, an almost uniquely Victorian air, possibly because his stern yet rounded features and his tonsure of whitening hair come straight from the sketchbook of Charles Tenniel.

One of the problems I had to deal with as Minister of State was that of polygamous wives, and it illustrates how punctilious is our civil service in affording to all what appear to be their full rights.

There had come to my notice a large number of cases in which men settled in Britain had brought into the country second wives by polygamous marriages. In each case the entry clearance officer at our post abroad had concluded that although the man had lived in Britain for years he was not domiciled in Britain because he had not demonstrated a fixed intention to abandon his domicile of origin in Pakistan. As polygamy was lawful in Pakistan, the marriage contracted there was valid under our law. I took the view that we should certainly scrutinise most carefully every such case.

As the general election drew near I made a speech on immigration, pointing out that every policy statement by Labour represented a weakening of the control. It provoked a letter of congratulation from the Prime Minister. Between 1983 and 1987 we made a lot of friends among the ethnic minority communities in spite of the difficult and often unpopular job I had to do. We were particularly friendly with Ashraf el-Doulah and his beautiful wife Jasmine – Ashraf being, I think, third in command at the Bangladesh High Commission in London. One Easter we had Ashraf and Jasmine to stay with us in Lancashire and on the first night gave a dinner party in their honour. Ashraf thoroughly enjoyed himself and at one stage a Lancashire friend of mine turned to him and said: 'I hope you don't mind my asking, old boy, but I thought Muslims weren't supposed to drink.' 'Quite so,' said Ashraf, 'but I look at it this way. I know there will be no port in the next life so I had better enjoy it now.'

Then there was the strange case of Professor Bedi, his wife Kuldip and little Piti. The professor was a great Conservative supporter in, if I recall, Ealing and he decided to stand for the chairmanship of the Anglo-Asian Conservative Association, sure of the support of conservative-minded Sikhs. Little Piti came for tea with his mother Kuldip and all I can remember of that occasion is that Basil, our Norfolk terrier, rushed out of the kitchen and jumped on Kuldip's lap, causing Kuldip to throw up her hands in terror and deposit her tea in the middle of the floor. Then Kuldip took off for India and went to visit in gaol a Sikh suspected of terrorism. For this heinous offence she was put in gaol herself. Terry Dicks, Kuldip's MP, set off to India to rescue her. He returned empty-handed but gave everyone in the House of Commons a marvellous afternoon's entertainment. He asked the minister, Lynda Chalker, whether she was aware that he had been to India to see the Indian authorities about his constituent Mrs Bedi and that on being shown into the Indian minister's room the latter had said: 'Now first, Mr Dicks, what is the present you have brought for me?' I thought the minister would have the vapours. The Foreign Office then got into a terrible fret because the Indian government started hinting darkly that Mrs Bedi and terrorists like her had friends in high places. One such was, they believed, a minister in the Home Office. I don't know whether a spy employed by the Indian government had reported that Kuldip had been to tea at the Waddingtons' or poor Kuldip had been talking in gaol of our friendship in the hope that it would do her some good. But perhaps at the end it did stand her in good stead; for a month or two later she was released from detention and reunited with her family.

CHAPTER THIRTEEN

Chief Whip

Much has been written about the 1987 general election campaign and conflicts between the Prime Minister and Central Office, but we never really looked like losing. I spent almost every day travelling from constituency to constituency in the north of the country. On one trip to Huddersfield some West Indians invited me into their home where they were watching cricket and drinking rum – more attention being paid to the latter activity than the former. On leaving I asked the detective who was keeping an eye on me, 'What are those curious plants in the front garden?' 'Cannabis, sir,' he replied.

The result of the election in Ribble Valley was very satisfactory:

D. Waddington (Conservative) 30,136
M. Carr (SDP/Alliance) 10,608
G. Pope (Labour) 8,781
Conservative majority 19,528

The Conservatives had won handsomely in the country, so the Friday after polling day, 12 June, was a day of anxious waiting. I had some idea of what might happen to me. I did not think for one moment that I would be sacked, but having been a Minister of State for so long I was bound to be moved. It seemed to me there were only two possibilities. I was going to be either Chief Whip or

Solicitor-General. John Wakeham had told me that after the 1983 general election he had motored home from his constituency on the Friday and had just got into the house at 10 p.m. when he received a call from No. 10, so I was expecting a call at about that time; and at ten precisely the telephone rang and the Prime Minister invited me to be Chief Whip. She asked me to get to London as soon as possible so that we could discuss ministerial changes the following morning, and I threw a few things in to a bag, said goodbye to Gilly and set off in the car. I arrived in London at about 1.30 a.m. and went to bed a happy man.

I later learned from Nigel Lawson that I was second choice for Chief Whip. The Prime Minister wanted John Major, but Nigel wanted him in his Treasury team as Chief Secretary and Nigel won the day. When I went in to No. 12 on the Saturday morning someone had forgotten to put away John Wakeham's notes and in those my name appeared as a possible Solicitor-General. Whether John Major would have become Prime Minister had he spent a sizable part of the 1987 parliament as Chief Whip is extremely doubtful. If I had been made Solicitor-General I certainly would not have become Home Secretary.

I saw the Prime Minister at 9 a.m. on the Saturday and then set to work with John Wakeham on the middle-rank and junior ministers. Later in the day we had another meeting with the Prime Minister. Willie Whitelaw was there and after a while he told the Prime Minister she looked tired out and should pack it in until Monday. She agreed, very reluctantly.

Two good tales about the 1987 election should be recorded: the first concerned Ian Gilmour who failed to turn up for his own count at Amersham. When asked why, he said he had forgotten the way to the Town Hall. The other story is of a misfortune suffered by Dr Alan (later Sir Alan) Glyn at Windsor & Maidenhead. He asked a group of Young Conservatives to come to his hotel in the morning to go canvassing with him. They duly turned up but there was no Dr Glyn. Eventually a search party went up to his room. There was no immediate sign of him, but there was an old-fashioned wardrobe lying face down on the floor and the team set about restoring it to an upright position. Underneath it they discovered the good doctor. In the middle of the night he had set off to go to the lavatory but instead of going through the door in to the bathroom he had found his way in to the cupboard. The cupboard had fallen over trapping him inside and he had spent the rest of the night there.

No. 12 Downing Street is at the far end of Downing Street from Whitehall at the top of the steps leading down to St James's Park. It was once the Colonial Office and in the anteroom is a copy of Elizabeth Longford's biography of Wellington in which she records that in that very anteroom took place the only meeting between Wellington and Nelson. Nelson was waiting to see the Secretary for War and for the Colonies, Lord Castlereagh, only a few days before he set out to join HMS *Victory* at Portsmouth and sail south for his last battle.

As Chief Whip I was following some very illustrious predecessors. Ted Heath had helped the Tory Party to survive the Suez debacle of 1956 and Francis Pym had masterminded Britain's entry in to the European Community in 1973. Disraeli had once remarked that the government Chief Whip required 'consummate knowledge of human nature, the most amiable flexibility and complete self-control.' I was not sure that that sounded like me.

My secretary and right-hand-man was to be Murdo Maclean. Murdo had become secretary to the Chief Whip in 1978 and only two others had held the post before him. The first was appointed in 1917 when Lloyd George was Prime Minister, and his salary was paid by Conservative Central Office. When, in 1923, a Labour government came along the Labour Party wanted to keep the same man on but could not afford to pay him. So by the stroke of a pen he was transformed into a civil servant.

The job of a Chief Whip's secretary is very unusual. He forms an important part of 'the usual channels' and has to spend much of his time frequenting the various bars in the Palace of Westminster trying to strike deals with the Opposition to facilitate the progress of parliamentary business. For two years before I arrived on the scene life had been complicated for Murdo because the Opposition Chief Whip with whom most of the negotiating had to take place was Derek Foster – a member of the Salvation Army who did not drink. Michael Cox, Derek Foster's predecessor, had been a very different cup of tea (if I may use a somewhat inapposite metaphor) and the business had been transacted in a most convivial atmosphere.

My team in the Office could not have been better. My deputy was David Hunt, very efficient and superb when it came to sorting out the detailed work of the office. After him came Bob Boscawen, the old soldier who hopefully could ensure the good behaviour of the old and bold on the back benches, and then Tristan Garel-Jones, known for his guile and subtle stratagems. There was not much subtlety about David Lightbown who came next in seniority. He was the heavyweight whom no troublemaker would willingly meet on a dark night.

Mark Lennox-Boyd was skilled in the handling of the well-born, and Tony Durant of those who had had fewer advantages. Michael Neubert was utterly dependable in any circumstances. Stephen Dorrell, Richard Ryder and Alan Howarth were the intellectuals of the office and Kenneth Carlisle, Peter Lloyd and David Maclean the workers. Altogether a very balanced outfit.

Throughout the Thatcher years the office had been used as a training ground for those whom it was thought had the qualities to become departmental ministers, and most of those I have named soon got promotion. We had some strange customers to deal with on the back benches and strange customers often need strange treatment. Nick Budgen, who in the 1983–7 parliament had for a short time been a whip, was invited to attend a whips' dinner. Before it took place he voted against the government. An outraged Lightbown told him he was no longer welcome at the dinner, and that, although he had already paid, late cancellation meant there would be no refund. We never quite got the measure of Elizabeth Peacock, another one who caused us trouble. Tristan suggested that we might get her vote one night if we used a bit of flattery. We all contributed to the purchase of a dozen roses. It did not do a ha'porth of good. Clasping them to her bosom she sailed off – into the wrong lobby.

At about the same time a little cartoon appeared in one of the dailies which neatly illustrated the public's idea of Whips Office tactics. Three MPs are entering the ARGHHH lobby with their arms behind their back plaited like rope.

One of our more unusual backbenchers was Anthony Beaumont-Dark. One of his constituents asked me how he was getting on as an MP. With a note of admiration, almost veneration in her voice she added: 'I knew him years ago you know, when he was plain Mr Dark.' She obviously thought he had been awarded the 'Beaumont', probably by the Queen personally. One night shortly afterwards I went to look at the tape before going into dinner, and there I read the ominous announcement: 'The pound has fallen against the Dark.'

The government Chief Whip has extraordinary influence with ministers, even Cabinet ministers. Shortly after I got the job my agent rang up and said that she had organised a big event in the constituency in July and badly needed a Cabinet minister to come and speak. I said that it was impossibly short notice but I would do my best. I sat down at my desk and extended an invitation to four Cabinet ministers, realising I had no time to wait for each to refuse in turn before writing to the next one. It was a long shot but perhaps one of the four might feel sorry for me and accept. By return of post I received acceptances from all four and had to think of good excuses for not wanting three of them.

Most troublesome from a whipping point of view was the Local Government (Finance) Bill which paved the way for the abolition of domestic rates and the introduction of the community charge. It seemed so right at the time to get rid of rates and introduce a system which would make virtually everyone who benefited from local government services pay something towards their cost. With only 20 million of the 35 million people who voted in local elections paying a penny towards its cost, it was not surprising that councils that spent like sailors were triumphantly re-elected. The poll tax (as the community charge came to be called) undoubtedly contributed to the downfall of Margaret Thatcher, but in my belief it was not the introduction of a flat rate charge which sunk us. It was a combination of Treasury-driven cuts in the rate support grant and gross overspending by local authorities. At the time of the 1987 election the level of community charge forecast for Ribble Valley was £178. That I had no difficulty in defending; but by 1989 the estimated charge had already risen to £300 and further increases were forecast. What at first had been marketable no longer was.

But these problems were still in the future. What we had to cope with in the 1987–8 session was not the fear that the Treasury would reduce its contribution to local government just when local expenditure was rocketing out of control. Our fear was that rebellious Tory MPs who felt that a flat rate charge was unfair and that there should be a charge that went up in bands according to the value of a person's property would derail the legislation. In April 1988 the so-called Mates amendment was debated at the report stage of the Bill and it was only with a lot of work that we managed to contain the revolt and see the amendment defeated. Even so,

I was not exactly happy that twenty-three Conservatives voted against the government and our majority sank from 101 to 25.

After the shooting at Hungerford in August 1987, Douglas Hurd introduced a very controversial Firearms Bill. The committee stage was taken on the floor of the House under a guillotine (or timetable) motion. At about midnight the guillotine came down with literally hundreds of amendments undebated. Michael Colvin rose and asked the Deputy Speaker whether the House was entitled to have a separate vote on each one of them. The reply from the Chair was in the affirmative and Dennis Skinner, who was as usual sitting in the chamber in the corner seat below the gangway looking for an opportunity to make a nuisance of himself, could not believe his luck. He proceeded to call for a division on amendment after amendment. Michael was a very nice man and his death was a great loss to Parliament, but on this occasion he had made himself far from popular and I told him that if he was wise he would go home. He made his getaway, but there was no getaway for us. For hours we were in the chamber voting on amendment after amendment and would have been there much longer had not the Deputy Speaker agreed after the first few divisions to implement the rule which enables an amendment to be declared lost on sufficient members rising to their feet to indicate beyond doubt their opposition to it. Chief Whips are not popular if they require the Parliamentary Party to spend the night bobbing up and down like this, and I was almost as unpopular as Michael Colvin as a result of this incident.

The most anxious exercise in my first year was the handling of Richard Shepherd's Private Members' Bill to reform the law on official secrets. He had come high up in the ballot so if his Bill got a second reading, it would go straight into committee. That meant that there would be the opportunity for prolonged and detailed debate on every aspect of the work of the security service. It was not being fanciful to fear that members might wittingly or unwittingly disclose details of the service's activities. But MPs are very jealous of their right to introduce legislation and nothing was likely to annoy our backbenchers more than the government setting out to destroy Richard Shepherd's Bill before it had hardly got started. I decided that I had no choice but to whip the Party to vote against the Bill on second reading and there was no point in half measures. We had to make absolutely certain that the Bill would be defeated in spite of the sympathy a large part of the Party had for Richard, if not for the Bill. So we did something which was almost without precedent. We imposed a three line whip which put the outcome beyond doubt. Of course, I had to take a fair amount of stick in the debate. At one point David Owen, who as an ex-Foreign Secretary should have known better, said in his elegant way: 'It is the day for the Patronage Secretary to get stuffed.' But stuffed I was not; and the Party soon forgave me. In due course the government introduced its own meas- ure to put the security service on a statutory footing.

In the summer of 1988 a reshuffle took place which infuriated the press and members of the lobby in particular. After we in the office had spread the story that there was to be no reshuffle until September we sprung one on them in July. Arrangements were made in complete secrecy and with the minimum of discussion with Cabinet ministers, and the announcement was made without a single leak. Martin Fletcher wrote in *The Times* that:

> David Waddington, the Chief Whip, kept it all so secret that even Lord Young, the Trade Secretary, was initially unaware that he was losing Clarke, his deputy (to become Secretary of State for Health). Indeed, some ministers first learned of the reshuffle through Whitehall's most reliable grapevine, their chauffeurs.

Also in that summer some crackpot decided that a government motion should be tabled incorporating a loyal address to the Queen drawing attention to the tercentenary of the Glorious Revolution of 1688. No one consulted me, the motion appeared on the order paper on a day on which the Party was not whipped – and the motion was debatable. Tony Benn seized what was an obvious opportunity to cause us maximum embarrassment and rose to speak on the motion, and after an hour or so it was clear that there was going to be a vote which could easily lead to a government defeat. Such a result would be construed as an insult to the Queen but would be even clearer evidence of the Chief Whip's incompetence.

But where were the Conservatives needed to support the motion? Everywhere it seemed, except in the Palace of Westminster. A lot had, I knew, gone to the Carlton Club for the One Nation Group summer cocktail party. I could not leave the House but ready at hand were Gilly and Paddy Hunt, my deputy's wife. Off to the Carlton Club they went and descended on the party goers. 'Back to the House,' they said, 'quick, sharp,' and back they came. One Tory MP was reported as saying: 'The wives were brilliant. They sorted out the problem and were more competent at it than their husbands.' Prudently he asked that his name should not be disclosed.

Leading up to the reshuffle Peter Brooke as Party Chairman and I had had three or four meetings with the Prime Minister over supper on a Sunday night. On one such occasion, we sat down to eat, but after a few minutes the Prime Minister said: 'It does seem unfair; here are we enjoying ourselves and poor Denis is having supper all alone upstairs in the flat.' Peter Brooke and I, taking what we thought was a pretty broad hint, told her to invite him down. The PM thanked us and said she could guarantee that Denis would not say a word when we were talking about the reshuffle. Denis then came down and on the whole was pretty good but at one stage he could not contain himself. 'Oh surely not so-and-so. You were only saying the other day, Margaret, what a complete wimp he was.'

When it came to discussing ministerial appointments one thing was quite apparent and that was that the Prime Minister liked a pretty face; once or twice she had to be discouraged when she wished to see some good-looking fellow promoted who was known throughout the Parliamentary Party to be pretty useless. Indeed, there was a time when her eyes lighted on a minister who for a time she talked of as a possible successor. He was a fine-looking chap but no one else thought that he was anything like up to the job. I am talking of an interesting foible; I am not suggesting, for one moment, that she was not perfectly capable in the ordinary course of events of picking competent people to fill posts.

One of the things I remember about the 1988–9 session was the great egg fiasco. Edwina Currie started a rumpus when she told the press that all eggs contained salmonella or something to that effect. Backbenchers were told by their chicken farmers that she was going to bankrupt the lot of them and there were many demands that she should be removed from the government without delay. Kenneth Clarke, her Secretary of State, argued strongly that she had said no more than the truth but eventually he recognised, like everyone else, that she had to go. I rarely made a note of anything that went on in Cabinet, but I did scribble down this exchange. Kenneth Clarke presented to Cabinet a report which comprised a very lengthy list of types of food which his department considered carried a health risk. Top of the list in terms of risk came precooked chicken, soft cheese and raw eggs. Nick Ridley, anxious as always to ridicule the experts, said this was very strange as he only ate precooked chicken, soft cheese and raw eggs. For once the Prime Minister, who was extremely fond of Nick, did not come to his support. 'You are not a pregnant woman,' she said sternly and we moved swiftly to the next item on the agenda.

In February 1989 I sat on the front bench as John Major in his capacity as Chief Secretary replied to a debate on economic policy.

He reminded the House of the state of the country ten years earlier in February 1979 and read slowly from a newspaper, holding it up carefully so that the Opposition could see what it was. 'Hospitals blockaded, docks closed by pickets,' he intoned, and then went on, 'food stocks running low, NUPE to select patients for treatment.' All the while he was barracked by the Opposition. 'The *Daily Telegraph*, ho! ho! Was that the best you could find?' 'Yes,' replied John. 'It was the only paper published that day. The rest were shut down by strike action.' I thought then that he was learning and one day might make it.

Meanwhile Gilly had established herself in the affections of the staff at No. 12 and was doing a great job 'supplying' in the words of one press article 'the laughter while her husband twists the arms.' She was also busy helping to found SANE (Schizophrenia a National Emergency).

On a Sunday at about the end of June 1989 Gilly and I went off to lunch at Chequers. It was quite a big party and when we went into lunch I found that I was sitting on the Prime Minister's left and a prominent businessman, who had donated a great deal of money to the Conservative Party, was on her right. On his right was Gilly. As soon as lunch started the PM leaned over the man's back and, tapping Gilly on the shoulder, signalled that she wanted her to keep the fellow entertained. She then turned to me and told me what was on her mind.

In his memoirs, Nigel Lawson says that Geoffrey was not expecting to be moved from the Foreign Office because right up to the last moment I was consulting him about the reshuffle, asking him whom he wished to have as his junior Foreign Office minister responsible for Europe. This is simply not correct. What happened was that Geoffrey rang me at my home to say that he knew a reshuffle was in the offing and was most anxious that Lynda Chalker should not be moved from looking after the European side of things in the Foreign Office. I, having been asked by the Prime Minister to say nothing of her intentions, could hardly have told him that there was no point in his worrying about Lynda because he would not be in the Foreign Office with her; so, having made one or two non-committal remarks, I got him off the line. Geoffrey later said that, in his view, I should have told him what was going on, but my first loyalty was to the Prime Minister and I was not free to do so. I do, however, understand what a shock it must have been when at nine o' clock on Monday morning (24 July) he was called to No. 10 and told he was no longer to be Foreign Secretary. I gather from what the Prime Minister later said that she offered him the post of Lord President of the Council and Leader of the House of Commons, but Geoffrey wanted time to consider and asked if he could have till mid-morning to give his reply. Eventually he returned to Downing Street and was offered and accepted the posts of Deputy Prime Minister and Leader of the House of Commons. The Prime Minister also agreed to his having the use of Dorneywood which was apparently not being much used by Nigel Lawson.

That evening, Norman Tebbit said the ministerial changes were disastrous – not because of the removal of Geoffrey from the Foreign Office, but because of the weakness of the DTI team, the inability of one minister to make up his mind about anything and the disloyalty of another. 'Otherwise,' he said 'the Party is pleased.' If he was right, he did not stay right for long.

The next day the storm broke. The talk in the lobby was all of Geoffrey agreeing to stay only when the Prime Minister had promised to take away Dorneywood from Nigel Lawson. That was a part of the story which I did not want to see come out. It made Geoffrey look petty, and it made the Prime Minister look mean in refusing to allow Geoffrey to remain at Chevening which she knew he loved. And it gave the impression to the world at large that there was too much interest in who was to have the grace and favour houses at the Prime Minister's disposal and not enough in the jobs to be done. Then Bernard Ingham did not help matters by telling the lobby, in response to questions, that the title of Deputy Prime Minister did not really mean anything at all. Geoffrey would have no powers as such and certainly would not be responsible for British government policy when Margaret was out of the country. Everyone knew from experience that Bernard's blunt answers echoed his boss's views. She was far too honest to pretend that the title of Deputy Prime Minister, which she had offered at my suggestion but against her better judgement, meant anything very much when it clearly did not.

In September 1989 Gilly and I went to Amalfi for a week's holiday. I soon learned that nowhere in the world can a Chief Whip escape his Prime Minister. The very first night I was called to the phone. Tony (Lord) Trafford, who in July had been appointed Minister of State in the Department of Health to pilot the NHS reforms through the Upper House, had died. The Prime Minister wanted to know who should replace him. We had a series of calls from her throughout the week and my reputation with those running the hotel was greatly enhanced. But Tony's death was a very sad event. He was the unflappable consultant physician at Brighton Infirmary who had looked after John Wakeham and Margaret Tebbit after the Brighton bombing.

I had an unnerving experience when I arrived in Blackpool for the Party Conference. I walked in to the Imperial Hotel and someone, shoving a microphone under my nose, said: 'Well, Chief Whip, what are your views on the collapse of the pound?' Having spent the earlier part of the day hard at work and having listened to a brand new tape of military marches on the journey from Sabden to Blackpool, I did not know what the girl was talking about but did not wish to admit my ignorance of the world-shattering events which had apparently taken place behind my back and without my permission. For a moment I wondered whether the best course might not be to fall to the ground in a simulated faint. Instead, I rambled on a bit and hoped for the best. The following week I got two rude letters accusing me of talking nonsense. I replied, agreeing with the writers.

When the House came back after the recess it was to face the television cameras. I had been against televising the House. It seemed to me that it was likely to encourage hooligan behaviour, not necessarily by members. After all, some lesbians had recently publicised their cause by abseiling from the public gallery in the House of Lords where cameras were already installed. I also doubted whether the Prime Minister would come over well on television. On the last point I was proved entirely wrong. On radio she sounded strident and unattractive, but for some reason, perhaps because one was seeing as well as hearing and not concentrating on the voice alone, she came over on television as a very much more sympathetic person.

Immediately after Cabinet on 26 October Norman Lamont came to see me and said a crisis was brewing. Nigel Lawson was in a state about Alan Walters's role as adviser to the Prime Minister. Would I go and see Nigel and try and dissuade him from doing anything rash? I said I would and when I got to Nigel's room, which was just through the door from No. 12, he said he was fed up and had made up his mind to go because of Alan Walters. The policies he was trying to pursue were constantly being undermined by Walters's gossiping. I told him that it would be very damaging to the government if he were to go and, having deployed all the usual arguments about loyalty, I flattered him by saying he was the best Chancellor for many years. But I made little headway and eventually fell back on begging him to stay his hand for a while so that we could all sit down and talk about his grievances. He said that he would think about it, and when I left I thought he was going to ponder before acting.

I went round to see Andrew Turnbull, then Principal Private Secretary to the Prime Minister, and we agreed that as the Prime Minister was about to have her first Question Time after the summer recess and also had to make a statement about the Commonwealth Prime Ministers' Conference in Kuala Lumpur, we would not interrupt her briefing. That afternoon in the House of Commons she was in top form. I could hardly believe it when told later that only minutes before leaving No. 10 to come across to the House, Nigel's letter of resignation had been handed to her. She must have been in some turmoil but appeared in complete command of herself and, as usual, of the House.

In mid-afternoon news of the resignation appeared on the tape. The business of the House was interrupted by points of order and then by requests for a statement from the Leader of the House. I was running between the chamber, the Leader's room and the Opposition Whips Office trying to get the Opposition to agree to make progress with the business on our undertaking that there would be a statement on the floor of the House as soon as possible. In the middle of all this I was told to get over to No. 10 to see the PM. As soon as I got into her room she said she wanted me to join the Cabinet but at that stage did not say in what office. She wanted my advice as to who should succeed me and who should be Chancellor. The second question was a lot easier than the first. John Major had not had a happy time in his few months as Foreign Secretary and would be a lot happier back in the Treasury.

I had a short conversation with the Prime Minister about who should be Chief Whip and, expecting to return to the matter in due course, I went back again to the Commons. I had not been there long, trying to cope with major trouble, when I was called back to No. 10 and the PM asked me to be Home Secretary. She then went on to say that Tim Renton was to be Chief Whip. I was surprised that she had made the appointment without further consulting me, and I thought that it was a mistake, made by someone who never did seem to have much of a clue about the workings of the office and had not the slightest idea as to how the Whips Office could watch the back of a Prime Minister in trouble.

I knew Tim to be a very decent, nice and honourable man but it was odd to make Chief Whip someone who had never served in the Whips Office and had no knowledge of how it operated. It did cross my mind that the Prime Minister had appointed Tim at Geoffrey's suggestion, to placate him, but on second thoughts that looked improbable in view of the way in which they were getting on, or rather not getting on, with each other. I only learned the truth a few years later when, again to my surprise, Kenneth Baker told me that it was on his advice that the appointment had been made.

Anyhow, I went back to the House to discuss with Geoffrey the statement he would have to make from the dispatch box about the changes. He was not in a happy mood, voicing outrage that he had not been properly consulted about them. Elspeth was with him just as she had been in the Foreign Office on the day he had ceased to be Foreign Secretary. I was not in the Commons to hear his statement, but this is how the *Daily Telegraph* described the scene:

There was a huge Conservative cheer for Mr Major when his appointment was read out, a smaller one for Mr Hurd the new Foreign Secretary, and a roar for Mr Waddington, the new Home Secretary. 'He's a hanger' came a loud observation from the Labour benches, as if to explain why the ex-Chief Whip's promotion had caused such joy opposite. 'There will be no change in our success- ful economic policies,' continued Sir Geoffrey, having had enough of the non-fiction. He did not specify whether these would be the successful economic policies of the Prime Minister or of the man we must now learn to call the Rt Hon. Member for Blaby.

My son James, his fiancée and her parents were due to come to the House of Commons for dinner. I met them in the Central Lobby, dragged them into my room, told them the news and then rushed again to No. 10 where we settled a few changes in the lower ranks. After dinner I went down into Speaker's Court to find my car. It had vanished and in its place was a shiny black armour-plated Jaguar complete with police driver and detective. Also standing outside waiting for me were Clive Whitmore, Permanent Secretary, and Brian Mower, press officer at the Home Office. They greeted me warmly and I arranged to meet them at the front door of the Home Office the following morning. I went home shell-shocked and slept like a log.

The next day Gilly set off for home in our own car while I was subjected to an enormous press conference and torture by camera. Eventually at 5 p.m. I set off in the Jaguar for Lancashire. The traffic, as usual on a Friday evening, was appalling and before long my exasperated police driver began to show his prowess. Siren wailing he used the hard shoulder as much as the road and by about eleven we were going up the drive to Whins House. To my surprise, the house was full of policemen including the chief constable. Someone had concluded that the appointment of a local lad as Home Secretary called for a party, preferably at the local lad's expense, and a party was in full swing.

The next morning I went to the back door to take Basil out for a walk and standing on the doorstep outside was an oversize and overweight policeman. 'May I ask what you are planning to do, sir?' he said. 'Take my dog for a walk,' I replied. 'I'd rather you didn't, sir,' he said. 'I have strict orders that you have not to leave the premises without a detective and the detectives are staying in a hotel, and they are not here yet.' 'Very well,' said I docilely, 'I'll just let the dog out on his own.' 'I'd rather not, sir,' replied the constable. I was beginning to think that things were getting out of hand. Orders were orders but I was not at all sure that Gilly would wish the beginning of my term as Home Secretary to be marked on the carpet by Basil; so Basil and I took the law in to our own hands. The rest of the day was spent watching the police drive large nails into the walls of the ironing room. There they set up a radio station command post which stayed there until a week or two later a rather smart hut was placed outside the backyard. This was my suggestion, a command post which could be moved as soon as a Home Secretary was replaced, and carted off to the home of the next one. In the past many days had been spent improving ministers' houses in order to accommodate the police.

CHAPTER FOURTEEN

Home Secretary

My appointment got a reasonably favourable reception from the press. There was a nice piece by Robin Oakley and Woodrow Wyatt – generous and thoughtful:

The Tory party has held its nerve better than may have been expected over the Lawson affair. The irony of the reshuffle forced on Mrs Thatcher by Lawson's resignation is that it may in the end actually strengthen her government. It has given her team greater coherence by fixing in the top jobs a group of people eminently suited to occupy them. The key to the whole affair was experience. Mrs. Thatcher installed in the three top offices of state men who had held the number two job in the same department. David Waddington enters the Cabinet probably more in tune with the instincts of rank and file Tories than anyone there already. A barrister whose days as a workaholic immigration minister gave him a keen insight into the workings of the Home Office and the human nature of his parliamentary colleagues (since put to good use as Chief Whip), he is an 'art of the possible' politician. He has one advantage over Hurd. As a natural right-winger on law and order, Waddington will be able to use the code words and to make those little growls in the back of the throat which assure the hangers and floggers at the Tory Party Conference that he is on their wavelength and that he understands their instincts even if he can never give them back the rope.

Gilly also got a very good and well-deserved write-up for all the support she had given me over the years, in good times and bad. One journalist quoted her as saying: 'I could gossip for Britain in the Olympics.' Another asked whether she was surprised at her husband's appointment? 'Not at all,' she said, 'if they made him Pope he would want to be God.'

There was no time to sit back and enjoy my good fortune. On the Sunday evening I was back in London and on Monday morning at my desk. There were some matters which had to be dealt with without delay. Not surprisingly the events in Tiananmen Square had had a very unsettling effect in Hong Kong and it was important to take steps to maintain confidence in the future of the place and stem the rising tide of emigration. To this end the Foreign Office had proposed a scheme to give a large number of key people British passports. Far from this being to encourage them to leave Hong Kong it was to give them confidence to stay, for they would know that if things went terribly wrong they would have somewhere to go. The Home Office could see the arguments in favour of the scheme but did not want to be accused of undermining the tough immigration policy which had been so successful in taking immigration right out of the centre of political debate. I looked at the list of so-called key jobs which the government of Hong Kong was suggesting should come within the scheme and soon concluded that it would leave us wide open to attack in the House. In essence Hong Kong wanted a scheme which, while heavily weighted against the unskilled, would still have given every category of worker, including the unskilled, some chance of success. But this seemed entirely inconsistent with the statements we had made in Parliament to the effect that highly-skilled people in Hong Kong would be selected. One would find it pretty hard to argue, I thought, that minor posts in the social services were key posts which, if left vacant, would undermine the stability of the territory; and I told the Prime Minister that in my view the list had to be revised and there had to be a strict limit – 50,000 – on the number of heads of families who could benefit.

The Bill was a short enabling measure to provide a framework for the operation of the selection scheme, with the scheme itself to be set out in an Order in Council. Norman Tebbit threatened to cause mayhem when the Bill was introduced, but he was not able to muster much support and I was greatly helped, not for the last time, by Roy Hattersley who did not find it easy to explain Labour policy, if any, on the matter. Perhaps I misunderstood him but at one stage he seemed to be saying that the government's scheme was 'wicked' because it involved 'a denial of basic justice' to the great majority of citizens of Hong Kong. All 5 million of them, or at any rate the 3.2 million British Dependent Territory citizens there, should have been given a passport and the right to settle in Britain. At another stage he seemed to be saying he would give the right to come here to some, not all, but he would not say to how many.

This was one exchange on BBC Radio:

Q: How many should have passports?
A: I don't know what the number is and I don't think about the number. I certainly think our figure will turn out to be less than the government's. But I don't know and I've not calculated our procedure on holding a figure down.

Nobody could be expected to make much sense of that.

When I got back into the Home Office, planning for a Criminal Justice Bill for the 1990–91 session was fairly well advanced. By an earlier Criminal Justice Act the powers of the courts to impose custodial sentences on young offenders had been strictly limited and it was thought it was now time to take the next step, and impose similar restrictions on the sentencing of adults. Many in the Home Office who were on the criminal justice side of the shop genuinely felt that judges and magistrates were still sending to prison offenders who could be better dealt with in the community, but many others wanted limits on sentencing powers for an entirely different reason. The Home Office had for years been faced with intractable problems on the prison side of the business. The government had, in 1979, embarked on a great new prison-building programme but the prison population had gone up and up and there was constant sniping at the government because of overcrowding. What better way could there be of tackling the problem than to make it more difficult for the courts to send people to prison? My own view was that there was no point in sending people to prison if there were other ways of dealing with them. There was not the slightest evidence that prisons taught people the error of their ways. Rather, they were universities of crime where people were, at best, confirmed in their antisocial behaviour and, at worst, learned even nastier tricks. But when I arrived on the scene little attempt had been made to work up a balanced package which would convince our own supporters that we were not just going soft on crime. We had, I believed, to balance the new proposals on sentencing with changes in the parole system on the lines of the Carlisle Committee's proposals so that when a prison sentence had to be imposed the sentence served bore a closer relationship to the sentence passed by the judge. There had then to be heavier sentences for crimes of violence, new policies to bring home to parents their responsibility when their children fell foul of the law, and more imaginative forms of punishment in the community. These could include curfew orders enforced through electronic tagging. Lastly there had to be a 'victims' charter' which recognised that those who suffered from crime also had rights.

The Green Paper published by my predecessor had proposed unit fines and I had been down to Basingstoke and had seen the pilot scheme in operation. It seemed to have many merits. What, after all, could be more sensible than a fine's size being related to the offender's means? But a few years later it was destroyed by the folly of politicians and the magistracy. At the behest of the Treasury the government had agreed on a unit scale so graded that at the top end wholly ridiculous penalties could be imposed on high earners for relatively trivial offences and some magistrates, who disliked the whole idea of unit fines, decided to make a political point by applying the scale in an entirely inflexible way, choosing to ignore the admittedly limited discretion given to them under the Act.

From the moment I arrived back in the Home Office the press wanted to talk of nothing else but capital punishment. I was, they said, the first 'hanger' to have occupied the Home Office since Reggie Maudling, and that, having marked me out as a very rare beast, was all that needed to be said about me. While I was certainly not going to change my views overnight to thwart the press, I was anxious to try and put the matter in perspective. I have to confess, however, that I was only partially successful in that regard.

I believed then and believe now that the first job of a Home Secretary is the protection of society and I felt then and I feel now that that protection would be reinforced by the restoration of capital punishment. Surely if a person knows that if he uses a gun in a robbery, he is likely to hang, he is less likely to take a gun with him. But I was a realist and I knew the way votes on capital punishment had gone over the years: not once since the War had there been a majority in the Commons in favour. The chances of capital punishment ever being restored were slight indeed. My job, therefore, was to do my best to give the public the greatest protection possible without capital punishment and do my best to ensure that those guilty of the worst types of murder stayed in prison, if necessary, for the rest of their lives. I did not believe that without capital punishment there was nothing I could do to improve public safety. There were plenty of worthwhile things to do within the system as it was. It was an uphill struggle trying to get this message across but I did my best.

The responsibilities of the Home Secretary were greater in the 1980s than they have now become. The Home Secretary was, for instance, concerned with the administration of criminal justice, criminal law, the treatment of offenders and the prison service – all matters now within the remit of the Ministry of Justice. He was also responsible for broad questions of national broadcasting policy; and in my first few weeks back in the Home Office broadcasting was another enormous headache. As Chief Whip I had for two years sat on a committee chaired by the Prime Minister which was working up proposals for radical change to independent broadcasting, but it still came as a nasty shock to learn that in a few days' time I had to address an important gathering of broadcasters on the government's plans – particularly the proposal that, subject to the passing of a quality threshold, television franchises should be awarded to the highest bidders.

Then it was Remembrance Sunday when I found my responsibilities even more alarming. My job was to review the police on parade in the quadrangle in the old Home Office building, then greet the members of the Royal Family attending the ceremony, including the then King of Norway who never missed. Finally I had to take the Queen through the building to the top of the stairs leading out into Whitehall. There stood an army officer alongside an ancient chronometer. 'It is 10.58 and twenty seconds, Your Majesty,' he said, 'and the time you normally set off.' And off went the Queen, arriving at her spot in front of the Cenotaph at precisely 10.59 and fifty-five seconds. I followed at a discreet distance and tucked myself in at the end of the line of Cabinet ministers. At the end of the service I had to set off after the Queen and take her back through the building, praying that I would not lose my way.

Later that morning I missed a trick. After the Queen had left, I was chatting with the Prime Minister and we got on to the beauties of the old Home Office building. 'Would you like it back?' said Margaret. 'I have other things on my mind,' I replied.

Soon, on 21 November 1989, we had the State Opening of Parliament and the debate on the Queen's Speech. The loyal address was moved by Ian Gow. In the course of it he said:

> We should send a message from this place, to friend and foe alike, that our resolve will never weaken, that those who choose the bullet and the bomb, will gain no concessions from Her Majesty's government and that their campaign of terror is as odious as it is futile. Terrorism flourishes where those who perpetrate it believe that one day terror will triumph. That is why all of us need to give no hint that it ever will.

Those words must have strengthened the IRA's belief that Ian was an inveterate foe, and in the summer of the next year he was blown up in his car by one of the brutes.

Shortly before Christmas we went to Paris and stayed with our Ambassador, Sir Ewen Fergusson. In his younger days he had been a great rugger player. He liked to show off his international caps to visitors male and female – which sometimes led to difficulties as he kept them in the gents' lavatory. We went to dinner with Pierre Joxe, then Minister of the Interior, and were most impressed by the magnificent palace which was his official residence. He did not believe me when I told him that a William Henry Waddington who was born in Britain had been Prime Minister of France in the 1870s, but eventually with the aid of reference books I proved to him that I was right. We went to see the David exhibition in the

Louvre and were suitably shocked by the pyramid placed therein with the connivance of President Mitterand. We went Christmas shopping to try to forget it.

One of my first jobs when the House met in the New Year was to deal with Lord Justice Taylor's Report on the Hillsborough disaster. The Report poured scorn on the football membership scheme which had been strongly advocated by the Prime Minister as the government's response to football hooliganism. I had no option but to go to the Prime Minister and give her the unpalatable news that the scheme had to be ditched. My statement in the House was eagerly awaited by the Opposition who felt that if ever there was a case of a government finishing up with egg on its face, this was it. But everything went incredibly well. Having announced that we were accepting the Taylor recommendation not to go ahead with the scheme because of the technical difficulties identified, I went on to highlight Taylor's support for all-seat stadiums, and to say that a football licensing authority would require an end to terraces on designated grounds by 1999. In addition, there would be improved arrangements for crowd control, and urgent consideration of the case for new offences and new powers to deal with those excluded from grounds by the Courts. Roy Hattersley, in his reply, jeered at the government for being forced to abandon the membership scheme but rejected the one proposal by Taylor which could also have a bearing on the fight against football hooliganism – all-seat stadiums. All-seat stadiums meant, he said, a ban on standing and 'could lead to people who leapt to their feet out of joie de vivre being slammed in gaol.'

Matthew Parris described the scene for readers of *The Times* with the headline:

'STRIKER DAVE PLAYS THEM OFF THE PARK'

On a football pitch tilted against the government by Lord Justice Taylor, and leading a team whose bootlaces had been tied together by their own Prime Minister, Home Secretary David ('Dave') Waddington yesterday snatched victory from the jaws of – well, not quite defeat – but Roy Hattersley. Labour's manager, Neil Kinnock, must have been as sick as a parrot.

Waddington has only just been put in Cabinet United's first team. New to the top division, this player's strike-rate was unknown. He had (before Christmas) been not so much talent-spotted as dragged on as a substitute at half time when 'bully' Lawson stormed off the pitch in protest at the appointment of a new physio, Alan Walters.

And now here he was, on a rainy Monday afternoon, kicking Labour viciously in the goolies whenever the ref. wasn't looking – and scoring time and again. Waddington was proving that, just occasionally, this country can still produce great strikers on the wrong side of sixty.

In the Distinguished Strangers' Gallery Taylor's demeanour was wholly un-partisan. Waddington's was anything but. Those who expect magisterial detachment from a Home Secretary will be disappointed in this magnificent old shin-kicker.

Mr Waddington speaks in the manner of an angry school master interspersing strokes of the cane with a point-by-point recital of the crimes of the errant boy.

Lord Justice Taylor, he said, had pointed the finger of blame at 'poor facilities' (thwack), 'hooliganism' (thwack), 'excessive drinking' (thwack) 'and poor leadership' (thwack). Furthermore, 'squalid conditions' (thwack) 'encouraging squalid' (thwack) 'behaviour'. In short, the real hooligans were the clubs.

It was shamelessly effective. By the time the Home Secretary sat down, we had quite forgotten that he had come to the House to announce that the government was abandoning the centre-piece of its Football Supporters Bill, the 'membership scheme', because an independent judge had said that the whole thing was a nonsense.

Curiously, Hattersley made little of this. After a few ritual insults hurled like soggy sprouts at the absent Mrs Thatcher, he endorsed the Taylor Report, which could be 'the basis of much-needed improvement to football grounds'.

Then he rejected the cornerstone of the whole thing. Labour could not, he said, support all-seater stadiums. After all, what if people wanted to stand up in their seats? Those MPs who do not expect the Princess of Wales to be dragged by police out of her box at Covent Garden next time she feels moved to give a standing ovation, felt that Hattersley exaggerated the problem here.

A most extraordinary incident occurred about this time which showed how utterly useless the football authorities were and explained why the game was in such an appalling mess. A near-riot had taken place at Bournemouth after the police had warned the football authorities that there was going to be trouble and had begged them to either move or cancel the match. They had refused. I summoned the chairman and gave him an imperial rocket after which cooperation with the police did improve a little.

If I had my time again I would organise my life a lot better, and certainly I should have arranged my life in the Home Office a lot better. For some reason civil servants are good at drawing up submissions and identifying courses of action available in a particular situation but quite hopeless at writing speeches, presumably because they themselves rarely make them and they cannot imagine how their words will sound when spoken. I wasted hours rewriting the most dreadful offerings when I should have (a) refused to go to half the events in the diary for which the offerings were intended and (b) made a few off the cuff remarks at the events which I did attend. One reform I did introduce which should be of lasting benefit: I flatly refused to motor across London in heavy traffic to have lunch with journalists. Those who wanted to see me could choose between a sandwich in my room or a quick meal in the nearest hotel to Queen Anne's Gate.

We stayed in Denny Street until the New Year, by which time the Hurds had left South Eaton Place for Carlton House Gardens. South Eaton Place had its advantages, principally a decent-sized dining room in which one could entertain. There was also ample room for visiting members of the family. But it was a dismally dark house with the basement occupied by the police, whom I was supposed to inform if I ever wished to venture out.

I was not sleeping well and one Sunday morning I got up at four o'clock to walk to Victoria bus station to buy the papers. There was a camera above the front door and I had to be very stealthy leaving the house, creeping along the wall to keep out of the camera's view. I made good my escape, bought the papers and prepared to re-enter the house in the same manner. Pressed against the wall and with latch key in hand I moved slowly towards the door-step. I then tripped over it and the papers went flying in all directions. The door was flung open from the inside. 'Hello, hello,' said a burly constable. 'And what might you be up to, sir?'

I got on well with the Metropolitan Police. The only trouble was their eating habits. I have never known people put away so much food at the multiplicity of lunches and dinners I was required to attend at Christmas time. Every rank in turn invited me to stuff myself – literally, I mean.

Douglas Hurd had introduced a War Crimes Bill to confer on the British courts jurisdiction to try people for war crimes committed in the 1939–45 war even though they were not British citizens or otherwise subject to the jurisdiction of the British courts at the time the crimes alleged were committed. The Simon Wiesenthal Centre had come up with evidence that a number of people who had found their way into Britain after the War as 'refugees' or displaced persons had been party to the most horrible massacres in Eastern Europe after the German attack on Russia in 1941, and we could not sit by and do nothing. We had either to send these people back to face trial in the places where the crimes were committed or give the British courts power to try them, and trying them here seemed the better choice. The Baltic states and Belorussia where the incidents had taken place were still a part of the Soviet Union and few had much confidence in the 'justice' meted out by the courts of those benighted lands. Furthermore most, if not all, the people under suspicion were now, by naturalisation, British citizens and legislation to deprive them of their citizenship and deport them would be at least as controversial as giving the British courts jurisdiction to try them.

The Bill got a huge majority on second reading and passed through the rest of its stages in the Commons at breakneck speed. The Lords took one look at the measure and threw it out; and now that I had taken over at the Home Office we had to decide whether to introduce the Bill again. I was sure we should. One could not just forget about a Bill which had received such a ringing endorsement from the elected House; and the Parliament Act, passed to resolve differences between the two Houses in favour of the Commons, was tailor-made to deal with the situation. If, after the Commons had approved the Bill a second time, the Lords again rejected the meas-ure, it would proceed to Royal Assent and become law without any further debate. In Cabinet I was surprised to find Douglas Hurd and Geoffrey Howe against reintroduction, but their objections were overruled and the Bill then went through the Commons again – as easily as it had the first time. What happened in the Lords the second time round I will describe later, because when I left the Home Office and went to the Lords, the Bill followed me there.

At Easter 1990 I was due to chair the World Summit on Drugs in London; I thought it a good idea to fit in a trip to America

before the summit to educate myself a little about the drugs problem in the States.

In Washington a police anti-drugs squad took us out late at
night to see the extent of drug trading on the streets and the way
the police were trying to cope with it. The police station from
which we started was austere in the extreme, a concrete floor, an
army-style trestle table and a few upright chairs. The police in
England would not have put up with it for a moment and it did
not suggest that Washington, the capital city of the richest country
in the world, was awash with money to maintain law and order.
Out on the streets a number of young people – some very young
– were searched, the method adopted being to spread-eagle the
suspect over the bonnet of the car and train a shotgun on him.
Some arrests followed.

It was interesting to talk to both the police and the politicians
in Washington. They all insisted that public attitudes towards
the use of drugs were changing and they were winning the war
against the casual or recreational user. But they were disturbingly
unwilling to face up to or at any rate voice the conclusion that the
drug problem in the States was now largely an inner-city problem
afflicting a black underclass and associated with urban decline
and poverty. What was very encouraging was the close working
relationship between the American agencies and our own drugs
liaison officer, Superintendent Trevor Cutts, who was attached to
the British Embassy.

We went to Quantico and saw members of the FBI in training
and then on to St Louis. We were entertained by an austere and
puritanical mayor at a river boat restaurant which served over-
cooked beef, and gravy with the consistency of porridge. Across the
river was East St Louis, almost a wasteland with only government
buildings looking habitable. We spoke to the US Federal Prosecutor
who said he liked to get his staff home early in the evening and

certainly before dark because in the evening the locals took pot shots at them from the roof tops. An FBI agent had been shot dead the day before when he had entered a house to execute a search warrant and had come face to face with a man high on crack. The house was full of weapons.

In St Louis the courts had been overwhelmed by a horrifying escalation in juvenile crime. In 1987, fifty juveniles had been arrested for drug offences. Since then there had been a tenfold increase. Ninety per cent of all crimes were drug related, with ninety per cent of drug offenders high at the time of arrest. Sixty-five per cent of other offenders were also high. It was not just a case of violence being used to feed the drug habit. Crack cocaine actually induced aggressive and violent behaviour. It was being sold for only five dollars a smoke.

We went to a school where children of only seven and eight were taught a WAR (We Are Responsible) programme. The teaching was jargon-riddled with much talk of resisting 'peer group pressure' when performing one's 'job functions' and all the teachers coupled alcohol and the smoking of tobacco with the use of hard drugs. I suggested that they were hardly likely to get the enthusiastic support of parents in the fight against drugs if they preached the message that perfectly lawful habits in which probably ninety per cent of the parents indulged were just as bad as the use of illegal substances. I got nowhere.

I also got pretty exasperated with the many criticisms of 'interdiction', the word the Americans used to cover prohibition. The Mayor of St Louis went so far as to say that interdiction forced up the price which led to the commission of more crime to feed the habit. More and cheaper drugs were apparently his answer to the ills of society.

We went on to New York and saw Mayor Dinkins who, unlike the Mayor of Washington, had not been arrested on drugs charges. The next day we visited an impressive drugs rehabilitation programme – Daytop. At the end of the trip I had learned some unpleasant lessons. (1) There was something especially destructive about crack cocaine. (2) The tougher the Americans got in the fight against drugs the greater the likelihood that Britain would face a flood of imports. (3) Jamaican gangs had a hold on the American trade and their links with gangs in Britain increased this likelihood. (4) There was a need for ever closer international cooperation in the fight against drugs. (5) Children in Britain should be taught about the danger of drugs, but the American approach would not do.

Things would have to get a lot worse before parents in Britain would put up with children chanting for hours on end 'Say "no" to drugs, say "no" to drugs'; and it was simply wrong to lump together in one's teaching legal and illegal substances, as if whether a thing is legal or illegal is neither here nor there. Things were serious enough in Britain but we could take some comfort in the fact that we had not yet the same lethal mixture of gang crime, urban dereliction, inner-city deprivation and freely available firearms. In Britain street dealers were still a rarity – in America commonplace. But there was nothing for us to be complacent about.

I made another interesting journey in the early part of 1990. I went to Brussels for a series of meetings and then on to Zeebrugge to see some of the key people there who did such a marvellous job when MS *Herald of Free Enterprise* sank. I then went on to the Menin Gate in Ypres to lay a wreath on the tomb of the Unknown Warrior. Nearby there was a beautiful cemetery in which were buried many members of the East Lancashire Regiment in which my father had served.

CHAPTER FIFTEEN

Trouble at Strangeways
and Elsewhere

Norman Harrison, a great Sabdener and the husband of our daily help Mary, decided that it was about time we took up fishing and on the afternoon of Saturday 31 March 1990 Gilly and I went with Norman to Churn Clough reservoir above Sabden to try and catch some trout. We had a lovely afternoon although it must have been pretty boring for our detective and our police driver who had to sit on the bank twiddling their thumbs.

When we got back home at quarter to five the telephone was ringing and moments later I learned that that afternoon there had been a riot in Whitehall and Trafalgar Square which had been instigated by demonstrators against the poll tax. I set off at once for London and the next morning saw many of the police officers who had been on duty. I also saw the considerable damage caused by the rioters in Trafalgar Square and the surrounding streets. There were a number of unpleasant characters still loitering about the place and at one point we got into difficulty when a gang of young men rushed at me, spitting and screaming and then attacked the car. The police moved with enormous speed and almost before I knew what was happening I had been bundled into the car and we were on our way. It was in the midst of all this excitement that I was told that a riot had broken out at Strangeways Prison.

The riot, I was told, had started during the Sunday morning service in the chapel and the number of men actively involved or caught up in the disturbances – in the region of 1,500 – had meant that all prison officers had been able to do so far was contain the men in the gaol and prevent a mass breakout. Rioters had at first taken almost complete control of the place but the staff were now being moderately successful in extricating prisoners who did not want to be involved and plans were already being made to move these prisoners to other gaols in the north-west.

The next morning I had a series of briefings to prepare myself for the two separate statements I would have to make to the House that afternoon – one about Trafalgar Square and the other about Strangeways. There was no detailed discussion of the tactics to be employed at Strangeways. So far as I was concerned the deputy director-general of the prison service, Brian Emes, had as his chief responsibility the handling of a situation like this and his first priority was to ensure that none of the 133 prisoners still on the loose escaped; his second was to transfer to other accommodation the rest of the inmates. They could hardly stay where they were because the rioters had already done enormous damage to every wing.

At that time I had no idea of tension, let alone disagreement, between the deputy director-general of the prison service and the governor of Strangeways. I assumed that Emes and the governor were in agreement that it was not practical to regain control of the prison at that time, that it would be too hazardous a venture and that the chances were that in the next day or so the number of rioters would be drastically reduced, making retaking the prison not too difficult.

The statements, before a sympathetic House, went quite well. On the Trafalgar Square riot I told the House that a team of a hundred officers had been set up to take charge of a major criminal investigation into the incident. There was plenty of evidence available in the form of photographs and film to identify those responsible. What had happened had nothing whatsoever to do with the right of peaceful demonstration. A large number of people had set out bent on violence and there could be no justification whatsoever for the savage and barbaric acts which millions had seen on their television screens. I infuriated the Labour Party by saying in answer to questions:

> It really doesn't help if MPs exhort people to break the law. Do they really expect those they seek to influence to draw a neat distinction between one sort of law breaking and another? Do they really expect the people they seek to influence to stop at trying to break the tax and abstain from breaking policemen's heads? Any member, and it has been said there are up to thirty of them, who has been exhorting people to break the law ought to be thoroughly ashamed of himself.

The statement on Strangeways was a calmer affair, but unwittingly I made one mistake. I said in reply to a question that there was nothing to suggest that there was a connection between the poll tax riot and the happenings at Strangeways. In fact, some weeks, not days, later I was told that on the Sunday when the riot broke out the ringleaders on the roof unfurled a makeshift banner which referred to poll tax. Why I was not told this on the Monday I really do not know.

In the next few days I was told over and over again by Brian Emes that the view of those on the spot was that it was far too dangerous to retake the prison. Landings had been made unsafe, booby traps laid and barricades built. The remaining rioters were in the rafters armed with scaffold poles and anyone who approached them from below would be horribly exposed. And surely, with the number of rioters falling each day as the lesser fry thought it politic to surrender, it was better to sit tight. On the Wednesday after the trouble started the rioters were still sixty-four strong, but the next day the number had fallen to forty-seven. On Wednesday 11 April there remained only sixteen. In these circumstances it was not just Emes who thought that the remaining rioters would not hold out very much longer and as all the Rule 43 inmates (segregated for their own protection) had been rescued we were not justified in risking the lives of prison officers retaking the place. The fact that nobody inside was in danger, that nobody had been taken hostage, also meant that there was no justification for asking the police to sort things out, let alone for bringing in the SAS.

The unsung hero of those early days was David Mellor, then the Minister of State in the Home Office responsible for prisons. Copycat disturbances were breaking out in other prisons, but he wasted not a moment in getting over to the governors the simple message that enough was enough and that he and I would back them up to the hilt if they took whatever measures were necessary to snuff out the disturbances and would be on them like a ton of bricks if they didn't. David's political career came to a premature end when John Major was Prime Minister and I had left the government for Bermuda, but I was immensely lucky to have him as a colleague, particularly during the prison riots.

For the first few days after the start of the trouble at Strangeways the press gave me a very easy time. A *Daily Mail* leader read:

David Waddington is the first genuinely right-wing Home Secretary we have had for years. He has no need to pay obeisance to anyone in the law and order lobby. Everything he has ever said and done shows that he is prepared to be as tough on criminals and law-breakers as any potential critic of the Tory right.

Because of this he has been able to take a cool and pragmatic view of the Strangeways and copycat riots which followed.

A so-called 'progressive' would have sent in the SAS days ago and probably ended up with a good deal of blood on his hands.

David Waddington has taken the eminently sane view that though prisoners on the rooftops of British jails may be very embarrassing to the government and galling to the prison service, these men are not endangering life.

Only if they were doing that, would there be justification to use force to bring them down. No doubt they will be punished when it is all over and they deserve to be.

David Waddington, by campaigning for years on issues of law and order, is at last someone at the Home Office who understands that if we are really to have law and order in this country we must have law and order for everyone and that sometimes includes the criminal.

While the *Mail* applauded our restraint the *Guardian* brigade, sharpening their pencils for the day, which they could not believe could be long delayed, when they could accuse me of being a murderous fascist, had for the time being nothing at all to say. The same was not true of the Prime Minister. She had plenty to say across the table in the Cabinet Room and said it. In this instance, as in so many others, she showed an uncanny understanding of what the British people were prepared to put up with and what they would not stomach. She had seen on television the film of the rioters capering around on the prison roof. She had seen, as the public had seen, the millions of pounds of damage done. She could see that the rioters were making fools of us all and she knew that the British people did not like to be treated as fools. At the same time we in the Home Office could see that the mood of the press was changing. Some of the papers were beginning to murmur 'enough is enough' and were no longer prepared to give us credit for the fact that the copycat riots at Dartmoor, Bristol and Pucklechurch had been dealt with robustly.

From day one I had been anxious to go up to Manchester, but

others argued strongly that I should stay away. The chief constable of Manchester did not want me to go because he felt he had enough on his plate and could ill-afford to take men off the jobs they were doing in order to guard me. He felt that my arrival could spark off trouble on the streets and Manchester could finish up with its own poll tax riot. My office did not want me to go because they feared that they and I would be accused of acting improperly by trying to take control of the situation, as Churchill was before the First World War when he went to see the Sydney Street siege. The deputy director-general of the prison service, Emes, was the man with operational responsibility, they said, and he should be left to get on with it.

Eventually I had had enough. I had been fobbed off with story after story as to why matters could not be brought to a conclusion. I was determined to see for myself what was going on. I got up early on Sunday 22 April and told my detective and driver that we were off to Manchester.

Brendan O'Friel, the governor, welcomed me warmly and was obviously delighted to see me. But he looked at me strangely when I congratulated him on the way he had handled things and eventually he told me that right at the start he had had a serious disagreement with Emes on the tactics to be employed. He said that he had wanted to go in and retake the prison on the first day and had assembled the necessary people to do this, but over the telephone Emes had vetoed the plan. Once that opportunity had been thrown away and the rioters had had time to fortify themselves in the rafters they had had little option but to sit it out. There were now only seven rioters left in the prison but they had built formidable defences and would be difficult to remove.

Back in the Home Office on the Monday I told the Permanent Secretary what I had discovered and that I was not at all happy at the way things had been handled. I think I convinced Clive Whitmore that he had got to get a grip on the situation himself and before long a plan was devised to retake the prison. A few days later a hundred prison officers in riot gear stormed in and nine hours later the last five prisoners surrendered. I flew up to Manchester by army helicopter to thank those who had carried out the good work.

From the outset, the matter was not handled well and I had to take responsibility for that. If I had known of the disagreement between Emes and O'Friel I would have stepped in and resolved the matter in favour of the man on the spot who was far better able to assess the situation than Emes sitting in London, and I am pretty sure that O'Friel would have snuffed out the riot. But I could take comfort from the fact that only one person had died (a remand prisoner) and he only indirectly as a result of the incident. Lives are more important than bricks and mortar and it would have been far worse if an early storming of the prison had resulted in a blood bath.

There is no doubt that the affair did great damage to my own reputation within the Parliamentary Party, and after it was all over Woodrow Wyatt was the only person to write in the press in supportive terms. Without, of course, knowing the whole story he said this in his *News of the World* column:

> Home Secretary David Waddington is not a sissy. The press and the media were full of lurid stories of mutilations and murders at Strangeways.
>
> The greatly exaggerated reports led to demands for the army to move in. That would really have caused a lot of deaths. It took courage on the part of the Home Secretary to stay calm. The ringleaders were desperate, evil men.
>
> Egged on by the TV coverage, they saw themselves as wild west heroes fighting to the last. But some good may come of it.
>
> The public will realise that more money has to be spent on prisons to stop overcrowding. And to make them fit for human beings, however wicked some may be.

John Carvel in *The Guardian* took a very different and damaging line:

> The man is neither particularly hard, nor naturally wimpish. Mr Waddington is an early victim of Home Secretary's disease – acute damage to reputation caused by inflammation of the media. Strangeways's wider political significance is that it may have stripped the Tories of an image on which they relied to cover their lack of a real law and order strategy. It would be unfair to blame Mr Waddington for the Strangeways eruption or the handling of the siege. It would have been outrageous had he overruled the professional experience of his deputy director-general of prisons and sent in the SAS on the crucial second day.
>
> In six months, Mr Waddington has got most of his decisions right by his own lights and ideology. There is no hard evidence yet that he was to blame for botching anything at Strangeways. His danger is that none of that matters any longer. If he is to be classed as a wimp by the right, his value as a front man covering for an inadequate Tory law and order policy may have been eroded.

A minister in the Home Office and the Home Secretary in particular often has to perform like a juggler. A number of balls are always up in the air at the same time and he can afford to drop none of them. While trying to cope with Strangeways I was also responsible for the World Summit on Drugs which had opened at the exhibition centre in Parliament Square; but it was very difficult to concentrate on this secondary task. The conference was useful but like so many of these international meetings it was somewhat spoiled by the determination of virtually all the delegates to read out lengthy statements completely unrelated to earlier contributions. At the beginning of one session I divided the time available by the number of those wishing to speak and told the assembled company that speeches had to be limited to seven minutes. The first person I called spoke for fourteen minutes and the second for eleven. I called for cooperation and self-control and the next person to rise spoke for seventeen minutes. I was fast losing my patience and when a Japanese delegate was still going strong after eleven minutes I rose and asked him to stop. His fury knew no bounds. He strode towards the podium and made as if to climb the two steps in order to upbraid or assault me. He tripped on the second step and fell on his neck. There was loud applause.

A week after the World Summit on Drugs I was once again at Buckingham Palace administering the oath for the swearing-in of a bishop. The oath which the bishop has to repeat line by line is not for the fainthearted, with tongue twisters such as 'all the spiritualities and all the temporalities thereof'. When it is all over the new bishop repairs to a downstairs lavatory to disrobe and is there given a glass of sherry. He badly needs it.

At about the same time I had to attend an investiture at the Palace, summoning forward those to be knighted. The day before I had told Alan Glyn, the Alan Glyn who spent a night during the 1987 election under a cupboard, that as he was in a state of decrepitude Her Majesty had let it be known that there was no need for him to kneel, but when I called his name he ignored my advice. There was much dithering and shaking and ungainly manoeuvres as he tried, vainly at first, to make contact with the stool; and watching him try to regain his feet was even more nerve-wracking for the onlooker. The Queen's face was a picture.

A week later there was a state banquet at Buckingham Palace in honour of the President of India, and the week after that an event which was far more difficult to endure. I refer to the BAFTA awards ceremony at which stars of cinema and television indulge in a prolonged orgy of self-congratulation. The event started at 6 p.m. and when, at about ten, the whole ghastly business seemed to be grinding to a halt I said goodnight to the Princess Royal.

She looked at me strangely and said "Oh dear, aren't you going to stay for my speech?' At which a well-wisher took me to one side to explain that we had only reached half-time.

In May I attended the Police Federation conference in Scarborough. It was going to be a difficult occasion. The police were up in arms about their rent allowances which were going to be cut, and we had learned that by way of protest the delegates were going to listen to my address in stony silence – not a cough, not a clap. My secretary had a stroke of genius. Immediately before I went in to the hall he said, 'What a colossal joke it would be if, at the beginning of your speech, you made some reference to their planned silence and treated it as an act of politeness.' So I opened my remarks by saying,

> I know it is the custom at these conferences to listen to Home Secretaries in complete silence and I would not wish you to deviate in any way from that custom today, as long as the public fully understand the custom and recognise that it is an indication of support rather than the reverse, etc.

The police had not a leg to stand on. Never once since 1979 had the government failed to honour the Edmund Davies formula and as a result police pay had gone up much faster than average earnings. On top of that the system of rent allowances had got completely out of control and we could not be expected to continue with a system which had led in the previous year to a 69 per cent increase in the allowances in Warwickshire and a 59 per cent increase in London.

At about this time, Gilly and I had an interesting and relaxing visit to the Channel Islands. When I addressed the States in Jersey I said that the UK government had no intention of interfering in the domestic affairs of the Islands, words which, had I remained

Home Secretary, I would shortly have had to eat. Within a year or so Kenneth Baker had to take action because of the shortcomings of the deputy bailiff who was not keeping up with his court work. I visited the new prison which seemed very short of customers.

During my time in government Gilly and I attended all sorts of formal dinners and sometimes they seemed a very mixed blessing. There is always work to be done and time at a banquet means less sleep that night as boxes still have to be gone through in preparation for the next day. But there were some glorious occasions, and Geoffrey Howe should be thanked for persuading the powers that be to allow the British Museum and the Victoria and Albert Museum to allow big diplomatic events, like the dinner on the Queen's official birthday, to take place on the premises. On one such occasion Gilly and I were in a V&A festooned with 'No Smoking' notices when from behind a statue emerged Princess Margaret with an inch of ash at the end of her cigarette. 'There you are,' she said, as she approached. I bowed, put out my hand to receive the ash and popped it in my pocket.

On 13 February 1990 a journalist and a photographer gained access to the intensive care ward of Charing Cross Hospital where Gordon Kaye, star of the popular television series *'Allo 'Allo!*, was lying in very bad shape after an accident. Although he was in no fit state to talk about anything, and quarter of an hour later had no recollection of the occurrence, the journalists purported to interview him and their paper later proposed to publish a report of that 'interview'.

The behaviour of the journalists was monstrous but when the matter came before the Court of Appeal the court ruled that Gordon Kaye had no right of redress. What had happened was an appalling abuse of press freedom but it was up to Parliament to create a legal right to privacy.

On 21 June the Calcutt Committee, appointed the previous year to review invasions of privacy by the press, produced its report. Its recommendations included the creation of a new criminal offence of invasion of privacy by the press and better self-regulation. This was to be achieved through a press complaints commission which would adjudicate on breaches of its code of practice and recommend how its findings should be published and how, in suitable cases, a correction, reply or apology should be made.

In the House I said that the government welcomed the committee's general approach and accepted the recommendation with regard to a press complaints commission. If the industry did not set up the commission within twelve months or if, after the commission had been set up, it did not prove itself, we would take steps to set up a statutory commission or even a tribunal. I also accepted in principle the recommendation that journalists or others entering or using surveillance on private property without invitation, in order to get hold of personal details for publication, should be guilty of a criminal offence. We would, however, have to consider the detail of the proposed offence of physical intrusion and the scope of the proposed defence of lawful authority and would announce our conclusions later in the year. In the event it fell to my successor to decide what, if any, further steps should be taken.

At about this time I had a protracted battle with Cecil Parkinson who wanted to introduce random breath tests for motorists. I pointed out that the police already had the power to stop any vehicle at any time without any reason and if, having stopped a vehicle, an officer formed a reasonable suspicion that alcohol had been taken, the breathalyser could be used. What more did the Department of Transport want? It seemed they had set their hearts on the police being able to set up road blocks at four o'clock in the afternoon in order to breathalyse every granny coming back with her shopping, and I was delighted to put a stop to what, at best, was mere window dressing and, at worst, would do great damage to relations between the police and law-abiding members of the public. I have to say that in a long life in the law and politics I have learned that there is one temptation to which the police find it easy to succumb – they would rather book for minor offences polite members of the middle classes not addicted to giving them lip than deal with crime among less salubrious members of society. We should help them to resist this temptation not give way to it.

In that summer my private secretary announced that the Prime Minister wanted what was called a 'bilateral' – a meeting with a minister on his own to sort out something worrying her. My officials seemed to be in a highly anxious state about the request, with one saying, 'You don't think she wishes to discuss the BBC licence fee? You will do your best, Secretary of State, to keep her off that.' Arriving at No. 10 I was surprised at the perspicacity of the official who had last spoken to me because the Prime Minister's opening shot was: 'I want to talk about getting rid of the licence fee.' I said that there should be plenty of time to talk about that but first I had to have her consent to a number of official appointments, and I made sure that took a fair amount of time. 'Now,' she said with relish, 'let's get to the licence fee. I am sure we discussed abolition in one of the committee meetings last session on the Broadcasting Bill.' I said I had no recollection of that but the Prime Minister's response was to call for the production of the minutes of the various meetings so that she could prove how faulty was my memory. After a little while a man staggered in with an enormous pile of paper in his arms. Margaret grabbed a fair amount of it and then, having flicked through a number of pages while sitting in her chair, flung herself on the floor to complete her search, bidding me to follow her. Her search proved, as I knew it would, fruitless, and when we had got to our feet someone came to the door and said: 'Prime Minister, the Israeli Ambassador has already been waiting for twenty minutes.' 'Infuriating,' said the Prime Minister, 'the licence fee will have to wait for another meeting.' Back I went to the Home Office and when I got there my private secretary said: 'Did she get to discussing the licence fee?' 'No,' I said. 'Well done,' said my private secretary.

Whenever there is a dearth of news, the press find a child which has been bitten by a dog. As all the dog biting stories occur in June and July I think you can take it that there is less news in June and July than in other months of the year. When the press start reporting that children are being bitten, the wise Home Secretary tries not to think about it. The dogs will stop biting in August, or rather the press will be on holiday in August and will stop writing about it. The unwise Home Secretary will introduce legislation when the press say dogs have started biting. The wise Home Secretary will do precisely nothing.

It does become slightly more complicated when it is the Home Secretary's dog which is doing some of the biting, and Basil let us down badly. On 23 July, Gilly tied Basil up outside a shop in Pimlico Road and then a little later, as she was paying her bill, she saw through the shop window a little boy about to put his nose close to Basil's teeth in a gesture of affection. Basil was a bit stand-offish with young people to whom he had not been properly introduced and before you could say teeth he snapped at and narrowly missed the little lad's nose. A brutish type who might have been the boy's father then commenced to beat Basil about the head with a bag loaded, Gilly suspected, with burglary tools, and then, having meted out a great deal of punishment, picked the boy up, saying he was going to take him to hospital.

Gilly reported all this to me when I returned home in the evening and I was not confident that we had heard the last of the matter. We had not. On 30 July we got a letter from the police saying that what had happened had been reported but because it was an isolated matter they were taking no action. We thanked our lucky stars but our luck did not last long. In the middle of August the *Mail on Sunday* rang and the next day a banner headline covering the two centre pages read: 'BASIL'S DAY OF SHAME'. Happily the story underneath was in fact not too shaming. The writer appeared to have accepted Gilly's side of the story and treated the man with the bag which may or may not have contained burglary tools as the villain of the piece, but it was not the sort of publicity my press office would have sought.

On 23 July came reshuffle day. The Prime Minister rang at nine in the morning and asked me if I would let John Patten go to be Minister for the Civil Service and the Arts. Reluctantly I said 'Yes' – reluctantly because John had done much work on the Criminal Justice Bill and I had been assuming that he would pilot it through the House after its introduction at the very beginning of the next session in October.

When I told John Patten what was afoot he protested that he knew little about the arts and hated what he did know. If given the job he would soon be found out to be the philistine he was. For instance, if asked when he had last been to the opera his reply would be: 'Never'. I rang Charles Powell at No. 10 and told him the difficulty. His reply was not unreasonable: 'If Patten won't do, who do you suggest?' I said that I wanted to keep my present team, but if I had to lose one or other of my ministers of state it was far better that David Mellor should go because he rather liked the arts. Charles said he would ask the Prime Minister and a little while later he phoned back and said she agreed.

I then had the unenviable task of telling David Mellor, who became quite apoplectic. It was an insult to offer him such a dead-end job. I went into a meeting and half way through I was passed a message that David Mellor wanted to speak to me urgently. I went outside and he was still waxing indignant and saying he was not prepared to take the job. I got cross and went back in to my meeting. Half an hour later when it ended I turned on the television and there was David before the cameras saying what a great honour had been bestowed on him – that Minister for the Arts was the job he had always wanted and he was the happiest man alive. I thought it very sporting of him in the circumstances and proved what a grand trooper he was.

That was not the end of my reshuffle difficulties. A moment or two later the Prime Minister was on the line saying she was glad I had been prepared to spare David but that she had now decided that I would have to part with John Patten as well. She wanted him as Paymaster General and offered me Douglas Hogg instead. I certainly had nothing against Douglas who was immensely able but I felt it was unfair to ask me to see my team completely broken up. Eventually she agreed to leave John Patten with me.

A week later on the morning of 30 July I had just got in to my office when I was told that a bomb had gone off outside Ian Gow's home near Eastbourne. In a further call a minute or two later I learned that he was dead. I had an appointment with the Prime Minister, and when I got to No. 10 she already knew about Ian and was very upset. She had always been very fond of Ian as he had been of her. 'Give me work,' she said to her private secretary, 'and I don't want any engagements cancelled. I have got to keep myself busy.' I went out into Downing Street and was caught by the press. I said that there were times when it was difficult not to hate. Ian was a good man and he had been blown to bits by the scum of the earth.

Gilly and I had planned a week's holiday in St Mawes and we travelled down to Cornwall with our policemen to find that the Devon and Cornwall Police were determined not to be left out of the show and had more or less taken over the hotel. They had also found someone with a boat who was detailed to guard us on the water. We went sailing on a yacht chartered by Gerry Neale, then MP for North Cornwall, and helped by a strong wind we zipped along in fine style with five policemen in a tiny motor boat bouncing along on the top of the waves beside us. Our chaps from the Met looked decidedly queasy.

After three days we came back to London and travelled down to Eastbourne for Ian's funeral. It was a very high church affair ending with a superb address by the Bishop of Lewes. We then had tea at the Dog House (Ian and Jane's home) before flying back to Cornwall.

Jenny, my elder daughter, was in Australia on a so-called working holiday and she had left a message at the hotel asking us to ring her the following Monday. When I got in touch she sounded rather quiet and pensive and the best I hoped for was that she wanted a thousand pounds to restore her finances. I asked her if anything was wrong and she said, 'You had better speak to Robbie.' Daughters really should not do that sort of thing to fathers, and I expected the worst. When, therefore, I heard what this Robbie had to say I was amazed but relieved. 'You will think this very odd, sir,' said a very Australian voice, 'but Jenny insists on my doing things properly. May I have your daughter's hand in marriage?' 'What a damn silly question,' said I. 'I haven't even clapped eyes on you.' Robbie's reaction was, however, so mournful that I immediately took pity on him. 'There there,' said I, 'if Jenny thinks you a nice lad I suppose it will be all right.' Thus was parental consent sought and sort of given.

It happened that in September we were due to go to Australia on a ministerial visit and these extraordinary family happenings proved to be of great interest to the Australian police and secret service, and to our own High Commissioner, Sir John Coles. The police and secret service wanted to check out Robbie to make sure he did not make bombs. Sir John said he thought it would be nice for Robbie and Jenny to be with him at Sydney Airport when we flew in and he would make arrangements accordingly. When we landed, however, only Sir John, looking rather bleak, was waiting at the bottom of the steps. I asked him where the lovebirds were and he explained that his driver had been sent to Jenny's address but as no one had answered the door, he had returned empty-handed. We went to our hotel harbouring murderous thoughts. An hour later there was a knock on our bedroom door and there they were; and pretty cocky too, in the circumstances. 'Oh, what a fuss, Dad. We went to a party in the mess last night and I overslept.' I told them in no uncertain terms that they had got themselves in deep trouble, and that as we were going on a trip round Sydney Harbour that afternoon with the top brass including the Premier and Chief of Police of New South Wales they had better use it as an opportunity to redeem themselves. They did. As soon as Robbie got on the boat, John Coles asked him what he did for a living. Robbie replied that he was in the army but had spent most of his life playing cricket. John Coles declared his addiction to the game and Robbie and Jenny were both forgiven.

After that near-disastrous start the Australian visit went very well. There were one or two scrummages in hotel lifts when the Australian police battled for ascendancy over our own detectives; but apart from that it was all sweetness and light. I visited various police forces, two police training establishments, at one of which I had to deliver a lecture, and a privatised prison run by a bluff Yorkshireman with an army background. The place seemed to be very well run but the key to its success might have been its size. Although there were a lot serving life sentences there were only 250 prisoners in all; the place looked manageable.

We stayed with John Coles in Canberra before going on to Melbourne and there we dined at the Melbourne Club as guests of Sir John Young, Chief Justice of Victoria. In those days I was still smoking small cigars and when I lit up over cocktails my host cried, 'Waiter, bring an ashtray.' Nothing happened for a few minutes and then the waiter returned and in a stage whisper said: 'Sir, there are no ashtrays in the club.' 'Don't be a fool,' said Sir John, 'bring a saucer.'

At the dinner table the Chief Justice let loose on Gilly a woman called Lady Derham. I could see from the other side that a furious altercation was in progress and when we rose Gilly told me that the woman had said: 'Every Britisher in Northern Ireland should be thrown out.' I thought that Gilly must have misunderstood and that what was being advocated was the usual 'troops out'; and I went up to Lady Derham and told her politely that our troops had gone to Northern Ireland in the first place to defend the Catholics and there would be mayhem in Northern Ireland if our troops were just to quit the scene. She said that she was not only advocating that our troops should leave but that every Protestant in Northern Ireland should be expelled and sent back to Scotland. At that stage Gilly intervened and told her that by that logic everyone in Australia who was not an Aboriginal should clear off and she should set a good example by booking her own passage the next day. All in all it was quite a lively evening.

Before going off to Australia I had decided to refer back to the Court of Appeal the case of the Birmingham Six. This was after receiving advice from the unit in the Home Office which then dealt with allegations of miscarriages of justice. Subsequently the Court concluded that the verdicts were unsafe and the convictions were overturned.

In October came the Party Conference. On the eve of the home affairs debate Robin Oakley wrote in *The Times* that I should survive the ordeal. 'Facing a conference audience Mr Waddington becomes generally heated. The Lancastrian growl and the "nowt for owt" style will come through.' He was kind enough to add:

'His short record as Home Secretary is in fact a respectable one for a man blinking in the light after a spell in the engine room murk of the Whips Office.' I was pleased with the way things went and afterwards the Prime Minister was embarrassingly kind about it.

I got a good write-up in the *Daily Telegraph* and could not complain about John Carvel's piece in *The Guardian* which read:

> David Waddington, the Home Secretary, yesterday woke the Conservative Conference from its mood of acquiescent lethargy by appealing to its atavistic instincts for retribution against violent offenders, including the death penalty for the worst types of murder. Mrs Thatcher applauded as he asserted the deterrent value of restoring capital punishment. And the first Conservative Home Secretary in a generation from the traditional Tory right was rewarded with the first standing ovation of the week which owed more to real passion than politeness.
>
> The paradoxical result is that the Home Office will be able to proceed in the next session of Parliament with an essentially liberal Criminal Justice Bill to keep thieves and vandals out of prison.
>
> Mr Waddington persuaded the Tories he shared their values and he is now free to pursue his policy for punishing petty criminals in the community.
>
> Mr Waddington's friends had feared he might get a critical reception because of the delay in ending the Strangeways riot in April and recent sharp increases in recorded crime, but he recovered his no-nonsense reputation with a well-crafted speech which touched all the buttons of Tory concern for law and order.

Robin Oakley wrote: 'Mr Waddington brought the conference to life with a well-judged performance in which he pressed all the right buttons to please the representatives, winning the most enthusiastic standing ovation so far.'

Simon Heffer in the *Daily Telegraph* said:

> Within moments of beginning his address it was clear that this
> was not the type of Home Secretarial imitation toughness we were
> used to. This was the real thing, though hardly anybody alive had
> been to a Tory conference when it had been displayed, so long ago
> did real old-fashioned Tory Home Secretaries cease to exist. Lord
> Whitelaw or Mr Douglas Hurd would never have referred scorn-
> fully to 'the mealy-mouthed claptrap of the left' that attributes
> every crime to unfortunate social circumstances.

As for Matthew Parris, I did not know whether to be pleased or
sorry about his effort:

> With the body language of an outraged greengrocer, the instincts
> of a cautious pragmatist and rhetoric of an angry headmaster,
> Waddington was the first Home Secretary I can remember who
> brought a Tory conference spontaneously to its feet. Standing
> by the backstage door as he and a delighted Mrs Thatcher exited
> together, I caught just the first half of her sentence: 'David, you're
> the first Home Secretary I can remember who...

Later in October there was a Council of Ministers meeting in
Naples. My main task was to make it plain that although in favour
of a convention to reinforce and harmonise entry and visa procedures at the Community's external frontiers, we intended to maintain checks at our national frontiers for the purpose of controlling
immigration from third countries. We knew that some governments, prepared as usual to sign anything, had not the slightest
intention of taking any steps to make the external frontier of the
community secure, although the whole idea of the convention
was that better immigration control at the Community's external

borders made safe the scrapping of controls between member states. Our partners told us that we had to abolish our controls on entry into Britain from the Continent. It was, they said, an obligation we had undertaken when we had signed the Single European Act. We, however, continued to argue that the free movement provisions of the Single European Act did not apply to nationals of third countries and we were entitled to have controls at, for instance, the Channel ports to prevent entry by such people. This was the advice the Prime Minister had been given by the Foreign Office before she agreed to go along with the Single European Act, and she was not best pleased when, subsequently, the law officers advised that in advancing this argument we were on extremely shaky ground. But on that ground, shaky though it was, we were determined to stand for as long as possible.

When we came out of our hotel the first night, the Naples Police decided to take the cavalcade of ministers' cars up a one-way street in the wrong direction. That meant forcing approaching cars into the ditch or onto the pavement. One car was slow to move and a policeman leapt out into the road and began to hammer on the windscreen with the butt of his revolver. The driver opened his window and got the pistol shoved in his face which so demoralised him that he was then quite incapable of moving his car at all and the police had to do the job for him.

A magnificent fireworks display was laid on for us after dinner. The frumpish Dutch Minister for the Interior said she did not like firework displays, particularly when they were as noisy as the one that night, and she told me why. As a girl she had lived in Arnhem and one day paratroopers began to drop out of the sky. The teachers at her school told her that Arnhem was about to be liberated and the war was soon to end, but first she and her classmates had to put on their coats and go off into the woods to wait until the fighting had stopped and it was safe to go home. They set off into the woods and for days, while the noise of battle rolled about them, they waited to be told they could return. Eventually, someone came to tell them what had happened and they walked back to their hometown to find it in ruins and the ruins still occupied by the Germans. That is why the minister hated fireworks.

I then had to go to a one-day conference in Rome. This was to celebrate the fortieth anniversary of the signing of the European Convention on Human Rights. In his opening speech the President of the commission said that there would be no cases brought to the commission or the court if all member countries of the Council of Europe observed the convention. He did not seem to realise that it was somewhat difficult to guarantee observance of the convention when its vague terms and generalities were constantly being reinterpreted by the court and it was difficult to know one day what was going to be the law the next. My comments to this effect were not well received. The proceedings groaned on and eventually I had had enough and set off down the grand staircase towards my waiting car. But my exit had been spotted and five delegates had set off in hot pursuit. When they caught me up they assured me that I was not going to be forced to listen to any more speeches. I was wanted for the group photograph.

Our Ambassador's wife, who was a Catholic, asked us whether we would like to go with her to mass in the Pope's private chapel at six the following morning, and there we went and met the Pope. I found him very much more spiritual and concerned with the saving of souls than any Church of England archbishop or bishop I had met, with the exception of the then Bishop of London, Dr Ellison. Dr Ellison left the Church of England a few years later.

Then came Geoffrey Howe's resignation from the government. In the statement he made to the Commons explaining why he had done what he had, he invited others to come forward prepared lead the Party in Margaret Thatcher's stead. It did not take long after that for Michael Heseltine to throw his cap into the ring, saying that he had a better prospect than the Prime Minister of leading the Conservatives to victory at the next general election. Sixty Conservative members had refused to support the Prime Minister in 1989 when Sir Anthony Meyer had stood against her, and now with a serious and very formidable opponent already campaigning hard to displace her, one might have thought it was time for supporters of the Prime Minister to get to work and launch a vigorous campaign on her behalf; but nothing of the sort happened. There was a feeling in No. 10 that the unthinkable could not happen, that the Party really would have gone mad if it sacked a leader just off to Paris to celebrate something she had done so much to achieve – an end to the Cold War. And Peter Morrison, the Prime Minister's Parliamentary Private Secretary, sat in his little den close to the Cabinet Room ready to offer visitors a hefty drink and tell them that all would be well on the night. He was going to busy himself flushing out of the clubs in St James's the very many members of the Parliamentary Party who, according to Peter, spent their time in such establishments.

It was not unreasonable to expect members of the Cabinet to vote for the Prime Minister and on the day I think they did. But earlier there had been rumours that there were senior Whips asserting the right to vote against her, which I thought was quite extraordinary. A firmer hand there and elsewhere in the Party, appealing for the loyalty which members of the Whips Office owed her, might have garnered the few votes necessary for her to win in the first round. But she failed to do so – by just four votes.

That night John MacGregor, Leader of the House, told me that he doubted whether the Prime Minister could win the second ballot. There were already stories of people who had so far kept their heads down now being prepared to come out for Heseltine. The next day, when I was away from London at a conference in Oxford, it was determined, I know not by whom, that every member of the Cabinet should have the opportunity to see the Prime Minister on his own and tell her his views. It was a barmy way of trying to determine whether a Prime Minister should stay in office and it would have been far more appropriate for the Cabinet to have met as one body. But the upshot was that when I got back to London and went round to the Prime Minister's room I found a queue at the door. At that moment Tom King was putting forward a weird idea that the Prime Minister should fight on but announce that if she was re-elected she would bow out in about March. Then out of the room came Chris Patten nursing his bottom like a naughty schoolboy who had been flogged by his headteacher. That did not endear him to some present.

In with the Prime Minister were Ken Baker, Party Chairman, and John Wakeham, who was going to be Margaret's campaign manager for the second round, if a second round there was going to be. Sitting on a sofa, Margaret looked thoroughly miserable. I had never seen her look like that before. I told her that she knew she could rely on my support if she fought on, but I had my own doubts as to whether she would win – or win convincingly enough to make it possible for her to continue in office. It was plain from her reply that she had already made up her mind to go. 'Isn't it unfair?' she said. 'I'll be sitting up all night preparing my speech for the censure debate when it will all be completely pointless.'

I sat for a while but, feeling so sad and distressed at the state to which she had been brought by people who, in my view, owed her loyalty and thanks for the great service she had done for the country, I felt I was doing no good there and left.

Early on the Thursday morning John Patten phoned. Douglas Hurd wanted me to propose him for the leadership. I told him I could not. I thought it had been a privilege to serve under

Douglas in the Home Office and knew him to be a man of great integrity and intellect, but I knew that John Major was Margaret's choice to succeed her and I was not in a mood, after all that had happened, to deny her what little consolation she might get from seeing the man she preferred become leader in her stead. I know that a number of other colleagues voted for John Major for the same reason.

When I got to No. 10 for the Thursday Cabinet meeting Norman Lamont asked me to nominate John Major. I told him that just then I could not bring myself to nominate anybody, but he could take it that in due course I would come out for John. In the Cabinet Room the Prime Minister began to read out the statement that was going to be released to the press, but she could not continue. James Mackay asked her if she would like him to read it for her, and at that she pulled herself together and said she could manage. By that time I was not the only one round the table close to tears, but eventually she got it all out. It read:

> Having consulted widely among colleagues, I have concluded that the unity of the Party and the prospects of victory in a general election would be better served if I stood down to enable Cabinet colleagues to enter the ballot for the leadership. I should like to thank all those in Cabinet and outside who have given me much dedicated support.

The Lord Chancellor then read a statement expressing the regret of the whole Cabinet and paying tribute to her enormous achievements. Douglas Hurd added a few words, as did Kenneth Baker. The normal business of Cabinet followed, and after reading out the business in the Commons for the following week, the Chief Whip finished by saying that the Prime Minister would have great sympathy at Question Time that day. At that Margaret recovered her old spirit and said with a snort: 'I prefer the business to the sympathy.'

That afternoon the Prime Minister delivered a speech in the censure debate which made her opponents look like novices. She enjoyed herself hugely as she tore the Opposition motion to pieces. Many who had so recently voted against her must have wondered how on earth they could have come to do it and what hope there could possibly be of the Conservative Party throwing up another leader with the same mastery of the House of Commons. Shortly afterwards, Norman Lamont rang to say that Norman Tebbit was thinking of standing. I rang Norman Tebbit and told him that in my view it would be a great mistake for him to do so. He would find it far more difficult than Douglas or John to unite the Party and, by standing, would harm John's chances. Norman replied that if he stood John would come last. He would think about what I had said but he did not like John Major's views on Europe and abhorred Douglas's.

On the Friday evening I went up to Manchester and spoke to the Withington Conservative Association. The chairman decided to conduct a leadership poll there and then, and John Major came out way in front. On the Saturday I was asked by the Major camp if I would declare my support for him on the following day. They had been keeping up the momentum of the campaign by each day getting a prominent member of the Party to say they were for Major, and I agreed to be next in line. I wrote to Margaret thanking her for everything and saying that I was sorry that ambition had led me to accept her invitation to leave the Whips Office and become Home Secretary. I could not help wondering whether, if I had remained in the job, she would have lost hers. I would have made pretty sure that the whips knew they had an obligation of loyalty to her and would have spread the same message among the backbenchers. She wrote back a very touching and generous letter in which she said I had nothing to reproach myself for. But I have never ceased to do so.

THE RT. HON. MARGARET THATCHER, F.R.S., M.P.

HOUSE OF COMMONS
LONDON SW1A 0AA

11 December 1990

My dear David

Thank you so much for your kind letter of 24th November — and forgive the delay in reply. You have nothing to reproach yourself with — you gave me support and unflinching loyalty throughout. Nothing gave me greater pleasure than to make you Home Secretary.

There is no point in going back over the past — we are fortunate to have John Major as our P.M. He deserves and must receive our wholehearted support. I hope you will enjoy the House of Lords.

All best wishes

Yours ever

Margaret

223

A review of her book *The Downing Street Years* contained this passage:

> One mystery remains. In her early years as Prime Minister Lady Thatcher was isolated in her own party and Cabinet: she was almost the only true Thatcherite. But more than a decade later the same remained true. Her last Cabinet contained only four genuine Thatcherites: David Waddington, Peter Lilley, Cecil Parkinson and, possibly, Michael Howard. Either she had systematically failed to promote Thatcherites up through the ministerial ranks, or she had failed to rally enough Tory Members of Parliament to her cause. These memoirs throw no light on this central question. Lady Thatcher seems willfully to resist it, as though frightened of its larger implications.

I am not sure that I can solve the mystery, but it is worth remembering that it was not always very comfortable to be a declared Thatcherite. In public it was far easier to portray oneself as part of the moderate centre, ever questioning the Prime Minister's decisions, always guarding the party's conscience, ever showing the compassion which it could be hinted 'the leader', for all her virtues, lacked.

Margaret Thatcher was not an easy woman to work with. On most matters she was convinced she was right, and that could be very irritating. But who can blame her for thinking herself right? She usually was. Three hundred and sixty-four economists said her economic policies could not work, but no sooner was the ink dry on their opinions than the policies were seen to be working. The Ministry of Defence doubted whether the Falklands could be retaken. She said they had to be, and they were. Everyone said that the government could not beat the miners. They were far too powerful. Margaret Thatcher knew better. She took them on and she won. The Chancellor of the Exchequer and the Treasury told her that Britain had to enter the exchange-rate mechanism. She felt in her bones it would end in tears and it did.

It is said that over the poll tax her political antennae failed her and she was over-committed before she realised that retreat was essential for her survival. I do not believe that the idea of a flat-rate charge for local services with rebates for those on low incomes sank her. I do think she failed to realise how grievously Treasury policy was affecting the level of the charge and, therefore, its acceptability. It was, however, her disagreements with the Foreign Office and the Treasury over European policy which provoked Geoffrey Howe's resignation and it was Geoffrey Howe's resignation which led to the leadership contest; and I have not the slightest doubt that over Europe she was right and the others wrong. In her refusal to go along with the pretence that Britain could continue to cede more and more power to the European Union – even to the extent of joining a European currency union and losing control of our own economic policy – and yet still remain an independent nation state, she was certainly more honest than her critics.

Margaret Thatcher was tough and did not suffer fools gladly. Diplomacy was not her strong point and the word 'compromise' did not feature large in her vocabulary. She knew what she wanted and she expected her ministers to deliver. Convincing her of a case was hard work. She tried to test your arguments to destruction, but when eventually convinced that what you wanted was right she supported you all the way. Indeed, so keen was she to show that support that she often attracted to herself the odium for unpopular policies when lesser Prime Ministers would have made sure it stuck firmly to their subordinates. So it was with the poll tax. Margaret Thatcher had great qualities of leadership which stood the country in good stead at times of crisis, and she was a giant on the world stage. It was sometimes difficult to describe her without using adjectives more familiar to the reader of *Jane's Fighting Ships* than the student of political biography – indefatigable, indomitable, intrepid and courageous.

Her determination to resist every threat to peace from the Soviet bloc, her willingness to face any amount of unpopularity at home in order to see her own country properly defended and the West secure, led to the deployment of the Cruise missile in Britain as a response to the Soviet deployment of the SS20 and to the massive build-up of forces behind the iron curtain. That in turn gave her the moral authority to speak for the west and made the Soviets realise that they had no hope with their own far more limited resources of forever preventing democracy in Eastern Europe, let alone extending their particular brand of tyranny further west.

When she was first Prime Minister Britain had lost her empire and was no longer a great power, but when she met George Bush Snr at the time of Kuwait there was no doubt who was the boss. 'All right, George, all right,' she is reputed to have said; 'but this is no time to go wobbly.' I doubt somewhat whether Tony Blair ever felt in a position to address an American President in such terms; and I fear it is inconceivable that David Cameron will ever speak in such terms to Obama or whoever succeeds him.

The trouble with high political office is that it is very difficult to leave it with dignity. Against the odds, Margaret Thatcher did just that. The British people owe her an immense debt and history will be kind to her.

It has no need to be kind to me. I felt that by leaving the Whips Office I had helped to bring about her downfall.

CHAPTER SIXTEEN

Leader of the Lords

On the evening of 27 November, John Major became leader of the Conservative Party. As soon as I had heard the news I had to leave for a dinner at which I was the guest of honour. I made my speech and then was passed a message. I had to go to No. 11 Downing Street at once. I went so fast that I got there before John Major who was still in the House of Commons for the ten o'clock division. Norma was at home and, having offered me a drink, invited me to sit at the end of their bed and watch on television the scenes in the House as John was congratulated by all and sundry. Eventually he arrived at No. 11 and, having talked for a little while on our own, we were joined by Andrew Turnbull and the Cabinet Secretary. We had a long conversation about who might fill various jobs and what I might do and, eventually, he offered and I accepted the leadership of the House of Lords. If I had had any sense I should have stuck out for remaining Home Secretary where my work was only half done, but I sensed that John wanted a change and I got it into my head that going to the Lords would be a more worthwhile challenge than stepping down from the Home Office and becoming, say, Leader of the Commons. I was wrong and I think my judgement was affected by the stressful time we had been through as a result of Margaret's departure.

Next morning I saw John at No. 10 after he had returned from the Palace. After chatting about other changes he said that he wanted Lord Denham (Bertie) replaced as Chief Whip by Alexander Hesketh, but I soon persuaded him that it would be a mistake to hurry the change. Bertie had said that he wanted to go in the spring in any event and the sensible course was to wait until then rather than make two key changes at the same time.

I went back to the Home Office to pack up my belongings, and some of the trappings of office of one of Her Majesty's principal Secretaries of State were then removed with astonishing rapidity. As soon as my move was made public I was told that my detectives were leaving as there were not considered to be any security problems connected with my new post. The next morning I went to the Palace and the Queen gave me framed photographs of herself and Prince Philip.

The next few days I spent in a state of black despair. I felt that in taking the job in the Lords I had let myself down badly. The children, not surprisingly, were not at all interested in becoming 'Hons.', and Gilly, whom I had expected to be delighted, was doubtful whether I had done the right thing. We went to a wedding and got stuck in a snow drift and I could not help thinking how nice it had been to be driven everywhere by the police. Gilly put a brave face on it publicly, telling the local paper: 'David finished his job as Home Secretary a success. He is still in the Cabinet and instead of sitting opposite the Prime Minister, he will now be sitting next to him.' But she then had to cope with the death of her mother, and both of us were miserable.

My move was, however, quite well received by the national press. Simon Heffer in the *Daily Telegraph* wrote:

Mr Waddington's imaginative appointment as Leader of the Lords is a great bonus. As a minister of long and varied experience and as a former Chief Whip, he should be able to defuse some of the myriad difficulties the government faces in the Lords, where its natural majority all too often acts against it.

One small consolation was the Leader of the Lords' magnificent room directly over the peers' entrance in Old Palace Yard; but my first job was not to get my feet under the desk, but my bottom on the red benches. This involved choosing a title and being introduced into the Lords as soon as possible. It did not take me long to settle on Waddington, of Read in the County of Lancashire; and Garter King of Arms did a fine job hastening on the formalities so that the introduction could take place before Christmas.

This was how the scene was described in the *Lancashire Evening Post*:

The 61-year-old Burnley-born Tory made none of the fuss that Baroness Castle caused when she was initiated as a life member of the aristocracy a year ago. There was no repeat of her objections to the red and ermine robes or her point blank refusal to wear and doff her hat.

Mr Waddington, the typical Tory officer and gentleman, was the soul of obedience and respect for tradition. At just after 2.30 p.m. he was led in by Black Rod – Air Vice-Marshall Sir John Gyngell and Garter King of Arms, Sir Colin Cole. His prime supporter, government Chief Whip Lord (Bertie) Denham, and his secondary supporter, Lord Carlisle of Bucklow – former Education Secretary Mark Carlisle – followed three paces behind. With an audience which included Baroness Castle in an autumn print dress, former Prime Minister Lord Callaghan in a grey suit and ex-Lord Chancellor Lord Hailsham with his inevitable stick, the three made their stately pace through the red and gold splendour of the Lords. The words that established the new Lord Waddington as a trusty counsellor of the Queen were read and he shook hands with the Lord Chancellor, Lord Mackay of Clashfern. Nodding his head in the direction of the Queen's chairman of the Lords, Baron Waddington and his supporters processed round the Chamber. They then took their seats at the side and respectfully put on their black hats, which date from the era when Wellington won Waterloo. With Garter King of Arms facing them, they doffed their archaic headgear three times to Lord Mackay, rose and, once more led by Black Rod, processed out of the Chamber. Mr Waddington – barrister and former Crown Court recorder of true Lancashire mill-owning stock – was now a peer of the realm for life.

I then got a bill from Garter King of Arms for £1,630, the fee for a grant of armorial bearings with supporters. The covering letter read like double dutch: 'You might care to suggest the tinctures which you would like to see employed and also such symbols and devices as are of appeal to you and would look well upon your shield or forming the crest.'

I soon discovered that my new job was far from taxing. Most mornings there was virtually nothing to do. I would call my private secretary and ask her to bring in some work and after a while one letter would appear and a notice of a meeting of the Dorneywood Trust of which I was chairman. If I had remained Home Secretary, I would probably have been about to occupy Dorneywood. Instead I was told, as if a great prize was being bestowed on me, that I could stay in South Eaton Place which I heartily loathed. John Major had told me that, as Leader, I would be his right-hand man, but within a matter of weeks it was obvious that that was not going to be the case – through no fault of the Prime Minister. Ninety per cent of the business management problems of the government were House of Commons problems and what happened in the Lords was small beer. Furthermore, with a general election not all that far off the Party Chairman's role was of great importance and time and again, when I saw the Prime Minister with John MacGregor (the new Leader of the House of Commons) on a Monday, our meeting lasted only a few minutes because the matters the Prime Minister thought important had already been covered in an earlier meeting with Chris Patten, the new Party Chairman.

I had to make my maiden speech from the dispatch box. Lord Elton initiated a debate on sentencing policy which gave me the opportunity to talk of the Criminal Justice Bill which I had introduced in the Commons the previous month. The debate was like most of those I had to listen to as Leader – well informed but sleep-inducing – with the Tory peers as critical of the government as the Opposition. Six former Home Office ministers spoke after me and a former permanent secretary; and I soon discovered that even in those days, when the hereditary peers far outnumbered the lifers, nearly all who took part in important debates had had distinguished careers in industry, the academic world or public service and made really well-informed contributions. Peers did not queue up at the Whips Office asking for a one-page brief on a subject down for debate, as sometimes happens in the Commons. Whips did not go around the place asking people to speak in order to keep a debate going until the hour at which a division had been arranged, as also happens in the Commons. People who knew what they were talking about put their names down to speak and their records entitled them to be listened to with respect. When I opened a debate during the Gulf War I was followed by two Field Marshals and after that experience I did not think I knew all there was to know about warfare.

Question Time I found a worry. It was not often that I had to answer any questions myself but I had to sit on the front bench worrying about the performance of others. There were few departmental ministers in the Lords, certainly not one in every department, so very often questions had to be answered by the Whips (entitled 'Lords in Waiting'). They did their best to mug up on subjects raised but they were either not particularly well briefed by the government department concerned (departments attached little importance to what was going on in the Lords) or they were not skilled enough to know what extra briefing they needed. As a result, they were always at risk of being caught out. Andrew Davidson, the deputy Chief Whip, provided a briefing for new whips in biblical language, part of which read: 'A Lord in waiting should stick to his brief. The further he strayeth from it, the deeper the pit he diggeth for himself to fall into; and if he knoweth not the answer, he should say so but not too often.'

In February 1991 there was the mortar attack on Downing Street. My room in the Privy Council Office overlooked Downing Street and I could see from my desk the usual group of photographers outside No. 10. Suddenly there was a loud bang and a cloud of black smoke rose above the roof of No. 12. I rushed down the stairs and out into the street and hammered on the door of No. 10. When I got inside a number of people were coming through the connecting door from No. 11. Nobody seemed to be injured and as there was nothing useful I could do, I went back into Downing Street and had a somewhat inconsequential conversation with a chap carrying a television camera on his shoulder. I was mightily surprised when I saw the news that night and found the whole conversation had been filmed. No harm had been done but I should have taken more care. I repeated in the Lords the statement on the incident made by Kenneth Baker in the Commons.

Gilly's father died in February. He could have been a great poet and would, I think, have made a more successful poet than he was a politician. He was a very intelligent man but his plain speaking, his refusal to suffer fools and his determination to fight marginal seats in Lancashire rather than seek a safe haven further south ruined his chances of rising as high as he deserved in government. His death left us a load of trouble. Under his will Whins House, where we had lived since 1965, had been left to Gilly and her two sisters equally so we could only stay there if we bought out her sisters.

We could not buy them out by selling our own house, The Stables, where the Greens had been living, because we would have had to pay a vast sum in capital gains tax as a result of The Stables not having been our residence. So a family arrangement made with the best will in the world twenty-five years earlier (the swapping of the two houses without transferring ownership) turned out to have been a monumental blunder. Eventually, we decided to do up The Stables and go back there. Gilly made a marvellous job of the alterations and it turned out all right in the end.

I was very worried as to what was going to happen in the by-election caused by my elevation. My advice to the Ribble Valley Association was that they should pick someone with previous parliamentary experience and local connections. There was only one person who fitted the bill, Derek Spencer, whose parents had a farm in Waddington, and he would have been excellent. The Association, however, thought nothing of my advice. They saw Derek and thought him boring, and chose a very worthy young Welshman, Nigel Evans. Nigel has, since 1992, served Ribble Valley extremely well, but he was a strange choice for a by-election in the middle of a parliament when even a local person was going to have an uphill struggle. The by-election came – and my 19,000 majority went down the chute. I had precipitated the by-election, I had lost it for the Party and what had I got in return? The leadership of a House in which one's own side had little idea of party loyalty and no compunction about embarrassing the government they had pledged themselves to support. I felt like cutting my throat.

There were some moments that brought me cheer. In the spring of 1991 Mikey Strathmore* asked me if I would give a cocktail party in my room in honour of Queen Elizabeth the Queen Mother who, being a relation of his, was coming to dine in the Lords' Dining Room. Queen

---

* The 18th Earl of Strathmore and Kinghorne.

Elizabeth arrived with her private secretary, Sir Martyn Gilliatt. It was rather hot and I thought Sir Martyn looked a bit vacant. The next moment he fell as if poleaxed. I thought he was dead. A number of people gathered round, someone went out to find a doctor. Queen Elizabeth, looking down kindly on him, said: 'He's always doing that,' and then carried on chatting with those around her.

I mentioned earlier that when Home Secretary I reintroduced the War Crimes Bill and saw it carried through the House of Commons for a second time with little dissent. On 30 April 1991, I had to move the second reading in the Lords. The Bill was word for word the same as the one the Lords had rejected in 1990. This was intentional. If it had been different in any material respect then, on rejection by the Lords, the Parliament Act would not have applied and the Bill would not automatically have become law. But the fact that the Bill was in the same terms did not mean that the government had made up its mind in advance to reject any amendments. I made this abundantly plain in my opening speech,* and it was absolutely obvious to me, and ought to have been just as obvious to the House, that it was in the interests of opponents of the Bill to give it a second reading. If it was rejected at second reading, it would become law immediately – warts and all. If, on the other hand, it got a second reading, the House would then have endless opportunities to either improve it by amendment or harass the government throughout a long hot summer and hope that eventually it would feel it had better things to do with its time.

---

* Hansard 30 April 1991 col. 621: 'This may be an appropriate moment to emphasise that the Bill being presented to your Lordships unchanged does not, of course, mean an unwillingness on the government's part to consider any amendments to improve it which this House may wish to make. Naturally, any such amendments would have to be considered by the other place where there has been, and no doubt will continue to be, a free vote.'

Luckily for the government the noble lords or, rather, a majority of them did not grasp these obvious points and the Bill was rejected and duly became law. The tactics of the Bill's opponents were plain stupid but their speeches were often brilliant. Douglas Houghton, who, having fought at Paschendale, must have known as much about the horrors of warfare as any man, and Hartley Shawcross, who prosecuted at Nuremberg, made truly magnificent contributions. Roy Jenkins mounted a most extraordinary argument – namely that it was perfectly proper for a Labour government to use the Parliament Act to bulldoze legislation through against the opposition of the Upper House but quite improper for the Parliament Act to be invoked in the case of a non-political measure like the War Crimes Bill. To me, the opposite view seemed much more attractive. It is surely very much more worrying to see the Upper House ignored when it is trying to put a brake on a dictatorial government bent on whipping its majority in the Commons to force-feed the public with unpopular legislation, than to see the Lords ignored when its opinion flies in the face of the views of the vast majority of members in the Commons expressed in a free vote. I put the point (tactfully) in my wind-up speech:

> There has been talk about abuse of power and of it being repugnant to bring the Bill back. However, most noble Lords will understand why the Bill was brought back. If one has a free vote in the other place, which supports the Bill so strongly, it would indeed be extraordinary if no opportunity was given to the other place to say once again, after the Bill had been rejected here, that it wanted this House to think again and bear in mind the strong endorsement that had been given to the Bill in another place ... It is not a question of the Parliament Act being held as a threat over your Lordships tonight. We all know that it is a matter of fact that

if this Bill is rejected by this House tonight, the Parliament Act comes into play by operation of law.

And I went on to say that the only result of accepting Lord Houghton's amendment (that the Bill be read a second time not now, but 'this day six months') would be that the House would lose its opportunity to improve the Bill. My words were, however, to no avail and the Houghton amendment, which under standing orders had to be treated as a rejection of the Bill, was carried by 131 votes to 109.

Lord Mayhew (of Wimbledon) was not on good form in the debate. Perhaps he was still suffering from a splendid put-down administered by Viscount Tonypandy at Question Time a week earlier. Lord Mayhew had asserted that in 1946 the Labour government of the day, of which he was a member, had decided that there should be no more war crimes trials. In fact, the Labour government had decided nothing of the sort; and Tonypandy drew attention both to this inaccuracy and to the fact that at the time Lord Mayhew was 'a very junior minister'.

At the beginning of June 1991 Humphrey Colnbrook* who, if Margaret had had her way, would have become Speaker in 1983 instead of Jack Weatherill, told me he was going to introduce a debate on defence. In my innocence I thought his idea was to give a helping hand to the government. Defence was hardly the Opposition's strong suit, and a speech strongly supportive of government policy coupled with a bit of knockabout fun at the Opposition's expense would not go amiss. Not for the last time I was in for a nasty surprise. There was precious little support for the government in Humphrey's speech or, for that matter, in any of the

---

* Before coming to the Lords, the Rt Hon. Sir Humphrey Atkins KCMG, MP.

other speeches from the Tory benches and not a glove was laid on the Labour Party. But I do remember the debate for an exchange between Lord Mayhew and Lord Boyd-Carpenter. The latter, in his reply to a completely fatuous comment of Lord Mayhew's ('the Soviets were building hundreds of submarines for purely defensive purposes') provided a perfect example of a particularly lordly debating style which can deflate the windbag in very quick time. 'My Lords, because it is the noble Lord's birthday today I shall wish him many happy returns. I hope that when he reflects on his intervention, it will not substantially diminish the pleasure of the occasion for him.'

The rules of order in the Lords require 'All personal, sharp or taxing speeches to be foreborn, and whosoever answereth another man's speech shall apply his answer to the matter without wrong to the person: and as nothing offensive is to be spoken, so nothing is to be ill-taken.' So if one wants to put down an opponent, a certain subtlety of approach is required.

A new session of Parliament was opened by the Queen on 31 October 1991. I carried the Cap of Maintenance. Matthew Parris wrote of the occasion: 'Not far from the throne stood a man I used to know as Mr Waddington, carrying a shower cap mounted on a broomstick.'

Andrew Rawnsley in *The Guardian* allowed his imagination to run riot:

If Margaret Thatcher's wildest nightmares about the Maastricht Summit come true, yesterday may have been our last opportunity to see Britain's parliamentary traditions in all their richly historical pageantry and gloriously hysterical absurdity. A final chance to see two blokes calling themselves the Rouge Dragon Pursuivant and the Beaumont Herald Extraordinary prance around in stockings while animated playing cards blow trumpets at duchesses wearing diamond mines on their heads. A final chance to lay bets on whether the Lord Chamberlain will manage to walk backwards around the throne without falling down the Queen's cleavage. Most of all, a final chance to watch Lord Waddington bearing aloft the Cap of Maintenance and speculate what that ludicrous velvet thing on a pole really is: Tudor night cap or Plantagenet condom?

By November 1991 the Maastricht Summit was imminent and their Lordships wanted their say. Colin Welch in the *Daily Mail* reported: 'Lord Waddington was his usual dry, semi-committed, cautious and circumspect self.' What I said was that Britain's view on the future of the Community did not tally with that of some other members of the community:

> A number of our European partners believe that the changes brought about by the Single European Act set us irrevocably on a predetermined path leading to political, economic and monetary integration within a federal Europe. That is not the case. Political union is an evolving process – not a goal – and the Community is a developing organism, the ultimate form of which none of us can confidently predict. We cannot set the final shape of Europe now. The most we can do is ensure that each step we take, each institutional change, is useful and workable in itself. We must consider the amendments proposed at Maastricht in this light; an end in themselves, not a means to a more distant goal.

In February 1991 I became a deputy lieutenant for the County of Lancashire, which pleased me greatly. Also in February I was given the job of representing the government at the funeral of the King of Norway in Oslo. I boarded a plane of the Queen's flight at Northolt and found myself in the company of various people who were connected with the Royal Family in some remote and minor way and had rung up Buckingham Palace asking if they could hitch a lift. A few minutes after take-off we seemed to be coming down again and I wondered whether we were in trouble; but we landed and the Princess Royal came aboard. We were somewhere near Sandringham. Up again and then Prince Charles appeared and asked if we were enjoying ourselves. He told us he was doing the flying. The funeral went off with many hitches. I had always thought the Norwegians were fairly efficient, but clearly ceremonial was not their strong point. After the service a lot of royals were left hanging around on the pavement. Their cars had been sent somewhere else.

There then came the enthronement of George Carey as Archbishop of Canterbury. It was a splendid occasion; but I felt the Cabinet rather let the side down. There were well-rehearsed processions of the clergy and civic dignitaries, and then, without any attempt to marshal us into some semblance of order, the Prime Minister and the rest of us shambled along. As we hunted for our seats we were not a pretty sight.

On 4 May I attended the Gulf service of remembrance and thanksgiving in St Mungo's Cathedral, Glasgow. The royal train broke down so the Queen was late.

In the same month Jenny was married. We had intended the ceremony to take place in the crypt of the House of Commons – more correctly the Chapel of St Mary Undercroft – but after all the invitations had gone out we were told that the maximum number of people allowed in the place had been drastically reduced on the introduction of new fire regulations. We waited for a few days hoping that the mail would bring masses of letters from people saying they could not come. Instead nearly everyone accepted so we decided to move to St Margaret's and notified everyone accordingly. All went well on the day. Walking from the church to the House of Lords for the reception we came across some morris dancers in Old Palace Yard. A man-horse descended on the bride and wished her fertility.

Back to work, and the task of getting through the government's legislative programme. Divisions I found pretty unnerving because rarely could a result favourable to the government be guaranteed. Whips worked hard to deliver the votes but the Conservative peers did not think twice about voting against the government. Some did not even think it their duty to tell us when they were unhappy with government policy and were minded to vote the 'wrong' way.

And I soon discovered that the built-in majority the Tories were supposed to have in the House simply did not exist. In 1991 there were, in fact, fewer peers who took the Conservative Party whip than there were members of the Opposition parties and the non-aligned peers together; but even the pure arithmetic exaggerated the strength of the Conservatives because a very high proportion of the peers on the other side of the House were life peers and dedicated party politicians, whereas the Conservative ranks contained many hereditary peers who called themselves Conservatives but did not feel under any obligation to be regular attenders and turn up for divisions.

Facing these difficulties I was bound to ask myself now and again whether the House of Lords as then constituted was worth preserving; but I always finished up answering the question with a resounding 'yes'. No one in his right mind, charged with the job of devising a constitution, would have proposed a second chamber remotely like the one we had got. But we were not devising a new constitution, and the question was whether anyone had come up with proposals for reform of the Lords which would result in anything better. A wholly nominated chamber? We had gone through all that in 1968, and it was a non-starter. An elected chamber? If it were elected on the same basis as the Commons it would be a mere carbon copy of the Commons and serve no useful purpose at all. If it were elected on a different basis it would have the same democratic validity as, and be a challenge to, the Commons. So my conclusion was that for all its faults, the House worked pretty well and no changes which up to then had been mooted would make it any better.

On 18 April 1991 the government suffered a defeat when peers voted by a large majority (177 to 79) for an amendment to the Criminal Justice Bill abolishing the mandatory life sentence for murder and allowing judges in murder cases to pass any sentence they wanted – from life to five years, to two years or, for that matter, to a fine or an absolute discharge.

In the debate I had pointed out that when the death penalty was abolished it had been decided that the sentence to be put in its place had to be one which continued to mark the unique wickedness of the crime of murder. The life sentence, the public were told, would not mean that every murderer would spend the rest of his days in prison, but that he would sacrifice his life to the State in the sense that he would only be released when the Home Secretary thought it appropriate. The Home Secretary would be responsible to Parliament if things went wrong; and, because the sentence was for life, the murderer would only be released on licence and for the rest of his life would be liable to recall to prison if he did not behave or appeared once again to have become a danger to the public. I also reminded the House that only a month earlier the House of Commons had once again voted not to restore capital punishment, that the vote had been taken against the background of there being the mandatory life sentence and, for that reason alone, it could not possibly be right to scrap it now.

Lastly, I made the point that it was highly unlikely that if the mandatory sentence was abolished, judges would pass determinate sentences which reflected the views of ordinary people. When some years before a proposal had come before the House for the abolition of the mandatory life sentence in Scotland, the Scottish law lords had made it quite clear that in certain well-publicised murder cases they would have passed sentences which in view of their leniency the general public would have thought quite inappropriate.

The Earl of Longford argued that the public reaction to sentences was irrelevant and should be ignored, but I thought it extraordinarily arrogant to assert that we knew better than everyone else what was and was not justice.

> Parliament has always paid regard to what ordinary people think in deciding what sentences should be passed in the courts. It will be a sad day indeed if we, from our Olympian heights, decide that ten years is an adequate punishment for murder. That could not possibly equate with the views of an ordinary man in the country. I should have thought that the public may have in mind, in the wicked beyond belief case, a penal term in the region of sixty years. After all, that would only be thirty years after the present or proposed system of parole has been brought in to effect. Sixty years would not be thought extraordinary at all. However, would judges in this country be comfortable with having to indicate sentences of that length? I do not know of a single sentence of that length ever having been passed by a judge.

The House was not persuaded, but the amendment was reversed in the Commons and that reversal was eventually accepted by their Lordships.*

---

* After the arrival of the Labour government in May 1997, Lord Ackner and others continued to argue for the abolition of the mandatory life sentence, but the government was having none of it, adopting many of the arguments I had advanced in 1991, which Labour had then treated with derision.

In January 1992 I led a Lords' delegation on a visit to the Pakistan Senate. We came back in poor shape and one of our number, Stanley Clinton-Davis, nearly expired. The trouble was a trip up the Khyber Pass. We had spent the night at Peshawar and the next day was brilliant with a cloudless sky. I did, however, detect a slight nip in the air and came down stairs carrying my overcoat over my arm. 'You won't need that,' said my host, snatched it off me and threw it to the hall porter. By the time we reached the top of the Pass it was perishing. A general stood by a sand model and as the wind howled off the snow-covered Hindu Kush he lectured us for an hour on the goings on in Afghanistan and we slowly froze. We then had to endure a flight home on Pakistan Airways via Moscow.

Shortly after I got back from Pakistan, Gilly and I had another chilly experience. I had been invited to speak in Perth in support of Nicky Fairbairn, a highly eccentric former law officer, and we went to stay with him and his wife at their home, Fordell Castle. On the first day, having been offered a somewhat liquid lunch, we had to repair upstairs to our tower bedroom and breathe hard under the bedclothes in order to thaw out. On the Sunday our host invited members of his Association to drinks in the middle of the day and was moved to address the gathering wielding a broadsword which I thought at any moment might free itself from his somewhat shaky grasp and shoot across the room to impale his chairman.

The general election could not now be long delayed. I told the Prime Minister that I thought there would be advantages in waiting until May, but it was clear he had almost decided on 9 April and in due course the date was announced and Parliament prorogued. Prorogation involved five peers, appointed commissioners for the purpose, sitting on a bench in front of the throne and taking off their hats as the Royal Assent to Bills was signified. The five on this occasion were the Lord Chancellor, myself, Lord Cledwyn (Leader of the Opposition peers), Lord Aberdare (chairman of committees) and Lord Jenkins (representing the Liberals).

The general election came and, in my view, was won (a) because Chris Patten never stopped hammering away at Neil Kinnock's obvious inadequacies and (b) because John Major used his soap box to great effect to show his courage, tenacity and ability to relate to ordinary people. But the press conferences held at Central Office each morning were a disaster. Each was supposed to begin with a Cabinet minister making a presentation about some aspect of policy for which he was responsible, and that was supposed to give the press something to chew on and set the tone for the day. Virtually all the presentations were appalling and the press showed no interest in them. Chris Patten seemed to go out of his way to invite the most troublesome journalists present to put questions to him. This had two disadvantages. One, he could not answer their questions. Two, friendly journalists who wanted to help got thoroughly fed up.

After each press conference my committee sat to answer questions from candidates, and only after that did I set off to campaign. I wasted a lot of time trailing round safe seats, but I did get up to Scotland to support James Douglas-Hamilton[*] and also to north Wales, Anglesey and the West Country, travelling in great style in a helicopter which had been lent to the Party by a wealthy industrialist. On 1 April I woke to hear Labour were between four and seven points ahead in the polls. Two days later I was in Bristol and was told by Michael Stern how badly things were going, but I myself could not detect a very sour atmosphere. On the Tuesday before polling day I was in Edinburgh and was well satisfied with what I saw in James Douglas-Hamilton's seat. I was most amused

---

[*] Then Lord James Douglas-Hamilton MP, now the Rt Hon. Lord Selkirk of Douglas.

by the respectful, indeed deferential, attitude of those attending the meeting I addressed. It was something I had never previously experienced. Perhaps the Scots reserve it for the sons of dukes. On the Wednesday morning I flew down to Manchester and then on to the East Midlands. That day I really did feel that things were coming back to us with John and his soap box having gone down well; and on the Tuesday Woodrow Wyatt, a wise old bird, said he thought we would win. On the Thursday, however, the exit polls were discouraging and Gilly and I sat at home expecting the worst. Then we heard the result at Basildon and soon after that it was clear Labour would not make it.

I was told that all Cabinet ministers should be available to see the Prime Minister on the Saturday, and on Saturday morning I was back in my office waiting for a call. It came just before 11 a.m. and, after I had congratulated John on his victory and we had had a short chat about the campaign, he said: 'I have something unusual to say. I am having to ask a number of people to leave the Cabinet for a big reconstruction. This is no criticism of the way you have led the Lords. You have done very well. But I need your place and I am offering you the Governorship of Bermuda. As far as I am concerned you can have it for the whole of the parliament.' I said I would like to talk to Gilly about that and after wishing him all the luck in the world I left. I rang Gilly and she said at once that I ought to accept the offer. And that was that. I had just become a grandfather and now was to become a governor as well. I felt very old.

CHAPTER SEVENTEEN

Bermuda

I was disappointed to leave the government, but I had known it was bound to happen sooner or later and I was grateful that I was going to have something useful to do instead. I got some nice letters which encouraged me to believe that I had played a useful part in the election campaign and had not been a failure as Leader of the Lords. I particularly appreciated a letter from Emily Blatch in which she referred to the 'sharpness and political edge' I had brought to the job of leader; one from Lord Simon of Glaisdale who had liked my speeches because they were 'wonderfully economical' and another from Roy Jenkins in which he said: 'I thought you were a good leader, crisp, quick to take a point and totally dependable.' One of the nicest was from Lord Jakobovits, the Chief Rabbi, who referred to the battle over the War Crimes Bill.

During the next few weeks I spent many hours wandering round the Foreign and Commonwealth Office attending briefings about Bermuda. I already knew a little, probably more than the Foreign Office which could not even run to earth a copy of the Bermuda constitution and sent me off on a number of wild goose chases. One thing I knew for certain: I had no responsibilities in the field of labour relations. But meetings with the TUC featured large in the Foreign Office's programme for me.

Bermuda was one of Britain's few remaining dependent territories and its recent history had not been trouble free. In 1973 the

Governor, Sir Richard Sharples, had been murdered and there had been serious rioting when the man responsible was hanged. I got useful advice from Viscount Dunrossil, who as plain John Morrison had been a friend at Oxford and had been Governor in the eighties. I discovered that the government of Bermuda, not Her Majesty's Government, was responsible for my salary and that once the British taxpayers had provided me with my uniform I was no longer to be a burden on them. I did not want to have to wait too long before taking up the appointment because it was not easy being without a salary; but I fully understood that Desmond Langley had to be given a reasonable amount of time to pack up and bow out. I did, however, begin to get anxious when the Foreign Office passed to me a message from Bermuda suggesting that I should delay my arrival until October as the Premier was going away on holiday in September and did not think there was any point in my coming until his return. I concluded that it was about time I asserted myself and a reply winged its way to the Premier saying that as he was going on holiday in September I would be arriving in August before his departure.

It was strange, after so many years as a minister, to have no official car in London; but I swiftly became an expert on the bus routes and got sore feet tramping hot pavements. I paid numerous informative visits to important personages like the governor of the Bank of England. I went to see various enterprises with a stake in Bermuda such as Cable & Wireless. I was to be chief scout in Bermuda so had to mug up on scouting. I was to be president of the Council of St John on the Island, so I went off to the headquarters of the Order of St John in Clerkenwell to be knighted. And at the behest of the Foreign Office I made a completely pointless visit to Brussels to speak to EU officials who might have wished to meddle in things Bermudian but, luckily for Bermuda, had not been given the chance.

I paid numerous visits to Mr Alan Bennett, tailor of Savile Row, and eventually took delivery of a blue uniform with black cocked hat for winter wear and a white uniform with pith helmet for the summer. Both hats were designed to sport a feather plume and Mr Bennett told the *Daily Telegraph*: 'Finding swans' feathers for these hats gets harder. The swan is a protected species, so we used to import them from Holland. That is now illegal. We eventually obtained about sixty from a swan factory in Norfolk. They follow the swans about, waiting for them to shed feathers.'

The press took a great interest in all this, asking why I was going to wear uniform when Chris Patten was not. I explained that there was no similarity between the situation in Hong Kong, where Britain was preparing to surrender sovereignty to China, and the situation in Bermuda, where Britain would remain the sovereign power as long as the people of Bermuda wished it. Presumably, at the present time the people valued the British connection and the traditions which went with it and many might look askance if I acted differently from my predecessors. Another matter in which the press took a great interest was the death penalty. In 1991 the British government had by Order in Council abolished the death penalty in the Caribbean dependent territories, but had not been able to do so in Bermuda, which in 1968 had been granted a consti-tution giving it complete control of its own internal affairs. The death penalty had been suffered by the man who had murdered Sir Richard Sharples and when the Island had had a referendum on capital punishment in 1990 there had been a four to one majority in favour of retention.

Under the 1968 constitution the Governor had the power, after consultation with an advisory committee on the Prerogative of Mercy, to substitute 'a less severe form of punishment' and my predecessor had used this power to substitute life imprisonment for the death sentence in the two murder cases which had come before him. Now another murder trial was pending following the brutal killing of a German tourist in Dockyard, and the question which kept on being asked was whether I would act as had the previous Governor or allow the law to take its course. I could only answer that I would carry out my duty in accordance with the constitution, which required consultation with the Mercy Committee and an examination of each case on its merits; and that my own views on capital punishment were irrelevant. I did not say, although I knew it well enough, that I could not ignore the fact that the death penalty had not been imposed for many years and when it had last been used civil disturbances had followed.

On 24 July Gilly and I went to Buckingham Palace for an audience with the Queen, and on the next day we flew to Singapore and on to Australia to stay with Robbie and Jenny. Back in England we had exactly one week to move out of our London house which we had decided to sell, do our final packing and leave for Bermuda, which for the next few years was to be our home.

I was to be sworn in on the morning after our arrival, so had to have with me in the plane both my uniform and my ceremonial sword. The carrying of swords on planes was, however, strictly forbidden, so arrangements had to be made for me to hand over the sword to the captain of the aircraft for safe keeping during the journey. Another problem was our dog Basil: somehow or other it was arranged that at Gatwick he could have a bit of exercise on the tarmac between two parked planes before he was put back in his cage and handed over to the chief steward on the aircraft bound for Bermuda.

Arriving at Bermuda, the plane landed on the American base which, along with other land on the Island, had in 1940 been leased to America but was available for use by civilian aircraft. Then, after being greeted by the Premier and members of his Cabinet, the Chief Justice, the Anglican and Roman Catholic bishops and sundry other dignitaries, we set out for Government House. Across the causeway which links the base and St George's to the main island there was a little knot of people holding a banner calling for independence. The children in the group had not been properly trained in the technique of protest and waved merrily. On we went for a few more miles and up the drive to Government House – a mansion in the Italianate style built of Normandy stone in the last decade of the nineteenth century. According to Jan Morris, author of three volumes describing the rise and decline of the British Empire, the explanation for there being such a magnificent Governor's residence in such a tiny place lies in a foreign office memorandum of the 1890s which reads: 'The keeping up of an outward appearance of power will in many instances save the necessity of resort to the actual exercise of it.' And the outward appearance of power certainly humbled us as we went up the drive and onto the forecourt, past the four cannons lined up opposite the front door. We were not too dismayed by the sight of the Governor's standard and the Union Jack bearing the Bermuda coat of arms flying upside down, and we knew as soon as we were inside that we would come to love the place. After a quick dinner we went upstairs to our magnificent bedroom with a balcony overlooking the sea and soon fell asleep in the four-poster bed. The next day I got into my uniform, and we set off down Langton Hill and into Hamilton, riding in the landau kept for such occasions. In Front Street there came a cry from one of the balconies: 'Hello, David, we are from Clitheroe,' and no longer did I feel a stranger in a strange land. On we went to the Senate House where, after I had inspected a guard of honour to the accompaniment of a seventeen-gun salute and music from the band of the Bermuda Regiment, I was sworn in as Governor by the Chief Justice.

Larry Mussenden, who had been the previous Governor's aide-de-camp, was to stay on with us for a month or two before going to the University of Buckingham to read law*. And after the swearing-in he took us on a tour of the seven islands linked together by bridges and causeways which make up Bermuda.

First we went to St George's Island and the town of St George, Bermuda's capital until the mid-nineteenth century, and from there along the coast to St Catherine's Bay where, on 28 July 1609, the *Sea Venture* was wrecked and the 150 on board struggled ashore. In St George's we saw a replica of the *Deliverance*, which in 1610 carried those who had been on the *Sea Venture* over to Virginia. We also visited the beautiful church in which, after the Island was formally settled, Bermuda's first Parliament met.

Close by in Tobacco Bay we met for the first time Jennifer Smith – later to hold a painting exhibition with Gilly and then, after the 1998 general election, to become Premier. Then it was on to Tucker's Town where, after the First World War, land was compulsorily purchased to build two hotels and golf courses and houses for rich Americans. A road built by the military in the nineteenth century then took us along the south shore to beautiful bays where the coral comes almost to the shore. And eventually as the islands curve back towards the north we came to Dockyard, built at the beginning of the nineteenth century as part of a chain of fortifications from Canada to the Caribbean to meet the threats posed by newly independent America and Napoleon.

We then had the chance to explore the Government House garden, thirty-two acres of it – big by any standards but particularly by the standards of Bermuda. A flight of steps took us from the top lawn to the first terrace and to the cedar planted by Winston Churchill in 1942 after he had travelled to America to meet President Roosevelt. This tree survived the blight which at

---

* He has done extremely well and became adjutant of the Bermuda Regiment and then Attorney-General.

the end of the 1940s killed off most of the cedars on the Island – a blight brought to Bermuda by an American who bore the curious name Carbon Petroleum Dubbs. Next to the Churchill cedar stood a princess palm planted by Haile Selassie in his last days as Emperor of Ethiopia. People in Bermuda will tell you that when the then Governor, General Gascoygne, who was a very tall man, was escorting the Emperor down the steps he had to bend low to converse with him. The result was that he tripped over his sword and shot down the remaining steps on his bottom. The general was one of Bermuda's most popular Governors which makes it hard to believe that this tale was told out of malice, but sadly I have to report that his daughter, Merida Drysdale, a neighbour of ours, says that there is not a scrap of truth in it.

At the bottom of the third terrace was the royal poinciana planted by the Duke of Windsor in 1940 when on his way to take up his appointment as Governor of the Bahamas. On the way down to the planting ceremony a member of the press asked the Duchess what she thought of her husband's appointment, and she replied: 'It is not so much an appointment as a disappointment.' There was then a royal palm planted by the Duke of Kent when honeymooning in Bermuda in 1934; and on the left of the drive on the way back to the house a grove of trees planted by American Presidents and British Prime Ministers when summit meetings had taken place in Bermuda. There had been a Bush/Thatcher meeting in 1990 and a Bush/Major one in 1991.

The drive from Langton Hill up to the house runs through a cutting in the rock and above and across the cutting bougainvillea grew in great abundance until the dreadful day when a dead rat fell from the foliage onto the lap of a Governor's wife riding in the landau on her way to the opening of Parliament.

In our day the garden was in the hands of Manuel and a team of five fellow members of the Portuguese community. When Gilly had the temerity to suggest to Manuel how a plant might be better tended, he replied: 'Lady, we know what we are doing,' and, for the next five years, she had to find other pastimes than gardening.

A barrier manned by the police stood across the drive as it turned towards the front entrance and, one morning after we had been in Government House for some time, there were found painted on the gate post on the house side of the police barrier a number of doom-laden messages. I remember in particular 'prepare to meet your doom' and 'the end of the world is nigh'. An investigation was launched. Clearly some villain had crept up through the garden, and without doubt, said my aide-de-camp, the messages were threatening and there was a real risk of my going the way of Richard Sharples if something was not done and done swiftly. It was some days before the investigators got round to questioning the policeman in the box that night, but he eventually declared with more pride than remorse that he had had a summons from heaven during the night and in accordance with a divine command had gone off to find a paint pot.

But now we were in the house, which proved far more comfortable and far less forbidding than we expected; and beyond the drawing room and dining room there was a swimming pool which was certainly well used in our time – not least by Basil who on particularly hot days would sit on the top step at the shallow end with water up to his neck. For the pool we were indebted to Lord Martonmere, a former Governor who was inordinately rich, having had the good sense to marry an American heiress.

Upstairs there were two fine bedrooms with balconies looking towards the sea and plenty of other bedrooms on that floor and in the towers. In one of those one of my predecessors had spent his time playing trains.

During the next few weeks, when many people including the Premier were away on holiday, I had plenty of time to find that, although small, Bermuda was home to some great people; and we soon got to know some of them. Harry Cox was one of the first to call at Government House and took us back to Sunnylands in Devonshire to meet his wife Jessica. Harry was an underwater treasure hunter, businessman, politician and raconteur and, with his barrel of white rum under a tangerine tree in his backyard, an exhausting companion. Geese guarded the rum and at the end of the garden in a shed now full to overflowing was what Harry had bought at the agricultural show as 'a miniature racing pig' but which had never stopped growing.

We also soon met Willie Frith, later Mayor of Hamilton, and his wife Sally. Willie's ancestors were privateers. His most famous forebear Hezekiah had sailed in a ship of that name to make his fortune on the seas off Hispaniola, but he was apprehended by the Spanish who sent him home with his head but without his sword. One of Harry's best stories was of Willie's ceremonial visit to St David's with his unofficial aide-de-camp, Colonel Craigen Curtis. As his hosts stirred the fish chowder with ceremony, the spoon met with an obstruction and eventually there emerged from the soup Ginger the cat who had gone missing some days earlier. Then there were Michael and Elaine Darling who, like Willie and Sally, never uttered an unkind word about anyone. Richard Thornton and his wife Susie also became great friends. They were on the Island temporarily having leased a house from Dick Butterfield, who was immensely kind to us, letting us have a mooring for our boat off the bottom of his garden.

Richard Thornton played golf almost as badly as I did but sailed with great competence his Scandinavian folk boat *Larkspur*. On one occasion Richard, who like all of us was getting old, was fussing about in the boat as we tried to make progress in the teeth of a roaring gale and while he searched for a piece of rope he handed me the tiller. He then tripped and disappeared headfirst into the scuppers. I tapped him on the nape of the neck to see if he was alive and when he responded with a whimper I begged him not to expire, explaining that I was not much of a sailor and knew not how to make land. As the storm raged about us I held the tiller with one hand and seized the seat of his pants with the other. I hauled and hauled and eventually Richard came upright.

Harry kept some of the treasure which he had picked up off the bottom of the sea in the Bank of Bermuda, and when Bishop (Bill) Down was due to leave the Island Harry said he would get the treasure out of the bank and, as a farewell gesture, show it to him. The Bishop and Richard went out to lunch at the Yacht Club and then turned up at Sunnylands at the appointed hour. They then settled themselves down on a sofa and to Harry's fury nodded off, missing any sight of the treasure.

The agricultural show in the spring was a great institution. The Governor and his wife were driven to the agricultural show in the landau, the Governor heralding the arrival of spring by wearing his summer uniform. Then on or close to St George's Day there was the Peppercorn Ceremony in St George's, when the Governor received a peppercorn as rent for the Old State House in the town: and in the winter months there were tennis tournaments, a rugby tournament, often featuring a team from the All Blacks, and golf championships with big names from America lured to Bermuda by the prospect of prize money and a mini-holiday in warmer weather. So there was no reason for anybody to be bored.

There were plenty of people on the Island having a lot of fun, but there were also plenty of people full of good works and public spiritedness making a great contribution to Island life. There was a National Trust, with a big membership and an income far greater per head of the population than in Britain, and with these resources able to keep in immaculate condition a number of historic properties. One of the leading lights was Patsy Phillips, sister of David

Gibbons, a former Premier. In the winter months there was an arts festival to both attract tourists and keep the locals amused, and there was never a shortage of people prepared to work flat-out to make it a success. Sir Edwin (Ted) Leather had founded the festival and he had also persuaded Yehudi Menuhin to lend his name to a foundation which helped pay for young musicians to come out from England and work in Bermuda schools. There was a Bermuda Philharmonic Orchestra, duly fortified by these teachers and other visiting musicians.

During our time Yehudi, then Lord Menuhin, came to stay at Government House. He wanted to see and perhaps give some instruction to a young Bermudian learning the violin, and one was chosen and brought up to Government House. Gilly and I sat on the terrace and could hear something of what was going on above us. Three or four hesitant notes were played, the violin was handed over to the maestro and a few haunting phrases followed. In the evening he went down to the City Hall and, up on the platform and bent almost double, he set about coaxing something like music out of the Youth Orchestra.

CHAPTER EIGHTEEN

Testing Times

Hail to Bermuda, my island in the Sun.
Sing out in glory to the nation we've become.
We go from heart to heart, and strength to strength.
The privilege is mine, to sing
'Long live Bermuda', because this island's mine.

Hail to Bermuda, my homeland dear to me.
This is my own land built on faith and unity.
We go from heart to heart, and strength to strength
For loyalty is mine, to sing
'Long live Bermuda', because this island's mine.

I t was now time to get serious and write my first dispatch to the Foreign Office. The Bermuda song did not, of course, state the constitutional position with accuracy, and the maps displayed in the schools showing Bermuda in the centre of the world might have been thought by some to be somewhat misleading, but both the song and the maps exemplified the enormous pride the people had in their tiny but immensely prosperous island home. And I wanted to try and reflect all that in what I wrote. At that early stage

I seemed to have grasped that independence was going to be the big issue throughout my stay. John Swan, the Premier, wanted it, I wrote, for a mixture of reasons. Being a man of considerable stature it was obviously galling for him to have to watch lesser men strutting on the world stage as full-blown Prime Ministers or even Presidents while he remained a mere Premier of a dependent territory, but it would have been grossly unfair to treat his motives as being purely selfish. He genuinely believed that with independence would come a spirit of national togetherness and a bridging of the racial divide which was very real – with the white Bermudians, a small minority, holding all the levers of economic power. And he wanted to steal the PLP's (the Progressive Labour Party's) clothes, they having for long had independence on their own programme for government. Rarely from 1982 onwards had John missed an opportunity to force independence on to the agenda. He had come close to losing the leadership of the UBP (United Bermuda Party) not long before by being over-enthusiastic about independence, but he had not abandoned his ambitions or conviction that eventually the whole Party would come round to his way of thinking. Many, however, feared that those running international companies, looking as they did upon the present constitutional set-up as a guarantee of Bermuda's stability, would in the event of independence soon lose their enthusiasm for Bermuda as a base and turn to places like the Cayman Islands – a very serious consideration when the number of international companies on the Island was continuing to grow and was replacing more and more of the revenue lost through a decline in tourism.

I finished my dispatch with some comments on race and said that I had felt somewhat discouraged when the white winner of the Miss Bermuda Islands contest was booed by the black audience (even though the unfortunate girl had been picked by a panel of judges all except one of whom were black). I had been at the event and not being one of the judges had had a relaxed evening, dressed, I think, in blazer and slacks, but a week or two later there appeared in the British press a story about how I had made myself a laughing stock by picking a white girl as the winner and then crowning her in full uniform complete with hat and feathers. A few weeks passed and then there was another story, this time about my having fallen in love with my Bermuda shorts to the extent that I had turned up in them at a white-tie affair to the fury of my host. It was only after a very much more serious incident following the recruitment of a new police commissioner in the early part of 1995 that we discovered that the purveyor of these falsehoods was a senior journalist on the *Royal Gazette* who was supplementing his income by 'stringing' for papers in London. The trouble with stories of this sort is that they find their way into the cuttings files of newspapers and incompetent and unscrupulous journalists regurgitate the inaccuracies from time to time. Much later, in May 1993, a piece appeared in *The Times* under the name of Michael Dynes which was supposed to be an intelligent contribution to a debate about the cost of British representation abroad. The article began:

> Shortly after his appointment as Governor of Bermuda, Lord Waddington agreed to judge the Miss Bermuda competition. Dressed in his plumed hat he presided over the choice of a white girl as the island's greatest beauty. Her Majesty's representative was immediately in trouble. The plumed hat made everything worse. Was this the image that John Major's classless Britain wished to display to the world?'

I wrote to Mr Dynes protesting at this nonsense and to my astonishment he wrote back saying that he was very much more aggrieved than I was because the paragraph about which I had complained had not been written by him at all. Without his knowledge or consent it had been tacked on by some sub-editor at *The Times* to add a bit of spice to his otherwise very serious piece.

A few weeks after my arrival Captain Eddie Lamb took over as aide-de-camp, and a fine one he turned out to be. He was a St David's islander and everyone in Bermuda will tell you that those who come from St David's are very different from anyone else. In the old days, before the arrival of the Americans, St David's was very cut off from the rest of Bermuda and there was a good deal of intermarriage between the comparatively few families with roots there. The best known surnames on the Island are Fox and Lamb and it was said that St David's is the only place in the world where the fox lies down with the lamb. Anyhow, Eddie decided that we must pay a visit to St David's, and as we were driven in the Daimler towards the centre of St David's there were quite a few people at the side of the road waving merrily. Eddie sat proudly in the front seat helping us to wave back; and it seemed that patriotism in St David's knew no bounds. Then we began to pay attention to what the crowds were shouting. 'Hi Eddie,' they cried as they welcomed home their favourite son. We visited St David's Primary School, and events followed a similar pattern. 'What would you like to ask the Governor, Malika?' said the headteacher to one child. 'Where's your hat?' said the little girl. 'Now, Raymonde, you've got your hand up. What would you like to ask the Governor?' and Raymonde replied: 'I don't want to ask the Governor anything. I just want to say "Hi, Uncle Eddie".'

At the far end of the US naval base was a NASA station from which in October 1992 we watched a space shuttle launch in the presence of an astronaut who had made a trip earlier that year. More memorable that autumn was a visit by Raine, Countess Spencer. I warned her that on the Saturday we were going sailing. She said she did not like sailing. I told her that I had accepted on her behalf an invitation to go sailing, that considerable offence would be caused if she cancelled, that it was a big boat and she could bring her knitting. She had to come. Reluctantly she agreed.

The day dawned and punctually at two minutes to nine Raine came down the stairs wearing a party frock, white lace gloves and high-heeled shoes, and carrying a parasol. I had not the energy to argue and off to the Royal Bermuda Yacht Club we went. The commodore looked at Raine in astonishment and queried whether she was in yachting form. He thought she looked nervous. 'Nonsense,' said I. 'If you have any trouble, lash her to the mast.' But a few discreet words were exchanged, and the next thing I knew she was tottering back along the jetty to the car; she and Gilly returned to Government House. At 3 p.m. I came back from my sail with a guilty conscience. What, I wondered, had they done for lunch? The staff had been told we were going out and had been given the day off. I need not have worried. They had had a wonderful time. Raine had talked all day about her romances, and Gilly had sat alongside open-mouthed forgetting all about food. But by then the Countess was peckish and I packed them in to our little Ford and took them to a pub in St George's for a ham sandwich.

Our next visitor was Prince Michael of Kent. He really did want to sail and although he could not come out himself Nicky Dill[*] provided his boat, *Dillightful*, together with a skipper. We bowled down to St George's for lunch, but by the time we set off back the wind had strengthened. In spite of that, the skipper gave the wheel to the Prince and directed him to round Spanish Point via Cobbler's Cut instead of steering out towards Dockyard and taking the longer but very much safer way home. A gust of wind hit the boat and drove it on to the rocks. For a moment I thought we were going over but the skipper turned on the engine and threw it into

---

[*]   Nicky was a barrister and a partner in Conyers, Dill & Pearman. He was also the Danish Consul and Chancellor of the Bermuda Diocese.

reverse; and we came off and righted ourselves. That evening a local police officer said to the Prince's detective, 'I hear you had a near miss today.' 'No,' replied the detective. 'The Prince never misses.' Very sportingly Nicky Dill protested that little damage had been done to *Dillightful*, but I have reason to think that that was short of the truth.

I opened Parliament at the beginning of November and it took me half an hour to read the speech from the throne. It would have taken even longer had I not spotted that at page eighteen there was a long passage identical in every respect with three paragraphs on the first page. I also excised a number of Americanisms. (The government had 'gotten' this and 'gotten' that.)

It was grand to learn that Bermuda still observed Armistice Day; indeed, it was a public holiday. A service took place at the Cenotaph below the Senate House and afterwards there was a lunch for the veterans in Number One Shed on Front Street. On parade with the veterans was a contingent from the Bermuda Regiment, a uniquely Bermudian institution. Young men of eighteen were liable for three years part-time service. They had to attend drills on one or two nights a week and while the first year's 'boot camp' was fairly arduous, in the second and third years the soldiers thoroughly enjoyed a fortnight's training abroad either in Jamaica or Fort Lejeune in North Carolina. The regiment performed ceremonial duties, but, more importantly, it was a disciplined force ready to help in national emergencies – hurricanes as well as riots. The camps in Jamaica did no end of good. Young men saw how poverty-stricken was much of Jamaica, and many must have realised how lucky they were to live in Bermuda even though it was not an independent country.

We were joined for Christmas by various members of the family and afterwards were due to go to Barbados for a Governors' conference. On the day we were due to leave for Barbados and Victoria was due to go back to university, Basil our Norfolk terrier, who had earlier distinguished himself playing the Government House piano, suffered a terrible misfortune.

I was looking for him after lunch to take him for a walk and found him sitting under a chair in the little drawing room. His ears were pricked and he seemed to be saying 'I don't know how to explain this, but something rather embarrassing has happened.' Indeed it had. His back looked like something on a butcher's slab. As we rushed him to the vet, I was thinking he had been run over; but, in fact, he had been savaged by a dog or dogs and thirty-five stitches were needed to repair the damage.

The news of his misfortune swept round the Island and the 'get well' cards began to arrive – scores of them. The *Royal Gazette* reminded the citizenry that St Basil – known as Basil the Great (330–379 AD), whose feast day is 2 January – was inclined to be headstrong and, among other 'biting' remarks, had voiced the opinion that a merciless attitude should be adopted towards bureaucrats; and the paper hinted that Basil possessed some of his namesake's attributes and that might have led to his downfall. His reputation was, however, vigorously defended by a body calling itself Basil's Press Office.

After the conference in Barbados we flew to St Vincent and then, with the British representative in St Vincent and his wife, sailed down through the Grenadines in a small yacht with a skipper and a so-called cook. On our way home we had an unfortunate experience in Miami Airport. The queues at immigration were immense and we were going to miss our onward flight unless something was done. When I got to the immigration desk I asked the immigration officer (a woman) to be as quick as possible as we were in trouble and before you could say knife she had called to some thug standing nearby who catapulted us into a room full of Haitians and Cubans. I complained to another woman who appeared to be in charge and demanded to ring the British Consul. That resulted in our immediate release. Most of the staff at the airport seemed to know no more than a smattering of English and were thoroughly unpleasant. We decided to avoid Miami in any future travels.

Easter was by tradition the time to send lilies to the Queen and in April 1993 off Gilly went to pick them. Then there was a St George's Day Service in the Salvation Army Citadel in Hamilton. The proceedings commenced with the Scouts coming up to the front and handing in their banners. At the end they knelt to receive them back and marched down the centre aisle towards the main doors. Suddenly there was the sound of circular saws and splitting timbers as each banner pole came into contact with the fans in the ceiling and was quickly decapitated. The Scouts' motto 'Be Prepared' may not have been observed but the Scouts themselves did not flinch. They picked up off the floor the shattered remains of their poles and with considerable dignity processed on to the street.

Later in the spring we visited our Consul-General in New York and then our Ambassador in Washington. I also had the opportunity to talk to American officials about issues affecting Bermuda. In Washington I was most anxious to get a feel on the future of the American base and do what I could to dissuade the Americans from a precipitate withdrawal: I spent some time talking to key people in the State Department, the Pentagon and Congress. I then received an astonishing phone call from an irate John Swan who asked me what right I had to be interfering in matters which were his responsibility. I pointed out that under the Bermuda constitution I had responsibilities for external affairs, but it made me realise that I was dealing with a Premier who previous Governors and others had encouraged to believe was in entire control of Bermuda's fortunes – which was nearly, but not quite, true. Without doubt he looked a national leader, capable of speaking with great sense and authority and he was a first-rate Ambassador for his country while travelling abroad, as well as a very able leader at home. It was, therefore, scarcely surprising that people like Ebersole Gaines, US Consul-General until the end of 1992, who probably did not understand the constitutional position, thought John of sufficient standing to deserve dinner at the White House. That might have helped to persuade John that matters like the future of the American base were his responsibility and his alone.

In July I visited London, principally for talks with Mark Lennox-Boyd, then the minister in the Foreign Office responsible for Bermuda, but I went to the Lords to see what was going on and in the Lobby was greeted by Lord (Oulton) Wade who cried out in his broad Cheshire accent: 'Hello, David. Are you brown all over?' Back in Bermuda my golf was going badly but my excellent aide-de-camp, Eddie Lamb, was beginning to perform for me the function Eb Gaines had performed for John Swan. He was a morale booster, and it was as a result of his efforts that I won my one and only golf trophy. Eddie set up a regimental golf championship. Sixteen agreed to play, four teams of four. Only fourteen players turned up on the day because the second in command of the regiment and Larry Mussenden were recovering from a hangover. My team was second and Eddie had arranged for everyone in the first three teams to get a prize.

In September I was asked to dissolve Parliament for a general election on 5 October. The campaign was not inspiring and when the result was declared, the UBP had survived with a reduced majority, winning twenty-two seats against the PLP's eighteen, with its lowest ever share of the vote (50% compared with 54% in 1989 and 62% in 1985).

The Opening of Parliament provided the PLP with their first opportunity to expose John Swan as a leader weakened by the election result. The Speaker in the 1989–93 parliament, David Wilkinson, had not stood for re-election. He was a splendidly laid back, some might say idle, figure from an old white Bermudian family and John Swan could not stand him. One reason for this antipathy was that on one occasion when in the Speaker's Chair David awoke from a deep sleep and feeling something was required of him announced 'this House is now adjourned.' Everyone got up and left except John Swan who was just about to deliver a great oration. John was determined that he would now have a Speaker of his own choosing and he decided on a black Bermudian, Dr David Dyer. On the day before the opening of Parliament I went down to the Senate House for a rehearsal and Dyer was there, also being put through his paces. That night there was the usual eve-of-session party at Government House and from the sniggering of some members of the Opposition I concluded that something was afoot.

The next day I arrived at the Senate House. My first duty was to inspect the guard of honour and I then went up into an anteroom on the first floor to wait for the members of the House of Assembly to answer Black Rod's summons and begin to process down the hill to the Senate Chamber to hear the speech from the throne. I waited and waited but there was no sign of the procession, and after ten minutes or so I began to worry. Perhaps the PLP had actually hatched some plot to boycott the opening of Parliament. So I sent a messenger up the hill to find out what was going on. And, just as in 1983 Margaret Thatcher's plan to install a Speaker of her choice had been derailed by Conservative backbenchers who thought the right man for the Chair was the Deputy Speaker – Jack Weatherill – so had John Swan's plan to install David Dyer. A group of UBP members had sided with the PLP and they and the PLP, a party not known for its sympathy for the Portuguese, had succeeded in getting voted in as Speaker the Portuguese Deputy Speaker – all for the sheer joy of annoying John Swan.

David Dyer of course had been made to look a complete fool and rather unfairly blamed it all on the Premier. It cannot be said that he at once set about engineering John's downfall but I have little doubt that from that time onwards he wished it most fervently.

CHAPTER NINETEEN

A Royal Visit

The UBP's election manifesto 'A Blue Print For The Future' had been a detailed policy statement about everything under the sun – from employment to the environment, from drugs to alcohol abuse, from crime to new steps to eliminate discrimination. There was no mention of independence and the matter was not discussed at all by the party leaders during the campaign. Furthermore, when John Swan had been asked about the subject by the *Royal Gazette* he had replied: 'It's not in the Blue Print'.

In the light of all this there was great surprise when, just before Christmas 1993, John told the press that Britain's announcement that it was to close HMS *Malabar*, the tiny shore station at the West End manned by just thirteen sailors, was a sign of the unravelling of Bermuda's ties with Britain. And also when, after Christmas, he blandly announced that independence was back on the agenda, 'Because of the withdrawal of the Americans, Canadians and British from the Island.' 'If I had made independence an issue in the campaign,' he said with commendable frankness, 'I would have lost the election.'

The decision to close HMS *Malabar* in April 1995 for a gross saving of £1 million per annum and a net saving which had not even been quantified was really stupid. Any sensible person could have seen the advantages for Britain in at least delaying any decision about *Malabar* until after the American withdrawal from Bermuda which was planned for 1995. As it was, people were able to insinuate that no possible blame could be attached to the Americans for deciding to leave Bermuda somewhat precipitately because, by resolving to do away with a Royal Naval presence on the Island, Britain seemed to be up to the same tricks.

None of this, however, seemed to be a particularly good reason for John Swan using HMS *Malabar* as an excuse for resurrecting the issue of independence, for the likelihood of the closure of *Malabar* had been known for some time. The truth was that rarely from 1982 onwards had John missed an opportunity to force independence onto the political agenda and here, after an election result too close for comfort and with demographic change working against the UBP, he could surely, he thought, persuade his Party that only by raising again the emotive issue of independence would they be able to avoid a UBP debacle five years on. And while commonsense must have been telling him that independence was a divisive issue within the UBP and might well dissolve the glue which held that precarious coalition together, one very influential member of the business community, Donald Lines of the Bank of Bermuda, was telling him that this time the furious opposition from Front Street which had followed the raising of the banner of independence in the past might well not be repeated.

In January 1994 the Premier talked to the press about the possibility of having a referendum on independence in the near future. He said this without the authority of Cabinet, and when Cabinet met, one of the members, Ann Cartwright DeCouto, complained, saying that if the Premier wished to raise these issues, things should be done properly and a paper presented to Cabinet for discussion. A paper was swiftly drafted and presented to the next Cabinet meeting, and by a majority the Premier's plan for the setting up of a Commission of Inquiry to explain the consequences of independence and for a referendum on that issue was approved. Ann DeCouto promptly resigned as a minister.

A Referendum Bill was then published, and in February it was passed by the House of Assembly by a majority of twenty to eighteen. At this stage, however, the PLP tabled a motion to halt the setting up of the Commission which, according to the Bill, had to report before a date was set for the referendum, and the Senate then also proceeded to put a spanner in the works.

The Senate was composed of eleven people. Five were appointed by the Governor on the advice of the Premier, three by the Governor on the advice of the Leader of the Opposition and three by the Governor acting in his discretion. So if the 'Opposition' senators and the 'independent' senators voted together, the government could be defeated; and this time it was defeated, first on a motion that the Referendum Bill should not be discussed in the Senate until the Opposition's objections to the Commission of Inquiry were resolved; and then when the Senate relented and did agree to discuss the Bill, it proceeded to vote for an amendment which provided that in the referendum a majority of those entitled to vote had to vote 'yes' for there to be a mandate for independence.

In the following weeks there were many rumours of plots to get rid of the Premier and one actual plot to install John Stubbs in his place, but Swan survived. The Referendum Bill did not. Having refused to accept the Senate amendment, John eventually announced that a committee of ministers was to be appointed to draft a Green Paper setting out the pros and cons of independence, that the existing Bill would be dropped but that in the next session yet another Bill providing for a referendum would be put before Parliament.

In March 1994 Bermuda had a well-earned rest from all the scheming and feuding over independence. After months of planning there was a state visit to the Island by the Queen and Prince Philip – the first since 1975. A committee had sat for months devising a programme which would suit everyone, and everyone's part had been rehearsed. We even had the whole Cabinet on parade on the Sunday before the arrival, learning where they were to line up and in what order, how a bow should be executed (from the neck not the waist) and how the royal hand should be taken assuming it was offered (not in a vice-like grip). We were prepared.

The Queen had left the royal yacht in the Bahamas and was coming by air, and at 2.25 p.m. precisely on Tuesday 8 March 1994 Gilly and I arrived at the airport. In a moment or two the plane had landed and was taxiing down the runway towards us. Miraculously out of the roof there appeared the Royal Standard and at 2.30 p.m. the doors opened and the Queen came down the steps. I presented Gilly and the Premier at the foot of the steps and after a twenty-one gun salute and the inspection of a guard of honour came the presentation of all the other dignitaries.

The plan then was for the Queen to go to St George's for a walk-about in the town square – travelling in the Daimler which was now twelve years old and temperamental. An American had offered us the loan of his Rolls-Royce and to ship the car from the States for the occasion, but the Queen had been adamant that she did not want that sort of fuss. If the Daimler had broken down, we would have been in a fix because the restrictions on car size in Bermuda from which only the Governor was exempt meant that the Daimler was the only big car on the Island: but it had been gone over from top to toe and was looking right royal, and we hoped it would not disgrace us.

After the walk about in St George's the Queen was supposed to get back in the car to go down the road a little way to the Tucker House, a lovely seventeenth-century National Trust property, but she delighted everyone by ignoring orders and striding off down the street on foot. Gilly and I then left for Government House, to be on parade there when the Queen arrived.

Government House was packed with Easter lilies and looked superb. For months workmen had been about the place carrying out repairs, redecorations, carpet cleaning etc. The Bermuda National

Trust had undertaken the refurbishment of the royal suite where furniture had been touched up, chairs reupholstered and the canopy over the four poster bed cleaned. We had been very lucky with the canopy. During the preparations for the visit a member of the recce party which had come out from London had insisted on Gilly lying on the bed and looking skywards. She did so and saw for the first time that the canopy was in an advanced state of decay. I, in my turn, had made a complete fool of myself over the lavatory. At a dinner party I had enjoyed myself explaining how hideous was the loo in the royal suite and how I had insisted on its replacement, but after dinner when I was invited upstairs for a wash and brush-up I discovered that our hostess was the proud possessor of a loo similar in every respect to the one I had had removed to please the Queen. On returning downstairs I had difficulty looking the lady of the house in the face.

The Queen arrived at Government House at 4.15 p.m. and there was an investiture in the dining room. A short time to change, and then we were off to the Speaker's banquet at the Southampton Princess. Trumpeters from the Bermuda Regiment had been assembled to blow a fanfare as the Queen entered the vast ballroom in which nearly 600 people were waiting to dine. The Speaker, Ernest DeCouto, had been told to pause at the door so that the trumpeters could prepare themselves; but Prince Philip who was two paces behind and getting impatient poked him in the back and asked him why we were all hanging around. Ernest lost his nerve and propelled the Queen into the room and straight onto the platform. The trumpeters lost their chance to sound a note and grumpily popping their instruments under their arms, slunk out of sight.

The food was excellent and the evening was voted a huge success even by those who thought it was rather offside for the Premier to make a speech which sounded very much like a bid for independence. 'Our destiny,' said Sir John, 'was once determined in part by our position as the Gibraltar of the West. Now we must face taking responsibility for our future by ourselves. I believe we are equal to the task.' Some of the Premier's colleagues denied that what he had said had anything to do with independence; but the *Mid-Ocean News* commented: 'If it looks like a duck, walks like a duck and quacks like a duck, it is usually safe to assume it is a duck – except in Bermuda, of course, when it is a Swan who has been misrepresented.'

Most people at the banquet missed a far more significant event than the Premier's speech. As the Queen rose to speak Ernest DeCouto decided that the microphone, which had been placed in front of her at just the right height, needed adjusting and as he leaned across to fiddle with it some of us could see disaster looming. Prince Philip shouted 'Don't touch the mike!' but it was too late. As the Speaker leaned across the front of the Queen his cuff collided with the Queen's glass of port and its contents descended on to her dress. With great presence of mind she covered the stain with her handbag and proceeded as if nothing had happened. The dress, I have little doubt, found its way into the dustbin.

The next morning the Queen and Prince Philip planted a tree each in the Government House garden, which was a blaze of colour with wild freesias in abundance. We then set off for the hospital. On the way up to the front entrance a little gathering of women were carrying placards which read:

'The corgis of Bermuda welcome Your Majesty' and there they were, all twenty of them, slavering in welcome – the dogs of course, not the women. On the way back down the drive the Daimler slowed to a halt and one of the women came forward and a few words were exchanged. Talking to Gilly about the incident later in the day the Queen said, 'That dog was called Lillibet. I was quite surprised. I thought it would be Queenie.'

Then it was on to the Bermuda College, the Dockyard and the

Maritime Museum before the party came back across the Sound by boat, accompanied by thirty or forty smaller craft. There was then a visit to the Yacht Club and, finally, to the Botanical Gardens for an entertainment by the young people of the Island.

That evening there was a banquet at Government House. Twenty-eight people sat round the main table which took up the whole length of the dining room, and thirty more guests sat at three tables on the terrace. A string quartet played as we ate iced tomato soup, medallions of beef stuffed with stilton cheese and brandy snap baskets with butterscotch mousse and fresh fruits. There were no speeches apart from my few words before the loyal toast, and the evening was rounded off with the regimental band beating the retreat on the front lawn. When it was over I told my aide-de-camp to ask the band to wait so that Prince Philip could thank them on behalf of the Queen, but Eddie had difficulty disentangling himself from the royal party and he did not catch up with the band until well down Langton Hill, the best part of a mile from Government House. Unabashed Eddie ordered an about turn and the band marched back up the hill for a 'Thank you' which I suspect the members thought they could have been spared.

The next morning had been planned as an opportunity for the Queen to thank those who had worked on the visit. Some were lucky enough to receive honours and I was particularly lucky to be made a Knight Grand Cross of the Royal Victorian Order (GCVO). The insignia included a collar of gold which I was told had to be returned on my demise and which the Duke of Edinburgh stressed I would seldom have the opportunity to wear; 'collar days', as they are called, being rare events.

Prince Philip was not going back to England with the Queen. He was due to set off for the Caribbean in the afternoon. But when it came to the Queen's departure he got into the Daimler as well. 'What are you coming for?' said the Queen. 'I am going to see you off' replied

Prince Philip. 'That's jolly kind of you,' said the Queen. And off they went, with plenty of people at the roadside to cheer them on their way. As usual we sent the Queen lilies at Easter and received a lovely letter thanking us for them and for the stay at Government House.

CHAPTER TWENTY

Trouble on the Island

From the moment when I had arrived in Bermuda the politicians had stressed the importance that they attached to 'Bermudisation', i.e. filling job vacancies with Bermudians rather than foreigners whenever that was possible. We were not doing much for that policy in Government House, with an English butler and English chef, an English Governor's secretary, a Portuguese maid and a Filipino maid, and five Portuguese gardeners. Indeed it was only the scullery maid, a downstairs cleaner and the woman who did the laundry who were Bermudian. When, therefore, the butler, Michael Schubert, was due to leave at the end of his contract I was determined to get a Bermudian replacement. The post was advertised but very few applicants put in for the job. One seemed reasonably good – a sergeant in the regiment whose wife was on the regiment's permanent staff – and Andre Nesbitt was duly recruited on a probationary basis.

It was soon clear that we had made a serious mistake. As the royal visit had drawn nearer Andre's nerves had got the better of him, and Eddie had to take away virtually all his responsibilities and bring in people from outside to do his work. After the royals had gone I had Andre into my room and told him that he had proved completely useless during the visit and, as far as I was concerned, he could leave there and then. But foolishly I then added that if he really wanted to stay I would give him a last chance and extend the probationary period for another six months. Andre agreed to stay on those terms. Unfortunately there was no improvement and the time came when I told him he would have to go. For that the PLP branded me a racist. I pointed out that it was hardly racist to dispense with an English butler so that I could recruit a Bermudian and the fact that I was now looking for another Bermudian did not look particularly racist either. But that got me nowhere, and soon the story had been sold to the English press where it appeared suitably embroidered and embellished.

Then the time came when I had to recruit a new commissioner of police and things went from bad to worse. There had always been difficulty in recruiting Bermudians for the police. In good times higher wages could be earned in other jobs and Bermudians were not particularly keen on doing a job which involved night work and might even make them unpopular in the communities where they lived. Consequently, many police officers were recruited from the Caribbean and from Britain. Often the Caribbean officers found it difficult to get themselves accepted and were heavy-handed in their dealings with the local community. The British officers, being white, were seen by young blacks as an alien element. Furthermore, these different groups in the police often did not get on with and did not trust each other. Jack Sharpe, a former Premier, told me that after the Sharples murder a very pleasant Bermudian officer showed up to give him personal protection. The next day he told Jack that he was going off duty for a while but was worried about his replacement: 'He comes from St Kitts and hates all white men.'

When I arrived in Bermuda Lennett (known as Lenny) Edwards, a black Bermudian, was commissioner of police and Alec Forbes, of Scottish origin who had acquired Bermudian status, was his deputy. Both were old-fashioned in their approach to policing and saw no need for change. Complaints against the police, if dealt with at all, were dealt with months after the event and then often not properly. Morale in the police was at rock-bottom. An exercise in crowd control was held at the US naval annexe. Members of the regiment were detailed to act out the role of rioters. The police approached the rioters carrying their shields. The 'rioters' lobbed a few missiles and the police broke ranks and fled.

The Foreign Office employed an overseas police adviser to go round the police forces in the dependent territories, carry out reviews and make suggestions as to how efficiency might be improved, and in May 1994 Lionel Grundy, the then adviser, visited Bermuda. His report was damning. There was no leadership or sense of purpose in the police and no attempt had been made to prepare people to fill the top ranks. Lenny could retire on full pension the following May on reaching fifty-six; Forbes was due to go on 1 March 1995, but there was no one to follow them. There were two assistant commissioners. One of them, Harold Moniz, was of Portuguese descent and was rated both unpopular and inefficient. The other, Wayne Perinchief, had only been promoted a month or two before and, having no experience at all of high office, could not possibly be considered a candidate for deputy, let alone commissioner at that time.

I discussed the matter with the Premier and with John Irving Pearman, the Minister for Home Affairs, and we decided to replace both Lenny (who had by then become ill and wanted to retire) and Forbes on his retirement, with a commissioner and a deputy commissioner recruited from abroad. Big trouble followed. The PLP declared that as there were two Bermudians qualified to be commissioner I had again been guilty of racism. The Leader of the Opposition, Frederick 'Freddy' Wade, and a number of his supporters brought a petition against overseas recruitment up to Government House, and in front of the cameras I made the mistake of telling Freddy that the decision to recruit had been made and there was no question of it being reversed. At the time I thought it right to be firm. If I had given the impression that I was prepared to reconsider, I would have been letting down the minister who had shown some courage in accompanying the deputy governor to London and seeing the applicants for the two posts. But it was a mistake to have been so forthright. According to the PLP I had not shown due respect towards the six thousand people who were alleged to have signed the petition, and there were calls for my salary to be cut. In due course the PLP tabled a motion in the House of Assembly reducing it to one dollar. It was rather discouraging that when such a motion had last been tabled it was a matter of hours before my predecessor Sir Richard Sharples was murdered. Indeed, the next day the *Royal Gazette* printed the report of the debate alongside the report of the assassination.

The motion, like the one in 1973, was, of course, really no more than a procedural ploy, a method of getting at the Governor as the symbol of British authority, and after a vote on party lines, with every government supporter voting 'no', the motion was defeated. But this did not deter someone on the *Royal Gazette* (who had earlier caused us trouble selling false reports to the British press) from telling this story in lurid and wholly inaccurate terms to the *Sunday Times* where it appeared under the headline: 'LOCALS ARGUE WADDINGTON WORTH JUST ONE POUND.' The article began:

It seemed an idyllic end to a distinguished political career. But David Waddington's reign as Governor of the sunshine island of Bermuda is in turmoil this weekend amid allegations of racism and deadly intrigue. Waddington, the former Home Secretary, is facing an unprecedented challenge to his rule after accusations that he despises the island's native population and is not fit to meddle in local political affairs. The tensions between Waddington and Bermudian Opposition politicians surfaced on Friday when he faced the indignity of a move to have his salary reduced to less than one pound a year, calculated on a performance-related basis.

Waddington narrowly survived the vote. Bermudian MPs voted twenty to seventeen in favour of continuing to fund Waddington's ostentatious ceremonial lifestyle.

The row arose after Waddington announced he was bringing two policemen from Britain to take the top jobs in the Bermudian constabulary. The move incensed Bermudians. Frederick Wade, the island's Opposition leader, received a cold reception when he travelled to Government House mansion, replete with servants and swimming pool, to hand Waddington the petition on Thursday. As the pair met beneath the chandelier in the Italian-style lounge, Waddington, sixty-four, was livid at the very idea of opposition to his decision.'

The article then went on to relate, with sundry embellishments, the story of Andre the butler before concluding:

Large sections of the black population see Waddington as an anachronistic throwback to the days of white dominated rule. The Governor's meddling in local affairs is raising their nationalistic passions. Ominously, Sir John Swan, the island's Premier, said this weekend that the row over the issue of white people taking plum jobs could place Waddington in grave personal danger. He recalled the assassination twenty-two years ago of Sir Richard Sharples, one of Waddington's predecessors, who was criticised over similar allegations of keeping the best jobs for whites.

Insofar as the article painted a picture of an island reduced to a state of turmoil as a result of a headstrong Governor meddling in affairs that were none of his business, it was a complete fabrication. But it was also a fabrication perpetrated by a journalist living on the

Island and employed by the *Royal Gazette* and his name appeared at the head of the article, along with someone called Andrew Malone. Imagine my surprise, therefore, when on the very day of publication I received a telephone call from another journalist on the *Royal Gazette* saying that the *Gazette* was going to publish the article and the paper would like my comments on the contents. I told the journalist that I had never heard such cheek in my life. If an article in a British paper was repeated in the *Royal Gazette* people were entitled to assume that they were being given the opportunity to see how other journalists in Britain were viewing the scene in Bermuda. When the article was nothing but a fabrication perpetrated by one of the *Gazette*'s own employees, I reckoned that I and their readers had something to complain about.

The only good thing about the whole incident was Peter Woolcock's cartoon in which Basil was pictured saying: 'Well, it was his constitutional right to choose the police commissioner and then this Mr Morton proposes cutting the boss's salary to one dollar, having just voted a nearly 28 per cent wage increase for himself – and so I bit him.' Well not quite the only good thing. Six months on and the politicians of the UBP were claiming that bringing in the officers was their own brilliant idea and the politicians of the PLP, while not going quite so far, were saying what grand chaps the British officers were and how successful they, the PLP, had been in building up a very special relationship with them. Colin Coxall and Michael Mylod did a splendid job and not so long afterwards were beginning to get a grip on crime on the Island and were the toast of those who had been so critical of the appointments.

CHAPTER TWENTY-ONE

The Referendum

The year 1994 began with Sir John Swan's surprise bid for independence. It ended with turmoil in the UBP following the withdrawal of the Premier's first Referendum Bill. Independence consumed so much of the government's time and filled so much of the papers, a visitor from outer space would have thought nothing else had been going on in Bermuda throughout the calendar year, and he would not have been far wrong. But one or two other things did happen. There was liberalisation of exchange control, and Dr John Stubbs managed to steer through Parliament a Bill legalising homosexual acts in private between consenting males. Those who voted for that Bill showed considerable courage in the face of a fierce campaign mounted by the black churches against the measure. Stubbs died shortly after the Bill became law and in the resultant by-election Grant Gibbons took his place as the member for Paget East. Grant Gibbons was the minister in charge of negotiations with the Americans following their decision to close the US naval air station and give up virtually all the land leased to America in 1940.

The American decision to close the base followed a report by Sam Donaldson, who made the place look like a holiday camp for retired admirals. Although withdrawal by the Americans was going to happen sooner or later, it would have been nice if it had been delayed for a little longer. It was certainly going to be a very costly business.

In 1992 the US, Canadian and British bases together generated income of $393 million and public service revenue of $14.1 million. In addition the US through their running of the airport provided $8.4 million in services free of charge. With all these additional burdens the Bermudians were determined that the Americans should have to pay to right environmental damage on the base caused by leaking oil tanks and the dumping of waste. The British government in supporting this was, of course, accepting its own responsibility to carry out a clean-up at HMS *Malabar* where oil had been discovered in underground caves. It had apparently been dumped by ships or leaked from the Shell oil tanks on the site. The MOD were very much less forthcoming when it came to the severance terms to be offered to the civilian employees at *Malabar* at the time of closure. The Bermuda Industrial Union (BIU) argued, I thought with force, that there could be no excuse for treating these employees differently from other government employees in Bermuda, but that was what the MOD were now bent on doing; and my warnings that industrial action might well follow if they ignored the workers' claim went unheeded. The date set for a parade on Front Street to mark the Royal Navy's 200-year presence in Bermuda and the closure of HMS *Malabar* was 18 February, and in a letter to the MOD I pointed out that if the dispute was not settled by then, there would be a countermarch and demonstration, reducing the occasion to a shambles. There was even the possibility of violence. I added that I thought it quite obscene that money should be spent flying a Royal Marines band out to Bermuda when the same money could be used to meet the employees' claim; and I gave notice that if the money to settle the dispute was not forthcoming, I would (a) cancel the parade and (b) withdraw my invitation to Vice-Admiral Tod to visit the Island and stay with me at Government House. That did the trick.

There was another little drama towards the end of 1994. In

1990 Bill Down, formerly general secretary of the Missions to Seamen became Bishop of Bermuda, having been appointed by the Archbishop of Canterbury after the Synod had failed to agree on a Bermudian. When, however, Bill arrived at the airport to take up his appointment he was somewhat dismayed to be handed a work permit valid for one year, and later learned with astonishment that the minister, Jack Sharpe, had ruled that the work permit could not be renewed unless the clergy of the diocese granted their support for the renewal application. A year passed and Bill was summoned to a meeting of the clergy and, after some discussion, was asked to withdraw while judgement was passed on him. Those present then graciously agreed to allow their bishop, appointed for life by the Archbishop of Canterbury, to remain. Bill told me afterwards that huge damage to his authority was done by this exercise and he vowed that he would not suffer the same humiliation again. So, in 1994, when the work permit had only six months left, he asked for my help. Strictly speaking work permits were nothing to do with me. They did not come within my reserved powers. But I did think the government was getting into very deep constitutional waters, and I told John Irving Pearman, the minister, that I thought it quite outrageous that bishops should be subject to work permits in the first place; and it was certainly unwise of the government to get involved in the politics of the Church. Eventually, the minister accepted what I had to say but Bishop Bill, while getting his work permit, was thoroughly sickened by the whole business and when a job in England came along he took it. I could not blame him.

Now back to independence. After his setbacks in the summer of 1994 the Premier had announced his plans for a Green Paper and in the autumn of 1994 a committee of ministers was appointed to be responsible for its production. Jack Sharpe, who in 1977 had had a hand in an earlier Green Paper, was to be adviser to the committee. If the new Green Paper was going to be anything like the earlier one, it was not going to point out any possible disadvantages of independence. So it turned out; and, as a result, attracted little but ridicule.

The committee's estimate of the cost of independence – between $800,000 and $2.3 million – was extraordinary, being similar to that put forward in the 1977 Green Paper without even an uplift to cover inflation in the intervening years. There was no mention of safeguards to prevent an independent Bermuda suffering from the abuse of power and corruption which had proved such a problem when other small island communities had gone independent. There was no acknowledgment that international business set store by the British connection, considering it some guarantee of political stability. There was a reference to Bermuda receiving 'expert advice and assistance from the United Kingdom' with regard to the Bermuda Regiment, but nothing about what might or might not happen after independence; and there was a wholly inadequate passage on citizenship, with no mention that the UK Parliament would be unlikely to pass an Independence Bill which did not give the right to Bermuda nationality to the very large number of long-term residents at present denied it.

On the police there was no acknowledgment that the sharing of power between the Governor and the government of Bermuda was a safeguard against political interference in police operations or discussion on how such interference might be avoided on independence. And when it came to Bermuda on independence 'assuming full responsibility for the conduct of its foreign affairs' the estimate of the cost of overseas representation was again little different from that put forward in 1977 with, as the newspapers noted with glee, no provision for a bicycle let alone a motor car for either Bermuda's Ambassador in Washington or its High Commissioner in London.

We had warned the FCO before the Green Paper committee went to London that there were bound to be questions about the possibility of a new relationship between Britain and the remaining dependent territories after the return of Hong Kong to China. Black people in Bermuda greatly resented the fact that, while most white Bermudians were British citizens, most black Bermudians were not and were subject to immigration control. There was a strongly held view that after 1997 and the return of Hong Kong to China the total population of the remaining dependent territories would be so small (about 160,000) there would no longer be any immigration control justification for people belonging to a dependent territory having a different citizenship from those who belonged to the mother country, and we could revert to a system not unlike that which appertained prior to the British Nationality Act when we shared a common citizenship of the United Kingdom and Colonies. That is what eventually did happen under the Labour government.

At this time, however, the government's attitude was that it was too early to consider what options might be available after 1997, and we painstakingly worked out and settled with the Foreign Office a form of words to go in the Green Paper to reflect this. It was decided that it should say that there had not yet been any discussions within government as to whether there might be a change in the relationship between Britain and the remaining dependent territories after the return of Hong Kong to China in 1997, that complex issues were involved; but there might well be the opportunity for a reassessment of UK/dependent territories policy at that time.

In February Freddy Wade, as Leader of the Opposition, set out for London to present the PLP petition against the police appointments and when there he raised the subject of the Green Paper. Tony Baldry, the minister, should have told him that insofar as the Green Paper purported to reflect British government policy, it did so correctly and he had nothing to add. But it seems that instead he said that, in spite of what was in the Green Paper, there was in his view no possibility of a change in citizenship post-1997, and his remarks were repeated by Freddy at a press conference.

That was embarrassing enough, but Freddy went even further and said that Tony Baldry had agreed with him that it would be most unusual to grant independence without a general election. If the minister had said anything like that, he would of course have been casting doubt on the appropriateness of using a referendum to determine whether the people of Bermuda wanted independence and was doing so in spite of our having, with the agreement of the Foreign Office, told the Bermuda government from the outset that a referendum was a perfectly legitimate way to determine the people's view. Worst of all, Freddy announced what I already knew – that the minister was planning to come to Bermuda at Easter to clarify a number of other matters about which Freddy had expressed concern.

Freddy at once seized on all this as an argument against the Referendum Bill being allowed to proceed until the minister came at Easter to explain Her Majesty's Government's position. John Swan was up in arms, and we thought it politic to advise the Foreign Office that it would be best if the Baldry visit was postponed.

At the end of March 1995, the Referendum Bill was due to have its second reading, but with two UBP members, Ann DeCouto and Trevor Moniz, saying they were prepared to abstain and another in hospital, John realised that if he wanted to get his Bill he would have to compromise, and after many comings and goings he agreed to it being amended along the lines of the Scottish and Welsh Referendum Bills. The referendum result would not provide a mandate for independence unless 40 per cent of the electorate voted 'yes'. Freddy Wade announced that the PLP would boycott the whole exercise and tell Labour supporters to stay at home.

As polling day, fixed for 15 August 1995, drew near, people began to sport button badges. One in great demand read 'Better Queen Elizabeth than King John'; but the progress of Hurricane Felix was attracting as much interest as the progress of the campaign. Gilly spent her time either taking the pictures down from the walls of Government House and putting them under the beds when Hurricane Felix was heading straight for us or putting the pictures back on the walls when Felix veered off to the left or right.

By noon on Sunday 13 August, Felix had become a category three storm with maximum winds of 110 knots and gusts of up to 135 knots. It would be within fifty miles of Bermuda at 3 a.m. on polling day, but in fact the storm passed the Island late on the 14th and although by 1 a.m. on the 15th the worst was over, the causeway to St George's was damaged and impassable. Early that morning deputy governor Peter Willis's secretary was up at police headquarters for the meeting of the Emergency Measures Organisation with Leo Mills, the Cabinet Secretary, and the Premier.

I was at Government House awaiting a report from the deputy governor on the damage from the storm and at 8 a.m. he rang. 'Things do not seem too bad,' he said, 'but the causeway to St George's has been breached and for the moment there is no way of getting across to St George's.' I then asked how the arrangements for the referendum were faring and, to my great surprise, he replied that it had been postponed indefinitely and that, after meeting with John Swan, Leo Mills had gone on the radio to say so. I told Peter Willis he had better get Leo Mills up to Government House at once.

To my mind the situation was dire. If the referendum was postponed for some months, not only had one to consider the economic damage that might follow, but months more campaigning with fiery speeches, demonstrations and marches might well end in violence. My job, therefore, was to make sure that by hook or by crook the referendum took place and the plain intention of Parliament was carried out.

Leo arrived and I asked him by what right he had postponed the referendum. He said it wasn't a question of legal authority but a question of whether the referendum could take place when one at least of the returning officers, St George's, simply could not get to his polling station. I asked why someone in St George's could not act as returning officer and why the polling station should not be opened later in the day when no doubt someone would be able to get from Hamilton to St George's. To that, Leo, a decent and honourable man, who had simply not thought the thing through, had no answer. I told him that in my view he should take whatever action was necessary to bring into play Section 44 of the Parliamentary Elections Act 1978 so that voting could take place next day. That meant ringing Marlene Christopher, the parliamentary registrar, and telling her to instruct the returning officers to get to their posts.

While all this was going on, a number of other people were arriving at Government House, all apparently coming to urge me to see that the law was obeyed and the referendum took place. Albert and Louise Jackson, Jim King and Eldon Trimingham were to the fore. Albert, they thought, should speak for them all and demand that if polling could not take place that day it must take place the next; and off he went to deliver that message over the air. Albert was by nature slow to stir but when he realised things were not being done properly he spoke out fearlessly; and he did so on this occasion in suitably sonorous and weighty tones. Meanwhile John Swan, who at Prospect had been protesting loudly that whether the referendum should go ahead was a matter for the civil servants, had at the same time been making it plain that his preference was for an indefinite postponement. He then had breakfast with his friend Edgar Wilkinson, who later told the waiting world what he had presumably been told by the Premier – that the referendum would be held in December.

That afternoon Ann DeCouto made an application in the High

Court for an order that the parliamentary registrar be required to carry out her function in accordance with the Independence Referendum Act 1995 and a declaration that the Secretary of the Cabinet's purported postponing of the poll was unlawful. The Attorney-General resisted the application and refused to give an undertaking that polling would take place the following morning, but even while he was talking returning officers were setting out from the government building on the way to the polling stations.

John Swan then summoned an emergency meeting of the Cabinet. What happened there is by no means clear, but just before 7 p.m. a formal announcement was made by the government that polling would indeed take place the following day.

The next day was a bit of an anticlimax. The polling stations opened promptly at 10 a.m. and voting continued in an orderly fashion throughout the day. Due to the crazy counting system (each individual voting paper was held up for inspection by the scrutineers and, when they had all had the chance to establish that it was indeed a voting paper and not an invitation to the vicarage tea party, was placed on the appropriate pile), the final result was not announced until 6.20 on the morning of the 17th. Even then there was a discrepancy between the total votes cast and the figure arrived at by adding together the 'yes' votes, the 'no' votes and the spoiled papers; but a clear enough question had been posed on the ballot paper (Are you in favour of independence for Bermuda?) and a clear enough answer had been given by the people.

Yes: 25.6% (5,714)
No: 73.7% (16,369)
Turnout: 58.8% (22,236)

Predictably, Freddy Wade claimed a victory for the PLP and his boycott. If, however, the turnout had been 80 per cent (and it was only 78 per cent at the 1993 general election) instead of 58.8 per cent and if every single additional voter had voted 'yes', the result would still have been 'no'. In fact, in comparison with previous referendums, the poll was high: in 1990 only 32.6 per cent of the electorate had turned out to vote in the referendum on capital punishment.

We had to leave the Island the same day and a short time later John Swan tendered his resignation to the deputy governor.

The attention of the press was focused not only on the result but on what one journalist described as the constitutionally jaw-dropping shenanigans of the previous two days. When asked if Bermudian democracy had gone off the rails on the Tuesday morning, Jim Woolridge, a senior and well respected UBP member opposed to independence said: 'I wouldn't say "off the rails", but it took a turn not in keeping with the best that civilisation has to offer.' Dr Dyer commented: 'The government is engaged in a crazy, banana republic-like activity. If there ever was an example of why this isn't the time to go independent, this is the example.'

After the result the reaction of the British media was interesting. Most commentators seemed genuinely delighted at what had occurred and reflected in their pieces the pleasure felt by people in England that there were some in the world who were actually proud of and wanted to maintain the British connection.

My own role received some praise. Under the heading 'GOVERNOR CATCHES THE BREEZE' Mandrake in the *Sunday Telegraph* wrote:

> Bermudians voted by three to one in last Wednesday's referendum to remain a British colony, after polling was delayed twenty-four hours by Hurricane Felix. News now reaches me that the hurricane caused such confusion about what happens when the gods strike in this way on polling day that those opposed to the colony remaining British were able to hatch a plot which very nearly stopped the referendum taking place at all. Had the Governor not mugged up

on his electoral law, and had those intrepid returning officers not done their duty, the referendum would have been cancelled – not just postponed – until a new Referendum Act was passed.

Martin Vander Weyer in the *Daily Telegraph* wrote:

It is difficult to resist a faint throbbing of emotion at the decision of a self-contained community thousands of miles away which was offered the chance of severing its links with Blighty but chose not to do so. That says something about the way Bermuda is seen in the world, and it must be worth at least three small cheers. What Bermuda clearly thought it would lose is that intangible sense of British stability. The risk for islands within reach of North and South America is that they may become offshore hideaways for giant sums of drug money and the gangsters that travel with it; to be a satellite of Britain is to have a measure of protection against such sinister influences. Independence may bring self-esteem and a seat, somewhere below the salt, at the table of world affairs – a wishful thinking element in the pro-independence manifesto of Bermuda's Premier, Sir John Swan, was that nationhood would allow the island to play a regional role in the UN. But for many new nations of the Caribbean, Africa and Asia, such trappings have hardly been worth the costs to citizens in terms of repression, economic mismanagement and rampant corruption, bringing in their train a decline of educational and social standards rather than the improvement which 'progressive' new regimes always promise, and a harvest of environmental damage.

At home in England I was surprised to learn a few days later that the dry, pedantic and white David Saul had been elected leader by the Parliamentary Party – by a clear majority of two to one over Jim Woolridge who had been billed as the people's choice. The anti-independence group then overplayed its hand, demanding far more in terms of offices than they could reasonably expect and, by lobbying as a team to get for their team what they thought was their due, they gave David Saul reason to say that he was not going to repeat the mistakes of John Swan and have a party-within-a-party. So at the end of the day, those who had won the referendum were almost entirely absent from the new government.

The PLP said they were determined to get to the bottom of the goings-on on polling day and as soon as Parliament met would move the setting up of a commission of inquiry. David Saul delivered a pre-emptive strike and advised me to set up a commission forthwith. I did so under the chairmanship of the Rt Hon. Telford Georges, retired judge of the Court of Appeal of Bermuda and Law Reform commissioner for the Bahamas, and when the commission reported I was relieved but not unduly surprised to find no criticism of my intervention on the 15th and, while there was comment on the failure of the government to make a public announcement until after the 5.30 p.m. Cabinet meeting, which magnified the suspicions that something devious was afoot, there was, the commission said, no evidence of political interference.

There was then a piece in the *Royal Gazette* on the 28 November about the outcome of the referendum in which there was reference to the work done by Governors' wives:

> There is now a long tradition of Bermuda paying the salary of a Governor and getting two hard workers for the price of one. Governors' wives have made an enormous contribution, especially to Bermuda's charities. Bermuda has a history of women who work hard for charity but governors' wives do not have to do so. Wives could well play hostess and chair a few charity meetings. Nothing says they have to work hard, yet governors' wives do work hard for Bermuda.

In the charity world it was estimated recently that the present Governor's wife has raised charity funds the equivalent of seven times the Governor's salary every year she has been in Bermuda. Lady Waddington has done that on top of a heavy schedule of public duties and endless demands on her time as the Government House hostess where incumbents operate a combination official entertainment centre and government guest house. Bermuda should have remembered all that when there was a recent suggestion to cut the Governor's salary.

Gilly deserved this recognition.

That autumn Rastafarians on the Island had started coming up through the garden from the north shore in order to smoke pot in the shade of the princess palm planted by Haile Selassie. The police wanted to clap them in irons but, thinking that that might have unfortunate repercussions, I made a bargain with their leaders. They could come up once a month and I, while not prepared to smoke pot with them, would join them in a prayer and a dance round the tree. This happened once, but I think they found my presence embarrassing and inhibiting and they faded out of our lives.

At about this time Gilly and I went to breakfast with Norma Astwood, one of the independent members of the Senate, at her house overlooking Flatts. It was a traditional salt cod breakfast, a reminder of the days when Bermudian ships used to rake salt in their de facto colony the Turks Island, trade it for rum in Jamaica and sell some of the rum for cod in Newfoundland before returning home with this most sought-after delicacy. Norma was one great public servant in the black community. Marjorie Bean was another and I was delighted when in my time Marjorie became Bermuda's first dame, with a tree in Government House garden to prove it. A teacher by profession, she was one of the first women to be appointed to the Legislative Council. Born in 1909, she did not look anything like her age and she spoke with a clipped upper-class accent. There was a very rough chap who when not in gaol worked as a caddy at Mid Ocean, and one day I asked him how he had acquired his most distinguished Oxford accent. 'From Dr Bean, sir,' he replied with pride.

CHAPTER TWENTY-TWO

Going Home

Thorold Masefield, High Commissioner in Nigeria, was named as my successor. He was to take up his duties in June after our departure at the end of April 1997. Meanwhile Gilly had taken off for Australia, Jenny having given birth to James Charles, and Victoria enjoyed herself riding in the landau to the opening of Parliament.

The regiment earned itself some bad publicity. A recruit at 'boot camp' who claimed to be a Rastafarian had his head shorn while handcuffed to a chair in the middle of the barrack square; a lawyer, who the previous year had himself escaped military service by claiming a conscientious objection, threatened to take the regiment to court. A hurried meeting of the Exemption Tribunal was summoned, and there the man was asked to explain why he objected to serving in the army when almost every photograph of Emperor Haile Selassie (whom the Rastifarians claimed as their leader) showed him in uniform. Indeed, when he had visited Bermuda, he had been taken to inspect a guard of honour of the Bermuda Regiment. The recruit's somewhat feeble reply was that he would be happy to serve in an army commanded by Haile Selassie but not an army led by the Queen. The tribunal, in spite of this, held that Private Harvey had a genuine conscientious objection to serving in the regiment and when the matter came before me I was advised that (a) I had to accept the tribunal's conclusion and

(b) I had no power to order the man to render some other form of public service.

The Mental Health Foundation (Gilly's baby) staged the second annual Dick Wilkie Memorial Lecture at Government House. The commissioner of prisons, Ed Dyer, was the speaker, and when at Question Time there was a deathly hush, I asked Ed whether he thought there was any connection between the behaviour of prisoners and their diet, commenting that: 'When we fill people up with junk food, hamburgers and all that rubbish, it would be surprising if there was not a connection.' The next morning I found my off the cuff remarks were headline news in the *Royal Gazette*, having unwittingly strayed into a debate about whether a company headed by John Swan should be allowed to operate a McDonald's restaurant on the Island. I was well on the way to being accused of taking sides on the issue.

At about this time there was an exchange between the Foreign Office and the UN decolonisation committee. The Foreign Office was rightly of the view that it was pretty cheeky of the committee not to accept that the remaining dependent territories were perfectly free to change their status if they wished and the dependent territories should not be on the so-called 'Committee of Twenty-Four' list. Officials thought that it might be possible to reach agreement with the committee that there should be one last visit from the committee to satisfy themselves that the people of the dependent territories had a free choice, after which the territories would be delisted. I was not happy with what officials proposed, fearing that we might not be able to control the agenda; and if public meetings were held, there would be an opportunity for malcontents to reopen what at the moment was a dead issue. No visit had been arranged by the time I left the Island.

The Bermuda Red Cross asked me to invite HRH Princess Alexandra to come to the Island to open their new headquarters and when she and Sir Angus Ogilvy arrived, Sir Angus took me aside and said that he had only just discovered that the Bermuda Red Cross had paid for their first-class tickets. He thought many people who had worked hard to provide funds for the Red Cross might not be happy at the money they had earned being spent in this way and he was giving me a cheque for £10,000 to cover the cost of the tickets. The next day I handed the cheque to Ann Spencer-Arscott, the Secretary of the Red Cross, with Sir Angus's instruction that only those who needed to know should be told what had happened. I fervently hoped that his wishes would be ignored.

We then visited Arcadia House which had been bought by the Mental Health Foundation which Gilly had helped to start. After that we went to Fair Havens, a home for young women who have fallen foul of drugs. There were nine residents, most still in their teens and virtually all of them with a background of prostitution. Princess Alexandra could not have handled the situation better. She sat down with the group and then questioned them, sympathetically but without any false sentiment or pulling of punches, as to how they had finished up homeless, destitute and dependent on drugs and how they were going to avoid drifting back into the mess from which they had so recently escaped.

It was a very successful royal visit and HRH could not have gone to more trouble talking to people and making them feel that she was interested in them and in Bermuda.

Then there was dramatic news on the political front. David Saul announced his intention not only to resign as Premier but to give up his seat. The hunt was on for a new leader of the UBP, but David Saul had prepared the ground carefully and it soon became apparent that a great effort was going to be made to avoid a contested election and have Pamela Gordon acclaimed leader without a contest. So it worked out. On the following Monday when nominations closed she was the only candidate. Pamela Gordon was articulate, friendly and tough and in my view an inspired choice as leader. Her father was Dr E. T. Gordon, the Trinidad-born civil rights and trade union hero, and the fact that she had surmounted difficulties in her life of the kind faced by many women in Bermuda – she had had a child when a teenager and then after getting married had quite quickly become divorced – helped her to relate to people and, with some justice, she put herself forward as someone who really understood Bermuda and the Bermudians.

My remaining tasks were social rather than political and enjoyable if exhausting. We went boating with Ray Moore and played *boules* on a cold beach. A special concert was given in our honour by the choir of St Mark's Church, the Thorntons gave us dinner, as did the Bishop and my splendid aide-de-camp Eddie Lamb and his wife.

We threw two parties at Government House – a buffet supper for 150 and, for the very old, a lunch. There was a golf match in my honour and a special game with the pros from both Mid Ocean and St George's. I was hugely embarrassed when off the first tee I really whacked the ball and holed in two. But the Lord was kind to me and the tut-tutting and suggestions that I was pretending to an incompetence which I did not deserve faded away when for the rest of the match my performance was abysmal.

The Town of St George then gave us a farewell reception, as did the National Trust and Masterworks. The Dinghy Club was not to be outdone and gave us dinner, and there followed dinner with Bob Farmer, the US Consul-General. That was kind of Bob who was still smarting from Gilly's refusal to sit down to dinner with Edward Kennedy who, as far as Gilly was concerned, was consorting with and apologising for IRA terrorists and was not a person to be indulged.

Tom Butterfield threw a marvellous picnic on Long Island; and the Peppercorn Ceremony at St George's was rather special as our friend Colin Curtis, in his capacity as Grand Master of the Lodge, was responsible for handing over the peppercorn as rent for State House. He coated the peppercorn in gold. The Premier gave a dinner for us at Camden and presented us with a fitted dinghy in a bottle.

We went out to lunch with Ann Smith Gordon and she showed us a very special walk over to the south shore. We paid our normal visits to the Agricultural Show and had a goodbye dinner with the Darlings. We were driven up to Government House in Patsy Phillips's donkey cart. The donkeys came to a sudden halt where a line of bricks crossed the drive and took some coaxing to finish the journey.

The last Sunday involved farewells at St John's in the morning and the presentation of a painting of the church, the St George's Day Scouts' service in the afternoon at St James's, Somerset and a visit from Malcolm and Debbie Butterfield and their horse-riding son Raymonde in the evening.

On Tuesday 29 April 1997 we went down to the Senate House in the carriage for the official leave-taking. After the inspection of a guard of honour from the regiment and speeches from Pamela Gordon and myself, Gilly and I said goodbye to literally hundreds of people who were formed up in groups on the grass – politicians, civil servants, workers for charity, our own Government House staff and personal friends. We then drove back to Government House, changed and set off for the airport, and at ten past eight we were in the air on our way home.

When given the chance to be governor I did not doubt that I was being very privileged; and as I prepared to go, quite over-whelmed by the warmth of the leave-taking ceremony, I knew what a lucky man I had been to have spent the best part of five years in such a place. Bermuda's history, quite apart from its present, will never cease to fascinate me. It seems so wonderful that the passengers and crew of the *Sea Venture* under the leadership of Sir George Somers never lost sight of their duty and that in two tiny new ships they should have struggled on to Virginia to get fresh provisions to the colony. After being formally settled Bermuda did not provide an easy living for the adventurers who had braved the perils of the sea to get there. They suffered many hardships and setbacks but no one can doubt that in building a great little country they achieved far more than most. Of course, there are bound to be strains when so small an island is shared by people with very different backgrounds. Of course, the scars of slavery will never be entirely healed, but I met plenty of people in the black, in the white and in the Portuguese communities who found no difficulty working in harmony with people of different races; Bermuda is a pretty successful multiracial society.

I was very lucky in the two deputy governors who served with me, John Kelly who went on to be the Governor of the Turks and Caicos Islands and Peter Willis who retired to play golf in France. I had with me a wife who carried a hefty burden of work and was a tower of strength throughout and, in particular, in times of difficulty. I look back on my time in Bermuda with great joy and thankfulness to the people of the Island.

CHAPTER TWENTY-THREE

Home and Back to the Lords

Apeacock had taken over our garden at Stable House. Its heavy landings did the roof no good. It was grand to be back; but if I was to take part in the work of the Lords, we needed somewhere to live in London. Very foolishly I had sold our house in Denny Street before setting out for Bermuda, thinking that by the time I got home I would be well past working in the Lords. Now I was anxious to get back into the swim of things as soon as possible, and we bought a flat in Chester Way, a few yards from where we had been before, but nothing like as nice. Gilly disliked Chester Way. She wanted to garden in the country and soon got fed up at having to come up to London every now and then to, in her words, 'muck me out'. So eventually we sold Chester Way and I moved into a club with many amusing companions like Bertie Denham[*] and Robin Ferrers[**].

Meanwhile, back in Lancashire it never stopped raining. Walking in the fields round our house with mud up to the top of our gum boots was a boring experience, and eventually the weather defeated us. A tree trunk was washed down off Pendle and lodged itself in a culvert under the drive. The culvert tired of the insult and burst open, making the drive impassable.

---

[*]   The Lord Denham, formerly government Chief Whip in the Lords.
[**] The Earl Ferrers, formerly Minister of State, Home Office.

We had been toying with the idea of moving south to warmer climes with better weather, and the flood made our minds up. But I am glad that before we moved I was President of the Royal Lancashire Show. It would have greatly pleased my father and grandfather.

New governments can usually endure a few calamities without their having much of an effect on their popularity. But it soon became clear after the election that sleaze was not just a Tory disease. Bernie Ecclestone gave £1 million to the Labour Party and then won for Formula One racing an exemption from the ban on tobacco advertising. The Welsh Secretary (Ron Davies) had a 'moment of madness' on Clapham Common, an explanation for his behaviour suggested to him by Alastair Campbell. Having trained for the job as a writer of pornography under the pen name Riviera Gigolo, Campbell was now press secretary at No. 10, and the following year he had to announce Peter Mandelson's departure from the government after dealings about his mortgage had been leaked to the press.

In the Queen's Speech we had also been promised a great programme of constitutional change, with referendums on devolution for Scotland and Wales and on a mayor for London; and the European Convention of Human Rights was to be incorporated into United Kingdom law. As to the last, I and only a few others spoke out about the dangerous territory into which we were moving. There was clearly the risk of clashes between Parliament and the judiciary, but few appreciated that the judges, who were going to have to interpret and then apply the very general words of the convention, might interpret them in the way most damaging for Britain and most likely, for instance, to undermine the country's security and our immigration control. It is really quite extraordinary that in February 2012 the Court of Appeal, in setting aside a ruling by a judge that a man from Nepal should be allowed to remain in the United Kingdom, commented that it looked as if the judge had been on 'a search for reasons for not deporting him.'

I raised in the Lords Basil's treatment in quarantine kennels. We had been persuaded to send him back to England in January 1997 so when we had got home ourselves we would not have to wait too long before being able to collect him. We were recommended a place in Deal and every now and then we used to get cheerful messages from the establishment telling us how well Basil was doing. Eventually we went to collect him and to our surprise he was brought to us in the arms of a kennel maid. 'You are not to worry,' she said, 'he has not had much room to move about and is a little stiff,' but in the car as we drove north he was whimpering, and that night as he lay in the basket I had put by our bed he was very distressed and having difficulty in breathing. First thing in the morning we took him to the vet in Clitheroe who, in accusatorial tones asked me how long I had allowed my dog to be in such a terrible state. I told him that I had only just picked Basil up from quarantine kennels, and his only response was: 'Oh my God!'

He said that he would have to carry out a thorough examination and it was agreed we would come back later in the day. When we returned to hear his verdict he said the dog was riddled with cancer and had to be put down. Back home I rang the kennels who protested that only a day or two before Basil had been seen by a vet who had declared him as fit as a fiddle. I made a formal complaint about the kennels, and I raised the matter in the Lords. And I like to think that the appalling way in which Basil had been treated did help Lady Fretwell's successful campaign to get rid of quarantine for pets.

I went to a police dinner at which Richard Wilson, later to replace Robin Butler as Cabinet Secretary, recalled that when Tony Blair arrived at Downing Street and the staff were lined up to greet him one lady was weeping copiously: 'Poor Mr Major, poor Mr

Major,' she wailed. The new Prime Minister, not knowing quite how to respond, said, 'I am sorry.' 'No you are not,' said the lady, 'you meant it.'

As the weeks went by, William Hague, the new Leader of the Opposition, proved himself nimble on the floor of the Commons but after getting on a waterslide at Alton Towers wearing a silly cap he went downhill metaphorically as well as physically.

At the end of the year there was a splendid Privy Counsellors' dinner in the Royal Gallery to celebrate the fiftieth wedding anniversary of the Queen and the Duke of Edinburgh. We then set off for Australia and in the New Year flew to Tahiti and sailed up to the Marquesa Islands.

By now so-called friendly hours had been introduced in the Commons. They were no doubt friendly for families but they were really nice for the government, with the Opposition losing one of its only weapons – the power to harry the government late into the night and wear down its troops. Now the timetabling of Bills was to be routine, which resulted in them coming to the Lords with great chunks that had not been considered in the Commons. A system of deferred divisions was also introduced, allowing MPs to vote on a Wednesday on matters debated after 10 p.m. during the previous week when they might not have been in London, let alone the chamber. We were confident that when, sooner or later, Labour was booted out, these abominations would be consigned to the parliamentary dustbin, but I am ashamed to record that they have all been adopted by the coalition.

In the summer of 1998 I represented Parliament at the Tynwald Day ceremony in the Isle of Man. That year the event was attended by a representative from the Faroe Islands and at dinner one of my hosts asked me if I had ever been to the Faroe Islands. I said I had not. 'Don't go,' came the reply. 'It's puffin for breakfast, puffin for dinner and puffin for tea.'

In the Queen's Speech for the 1998–9 session it was announced that: 'A Bill will be introduced to remove the right of hereditary peers to sit and vote in the House of Lords. It will be the first stage in a process of reform to make the House of Lords more democratic and representative.' When the Bill arrived on the scene there were some acrimonious debates and veiled threats that if the government pressed ahead without revealing its plans for a more democratic house its whole legislative programme might be at risk. At this stage I received a mysterious invitation to dine with Robert Cranborne*, then Leader of the Opposition in the Lords. At his London house I found myself with Janet Young**, Bertie Denham and one or two others who had been involved at some time or other in the business management of the House; and Robert proceeded to tell us what he had been up to. He had had meetings with the Lord Chancellor, Derry Irvine***, and had reached agreement that a number of hereditary peers should remain in the House pending long-term reform and as a guarantee that such reform would take place. Jack Weatherill, the former Speaker of the Commons, had been persuaded to introduce the necessary amendments to give them cross-bench respectability. When it came to the question of the shadow Cabinet's attitude towards all this, Robert was noticeably reticent: but under the impression that there would be little trouble, if not great enthusiasm, at the other end, we all said we would go along with what was proposed. What we certainly did not know was that when Robert had put his plan to the shadow Cabinet William Hague had given it an unequivocal thumbs-down.

The next day there was a meeting of the Association of Conservative Peers in the Moses Room and Robert told colleagues

---

* The Rt Hon. Viscount Cranborne, now the Marquess of Salisbury.
** The Baroness Young, formerly Leader of the Lords.
*** The Lord Irvine of Lairg.

of the agreement he had reached with the government. He had asked me to get to my feet after he had spoken to express my support, and up I duly got. But I had hardly got into my stride when William Hague and a clutch of minions burst into the room. There was an awful pause after I had finished my remarks and then William set about me, because I was in the firing line, and then Robert. I cannot remember what he said but it was not complimentary, and outside the Moses Room there was an exchange between him and Robert which finished with Robert being sacked. The deal, however, had been done; the Weatherill amendment was carried, and in 2011 there were still ninety-two hereditary peers in the House. There have been a few deaths among the original ninety-two, but Derry, no doubt imagining that the promised changes to make the House 'more democratic and representative' would not be long delayed, had also agreed that there would be by-elections to provide replacements when deaths occurred.

In the 1999–2000 session the government introduced a Bill to lower the age for consent to buggery and homosexual acts from eighteen to sixteen. I found very offensive the suggestion that the Bill was extending the rights of 16–18-year-old boys. That, I pointed out, was rather like saying that a railway company bestows rights on its passengers when it leaves the train doors unlocked. The Bill was about removing from young people aged between sixteen and eighteen the protection they then had had against older people minded to prey on them.

The session also saw the scrapping of Section 28 of the Local Government Act 1986 which prevented a local authority from intentionally promoting homosexuality and from promoting the teaching in any maintained school of the acceptability of homosexuality as a pretended family relationship. At that very moment the Lambeth, Southwark and Lewisham Health Authority was funding a guide to the etiquette of 'cruising and cottaging' so it did not seem that after the introduction of Section 28, those minded to advertise and applaud promiscuous gay sex had learned the error of their ways. The North Bristol National Health Service Trust had certainly not, for it had just funded a so-called educational pack which encouraged children as young as fourteen to act out homosexual scenes, including pretending to be a married man addicted to having sex with other men in secret. 'Allowing councils to promote homosexuality,' said the Chief Rabbi, Jonathan Sachs, 'would run counter to a moral code shared by all the world's great religions. There is a great danger that lifting the existing ban could lead to the promotion of a homosexual lifestyle as morally equivalent to marriage.' And he has, we now know, been proved right.

The scrapping of the section proved to be the first of a whole raft of measures presenting a gay lifestyle as valid as any other and devaluing the institution of marriage. No sooner was the ink dry on the legislation licensing civil partnerships than people were demanding that civil partnership ceremonies should be allowed in churches, and soon after that there were even demands that gay marriage be legalised. Legislation was then introduced to ban the mere criticism of homosexual acts and preachers were being arrested, tried and convicted of offences under the Public Order Act after being assaulted by hooligans pretending to be offended by the preachers' biblical quotations. But it did not even stop there. Soon there was legislation ostensibly to stop discrimination against persons in the provision of public services, but used instead to drive out of business Catholic adoption agencies, to ban employees from wearing crucifixes, to deny a registrar the right not to have to conduct a gay civil partnership ceremony and to punish a couple running a B&B for turning down a gay couple. In short, in this brave new world people were being persecuted for sticking to their Christian beliefs and acting according to a moral code which only a few years before had been accepted as the proper guide to behaviour by the vast majority of people. I spoke out against the government's proposals on all these matters, with some others of a like frame of mind, and some good came to me from it.

First of all I got involved with the Christian Institute which was deeply concerned at what was going on, and I began to work with Baroness (Detta) O'Cathain when issues were raised which touched on the right of Christians to follow their beliefs. Detta's Christian belief was rock-firm, and she was also firm in muscle. My legs were in a poor state and there came a day when they gave out on me. Lord (Ian) McColl was in the House and fearing something might be seriously amiss rang for an ambulance to take me to St Thomas's. After a while a flustered ambulance driver appeared at the peers' entrance and explained that everyone in London seemed to think they had got Asian flu and there was not an ambulance to be had, but he would wheel me to St Thomas's. That he duly did, but by the time I had been checked over and deemed fit to return to Parliament, although still unable to walk, he had gone off duty and very sportingly Detta wheeled me all the way back to the House.

Few MPs and peers fail to find themselves involved in voluntary work of one sort or another. When I was MP for Ribble Valley I used to be asked by the then president of the East Lancashire Scouts to take the salute at the parade and march-past of the Scouts on St George's Day. He then died and, not only did he in his will leave all his property to the Scouts, he included in the will a request that I should succeed him as President. It was a cunning move and when a delegation turned up at Stable House to seek my acceptance of the honour I could think of no reason to refuse. In fact, it proved a very worthwhile experience and I treasure the silver acorn I was awarded for my endeavours. I had to resign when we moved south but used all my powers of persuasion to get Lord Patel of Blackburn to take over from me in the hope that that might encourage more Asian boys to join the movement.

I was then also President of the Hertford Society which promotes the interests of Hertford College, Oxford. Many years earlier the college had refused my son James a place, but eventually I forgave them and was mollified when I was made an honorary fellow.

I was for a number of years a trustee of Natural Justice, a charity concerned, among other things, with the effect of diet on criminal behaviour, but eventually gave up when my ears packed up and I could not hear what was going on at meetings.

As to the Overseas Service Pensioners' Association (OSPA), of which I have for many years been President, it has among its members many former servants of the Crown who had worked in Southern Rhodesia and stayed on when it became Zimbabwe. It was a very serious matter for them when, first, run-away inflation reduced the value of Zimbabwean pensions to a pittance and, then, Mugabe and his government ceased making any pension payments at all in contravention of the terms of the independence constitution agreed at Lancaster House. At that juncture, the British government should have stepped in and assumed responsibility for payment of the pensions in the same way that they had done when the governments of other former colonies had defaulted. But, to its shame, the British government said it was under no obligation to help because Southern Rhodesia had been 'an internally self-governing colony with its civil servants recruited by Rhodesia House in London rather than by the Colonial Office'. Those Crown servants were to be abandoned even though Rhodesia had been thought so much a British responsibility that Mr Smith's unilateral declaration of independence had been resisted in every possible way. It seemed pretty daft and downright immoral to me, but I have got nowhere when I have raised the matter. That is not quite right. I did get somewhere with Lord Malloch-Brown who, having heard my pleas, seemed entirely persuaded and went away to tell the Foreign Office so. But after a month or two he came back and said most apologetically that he had failed to persuade his superiors.

I have been President of OSPA for far too long, and have asked them to look for someone to take on the Presidency – a step I was reluctant to take because, with the days of Empire fading into history and the last of its servants trooping to the grave, the winding up of the organisation might not long be delayed. There is, however, still important work to be done by the organisation. It is surely our duty to see that the good name of the Service is not sullied and that the public understands that those who went out to the colonies were motivated by a sense of public service and were there to help prepare the people for independence, not (as left-wing propagandists pretend) to bully the people and profit at their expense.

A few years ago there was a service in Westminster Abbey attended by the Queen to celebrate the work done by the Colonial Service over the years, and I asked Richard Luce to give the address. I remember the Queen listening with rapt attention as he described how, as a young district officer in Kenya, he dispensed justice under a tree; and I like to think that when a short time later he was appointed Lord Chamberlain I might have had a small hand in it. OSPA is very lucky to have Lord Luce at hand, always prepared to take a keen interest in its affairs.

Lastly, I seem to have spent an inordinate amount of time supporting the National Council of Resistance of Iran which works tirelessly to hasten the day when Iran will be rid of the present tyrannical regime. Numerous articles under my name have appeared in American and other newspapers, and I was one of those who brought proceedings to have the People's Mujahedin of Iran (PMOI) removed from the list of organisations proscribed under powers in the Anti-Terrorism Act 2001. When Gilly and I went to Paris to meet Mrs Rajavi, the President of the NCRI, and attend a rally I found myself addressing 70,000 people in a gigantic hangar-like building somewhere in the northern suburbs. For me that was a record.

So I find it quite difficult to be bored and rarely succeed.

In the general election of 2001 William Hague led the Conservative Party to defeat after a lacklustre campaign in which he said that there were only a few days left to save the pound. The claim was not convincing, the government having promised a referendum if they concluded that the time was ripe to join the euro. When the votes had been counted William resigned and the Party had to set about electing a new leader. The obvious candidate was the one with vast experience of government, Kenneth Clarke, but I could not support him because of his pig-headed refusal to compromise in the slightest over Europe. Various people begged him to say that he would not force-feed the Party with his views and would listen to the opinions of others, but he went down to defeat having steadfastly declined to say anything of the sort. So Iain Duncan Smith won, but there were soon doubts as to whether he was up to the job.

John Prescott was now busy cooking up plans for elected regional assemblies. In the debate on the Queen's Speech I expressed surprise at the extraordinary interest being taken in these developments by the bishops. 'Perhaps,' I suggested, 'unbeknown to me the synod has just slipped through an addendum to the creed: "I believe in the Balkanisation of England, another layer or two of local govern-ment, a multiplication of councillors and a Europe of the regions".' The Bishop of Bristol talked about bringing decision-making closer to the people, but that was not for one moment what the govern-ment's plans meant. As I pointed out in the debate on the address, the plan was for powers devolved from Whitehall to go to regional bodies, not to existing local authorities which really were close to the people. Happily, the bishops did not get their wishes.

There could be no better reminder of our Christian heritage which some are trying to airbrush out of our island story than the fact that we have an established Church of which the Queen is Supreme Governor, with bishops of the Church sitting in Parliament. I do, however, confess that the bishops do sometimes try my patience – as I no doubt try theirs. They are very quick to talk of things like regional government where they have no special expertise, but in recent years they have been remarkably reluctant to speak out on matters of faith. It is ridiculous that it should have been for me, Detta and a few others like Rodney Elton* to defend the right of people to live by their Christian beliefs and practise their faith in the face of the rising tide of atheism, while the Bishops' Bench has for most of the time stayed silent. The bishops, with one or two honourable exceptions, seemed to have become quite reconciled to 'equal rights' prevailing over the rights of people to practise their faith even when the result has been, as it was in the case of the Catholic adoption societies, reducing the chance of young children finding a good home and loving parents. Perhaps now after the spirited defence of the Church by the excellent Lord Carey and the intervention of the Queen, some of these bishops and other churchmen will at last wake up to the great danger the Church is now facing as a result of their not having faced up to the threat from secularism and atheism long ago.

In the early summer of 2003 when the government, grappling with the grizzly consequences of the invasion of Iraq, might have been thought to have something better to do, Blair decided to embark at home on a blatant and preposterous piece of constitutional vandalism. On 12 June 2003, there was an announcement on

---

* The Lord Elton, for many years a minister in Margaret Thatcher's government.

television that the office of Lord Chancellor was to be abolished and the Earl of Onslow interrupted a debate in the House of Lords to say that it was an outrage that this should have been decided without debate. Lord Cope of Berkeley, the Opposition Chief Whip, intervened to say that one of the things the government was doing was taking away from the Lords the services of the Lord Chancellor as their presiding officer, which led Lord Williams of Mostyn, Leader of the House, to rise and refer to what appeared to be a press release entitled 'Reform of the Speakership of the Lords' which talked, he said, of a new Speaker for the Lords being in place after the recess. Lord Onslow's motion that the House adjourn was lost, but the cat was out of the bag.

Although the office of Lord Chancellor was older even than Parliament, Tony Blair had decided to abolish it and create instead a Ministry for Constitutional Affairs – and to do so without consulting Parliament or even the Queen. The Prime Minister seems to have thought that all that was involved was a change in the machinery of government and he had to be told that there were about 5,000 references to the Lord Chancellor in primary and secondary legislation and there would have to be a huge 'transfer of functions order' to allow others to exercise functions then exercised by the Lord Chancellor. Furthermore, those of his functions which were judicial could not be transferred to any old Secretary of State, but would have to go to a 'residual' Lord Chancellor until legislation was passed creating a new head of the judiciary. At the eleventh hour Lord Irvine had put forward a compromise plan under which he would stay in office until these necessary changes had been made, but this idea was not acceptable to the Prime Minister and Irvine's services had been dispensed with. A more pliable Lord Falconer of Thoroton had then agreed to serve as Secretary of State for Constitutional Affairs and was apparently under the impression that, there being no longer a Lord Chancellor, someone else would be found to sit on the woolsack when the House of Lords met in the morning. He was in for a rude awakening.

The Opposition Chief Whip let it be known that the Lords' Standing Orders required the Lord Chancellor to be present and made it plain that there would be a most almighty row if he was not there. 'But,' said Falconer's private office, 'he has not got the uniform.' 'He had better find one,' said Cope: and he did. Furthermore, he found himself compelled to continue to sit on the woolsack for many, many months while legislation creating a Ministry of Justice and a Supreme Court ground its way through Parliament.

Altogether it was a shocking tale of constitutional meddling and the arrogance of power. It also cost the public a mint of money: the Lords had now to elect a Speaker to replace the Lord Chancellor, and the new Supreme Court had to be found a lavish building in which to perform functions, which up to the time of Blair's brainstorm the Law Lords had had no difficulty in carrying out in a modest room on the committee corridor in the Palace of Westminster.

Meanwhile, Valéry Giscard d'Estaing was presiding over a commission charged with drafting a constitution for the European Union and the excellent Gisela Stewart, Labour MP for Edgbaston and a member of the commission, was being told by the great man that she had better shape up and agree with what he proposed or she would not get an equestrian statue of herself in her village square. Eventually the constitution was published and was found to contain 67,000 words with another 60,000 words in the appendices. Critics were not slow to point out that the Lord's Prayer contains sixty-six words, the Gettysburg address 179 and the Ten Commandments 179. I spoke out against this piece of constitutional vandalism.

In November 2003, the government reclassified cannabis as a Class 'C' drug. I spoke against the order making the change and pointed out that downgrading cannabis and the decision to let off offenders with a caution sent out entirely the wrong signal to young people and made things almost impossible for parents. 'Not only,' I said, 'does smoking cannabis all too often lead to the use of heroin and crack cocaine, traded by the very same dealers from whom the cannabis is obtained, it is a very dangerous drug itself. It is a mind-bending substance.' And I then went on to quote what Professor John Henry, a toxicologist, had said at The Royal Society of Medicine conference in London: 'Regular cannabis smokers develop mental illness. There is a four-fold increase in schizophrenia and a four-fold increase in major depression.'

I felt I had to explain why I felt so strongly about the matter, my son Matthew having had to leave Cambridge because of mental illness brought on by cannabis use. 'I have to tell Your Lordships,' I said, 'that I know personally only too well that cannabis does ruin peoples' lives. It has come close to ruining the life of someone very close to me who has suffered from schizophrenia as a result of cannabis use. That is the diagnosis so don't tell me that cannabis is pretty harmless.' The government got its order but in 2008 realised how foolish it had been and restored the original classification.

The beginning of 2004 saw the publication of the Report of the Inquiry into the circumstances surrounding the death of Dr David Kelly. We on the Opposition benches in the Lords had prepared ourselves well before is publication. Clearly there was no way in which Alastair Campbell was going to wriggle out of this one, no chance of Geoff Hoon and officials in his Department having been able to persuade Lord Hutton that they had treated Dr Kelly properly, and Tony Blair was clearly in for a roasting for having remained silent when papers reported that Saddam Hussein's weapons of mass destruction could be used against us at forty-five minutes' notice. Obviously it was going to be difficult for Michael Howard, Leader of the Opposition, who was not to see the report until the morning of the day on which it was to be presented to Parliament, but as it was so obvious that the government had misbehaved he would have in his head already the arguments to be used in the House. When, however, Michael read the report he must have been absolutely astonished, and a weaker man might have had all the stuffing knocked out of him. For the report was a complete whitewash.

A few days later there was a debate in the Lords. It was opened by Lord Falconer, still Lord Chancellor, and I followed. The report's conclusion was that there was nothing wrong in the way Dr Kelly was revealed as the source for what Andrew Gilligan said on the *Today* programme. But that seemed quite bizarre. I reminded the House of what was said in Alastair Campbell's diary: 'GH (Geoff Hoon) and I agreed it would f*** Gilligan if that was the source – the biggest thing needed was the source out – spent much of the weekend talking to TB and GH re the source.' Campbell had, in fact, said at the inquiry that in government circles it was recognised that it would indeed assist them to get Kelly's name out in the open. 'How on earth, in the face of all that,' I said, 'can one take seriously Mr Hoon's statement that he made great efforts to ensure Dr Kelly's anonymity? Far from doing anything of the sort, he agreed to the issue of a press statement and a course of action which he knew would lead to the naming of Dr Kelly. He did not even tell Dr Kelly what he was going to do.'

I continued:

As for the Prime Minister, he may not in the strictest sense have authorised the leaking of Dr Kelly's name, but he presided over the meeting where it was decided to issue a press release that led, inevitably, to the naming of Dr Kelly. Campbell's diaries show that neither he nor anyone else in No. 10 were the slightest bit interested in Dr Kelly's welfare. On the contrary, they spent hours and hours in unminuted meetings, making unrecorded phone calls and plotting not how Dr Kelly's interest might be protected, but how his being thrown to the media might be turned to their advantage. Campbell decided to wage war on the BBC, a war with no holds barred, and he was happy to use Dr Kelly as a weapon in that war. Dr Kelly, already under intolerable pressure, was given no support, but instead was thrown to the media wolves and in that situation of mental turmoil, largely created by others, he took his own life.

Finally I reminded the House that the Prime Minister himself signed the foreword to the dossier which contained the words 'His (Saddam's) military planning allows for some of the weapons of mass destruction to be ready within forty-five minutes of an order to use them.' The Prime Minister knew perfectly well, from the intelligence reports, that this did not mean that Saddam had long-range weapons at his disposal; but when newspapers took those words of his to mean that there was a threat to Britain from long-range weapons – when there was a headline in *The Sun* reading: '45 MINUTES TO DOOM' and the *Evening Standard* wrote '45 MINUTES TO ATTACK' alongside a photograph of a London street – Tony Blair did absolutely nothing to correct the false impression he had given.

There must have been thousands of people wanting to say what they thought about the government, Alastair Campbell, poor Dr Kelly and the Hutton Report. I *could* say what I thought and realised as never before how lucky I was to be a member of the Lords and able to debate great issues.

I was off work for quite a long time having a new knee; and on my return introduced a debate on immigration and asylum. I pointed out that by the latter part of the 1980s, with firm and fair immigration control established, immigration policy had ceased to be a very contentious matter, but Labour had allowed what was to all intents and purposes a free-for-all – with work permits handed out in ever increasing numbers. And with most immigrants going to the same parts of the country, an intolerable strain was being put on public services. Sham marriages, bogus students and fraudulent visa applications had made matters worse. Total net immigration to the UK, which in 1997 was 46,000, had over the previous five years averaged 157,000 a year. And it was estimated that over five million of the six million increase in population expected in the next thirty years would be due to new immigrants and their offspring. That was enough to populate six cities the size of Birmingham.

It does not seem that on this occasion my oratory was very persuasive, for in the years that followed things got even worse. When Brown got into office he proudly talked of his determination to cover great tracts of the country with concrete to house the growing population. Some were brave enough to point out that if we could limit immigration so that there were no more people entering the country than leaving, there would be no need for any of this massive housing development; but they, of course, were branded racists.

In the 2005 general election Michael Howard fought valiantly. The Tories won a number of seats but Blair was still left with a thumping majority. In the summer of that year my great friend Mark Carlisle died. For a long time he had suffered from ill-health but he never lost his zest for life. He was the most gregarious of men and my only complaint is that he liked drinking standing up. Because of the difference in height this used to give me a stiff neck. I felt it a great honour to be invited to give the address at his memorial service in St Margaret's.

I will spare the reader an account of all I was up to in the next year or two but one matter is worth mentioning. A Bill to give effect to an agreement on European finance does not usually hit the headlines but in January 2008 I had the chance to put on record one of the most extraordinary betrayals of our country's interests.

The rebate on the UK's contribution to the EU, hard-won by Margaret Thatcher, was protected by our veto and could not be taken from us without our consent, but Tony Blair surrendered a part of it for precisely nothing. It all started honourably enough with Blair championing the expansion of the EU into eastern Europe; and he seems to have convinced himself that the French would be prepared to agree to reform of the farm budget to pay for expansion if Britain sacrificed at least part of the rebate. That was inherently unlikely, Blair himself in 2002 having signed up to a CAP settlement to last through to 2013, but when the French gave the inevitable '*non*', there was not the slightest need for the Prime Minister to do what he did which was, with great alacrity, to abandon his call for a budget freeze, abandon his call for a fundamental reform of Europe's finances and hand over part of our rebate on a plate. What he ought to have done was take the rebate off the table, pack his bags and return home. The tale told of course was that all this was necessary to secure enlargement and we could not 'will' enlargement without being prepared to pay for it, but that is simply not what happened. When enlargement was already a done deal Blair had told the Commons: 'the UK rebate will remain and we will not negotiate it away.' That was the promise; and the promise was broken. We had by then got used to surrenders and with each one came the same lame excuse: 'We had to surrender; failure to do so would have precipitated a crisis and, even worse, shown our lack of commitment to the EU.' We can only hope that a new government has really learned a few lessons from Blair's deceit over Lisbon and from this particularly dismal story about EU finance.

The Criminal Justice and Immigration Bill which arrived in the Lords in January 2008 contained a clause which made it an offence to incite hatred on the grounds of sexual orientation. It seemed clear to many of us that if there was to be this new offence, it was important that it did not damage free speech; and in due course I moved an amendment to ensure that the police did not construe criticism as threats or confuse strong criticism of a person's conduct with incitement to hatred. There was, I said, nothing in recent history to show that the police were good at distinguishing between legitimate comment and language calculated or intended to stir up hatred. I cited the case of the Bishop of Chester who was the subject of investigation by the Cheshire Police after he had made some comments about research showing that some homosexuals could be reoriented to heterosexuality. I also cited the case of the Fleetwood couple interrogated by the police after doing no more than complaining about their council's gay rights policy and the case of Lynette Burrows who was questioned after saying on the radio that homosexual men might not be the right people to bring up children.

The amendment was reached very late in the day but we won by eighty-one to fifty-seven. The decision was reversed in the Commons but when the matter came back to the Lords we won by 174 to 164 and the government did not make another attempt to reverse the decision.

One might have expected that to be the end of the story but, to my astonishment, into the next session's Coroners and Justice Bill the government slipped a clause repealing the free speech provision. Lord Bach, in moving the second reading of the Bill, sought to justify the government's strange behaviour, suggesting that in allowing the free speech safeguard to reach the statute book in the previous session the government had made clear its intention to return to the issue when circumstances allowed. In fact the government had not said anything of the sort and had merely intimated that if Parliament at any time wanted to return to the issue it would be able to do so.

In July 2009, my motion that the clause repealing the free speech safeguard should not remain part of the Bill was carried by a majority of fifty-three, but the decision was reversed by the Commons, and did not come back to us until 11 November. Lord Bach argued that we should not take our disagreement with the Commons any further and should bow to the will of the elected House, but rather overdid it when he referred to the 'clear and unambiguous view of the Commons'. That gave me the opportunity to point out that not a single Labour member supported the government's case, except of course the minister speaking from the front bench.

> Indeed, almost the only person on the Labour benches throughout the debate was Mr David Taylor who, in spite of the government having refused to allow a free vote on this matter of conscience, stuck to his guns and voted for free speech. Before doing so he had said, 'I thought that free speech, civil liberties and human rights were exactly the sorts of things that we were supposed to be in favour of.'

We won the division by a majority of forty-four, but then had an anxious night and an early start in the morning preparing ourselves against the possibility of the decision being reversed in the Commons and our having to debate the matter yet again. But when the Commons met, a government motion that the House should not insist on its disagreement with the Lords was agreed without debate. Mr Edward Leigh (Gainsborough) (Conservative) did, however, rise and say:

> On a point of order Mr Deputy Speaker, it would be useful if the Secretary of State could make a statement on the fact that the government appear to have run up the white flag on Lord Waddington's amendment. This a great victory for free speech, and we should know more about it.

Not surprisingly the Deputy Speaker said it was no point of order and that was that.

After we had successfully amended the Criminal Justice and Immigration Bill in April 2008 I had been astonished to receive a telephone call from one of our shadow ministers in the Commons saying that they were not going to support our amendment, but were going to put down their own amendment in lieu – the terms of which, I then discovered, would completely undermine the case I had been deploying. It was only after furious protests from Detta and myself and threats to resign the whip that these shadow ministers were eventually prevailed upon to change their minds. I thought it monstrous that they should think for one moment that it was right not to support colleagues in the Lords who had inflicted a very significant and wounding defeat on the government. But what I suppose was even more monstrous was that people who considered themselves Tories should not think it important to protect free speech and guard against people being prosecuted as a result of the authorities assuming that any criticism of sexual behavior must be motivated by hatred.

It was a notable victory achieved because of the marvellous support I received from the Christian Institute and Simon Calvert, in particular, and the heroic help I had from Detta O'Cathain.

CHAPTER TWENTY-FOUR

Bowing Out

The House of Lords is not always the place to go to for polite and well-informed debate. There was an occasion recently when Lord McNally from the Liberal Democrat benches accused Lord Pearson of Rannoch of being a ranter with militant tendencies and that he was using tactics drawn from a Trotskyite handbook. Lord McNally is a Europhile and Lord Pearson a member of UKIP, and it has to be said that Lord Pearson's frequent exposures of the goings-on in Brussels often give great offence to the apologists for the EU who seem to form a majority of members of the House. I do not know how it has happened but peers of a Europhile persuasion dominate the committees dealing with European business and have often shown little respect for the views of others who do not feel as they do. I witnessed the proceedings in the committee which heard evidence from Marta Andreasen, the brave woman sacked for criticising the EU's accounting system and the way in which it was exposed to fraud. She was listened to with scant respect. Neil Kinnock, who had had a hand in her dismissal, then gave evidence and was treated like a conquering hero.

All this has caused me much irritation, but I still view it as a great privilege to be a member of the place and be able, when the spirit moves me, to take part in debate.

A few years ago Miles, the late Duke of Norfolk, was attending a ceremony with me for members of the Royal Victoria Order. 'Tell me, old boy,' he said, 'have you had your first stroke yet?' With some surprise at such a delicate subject being raised so early in our conversation I answered in the negative. But not long afterwards my first stroke did arrive, and it has slowed me down a bit. But I still attend the House from time to time, and I am then greatly rewarded by being able to travel home and be greeted by a wife ready to listen patiently to my account of what is going on in the Palace of Westminster. I am a lucky man and am often reminded of those lines of Dryden:

> Happy the man, and happy he alone,
> He, who can call today his own;
> He who, secure within, can say,
> Tomorrow, do thy worst, for I have lived today.

> Be fair or foul or rain or shine
> The joys I have possessed, in spite of fate, are mine.
> Not Heaven itself upon the past has power;
> But what has been, has been, and I have had my hour.

Index

Coming soon to Biteback

WHATEVER NEXT
EARL FERRERS

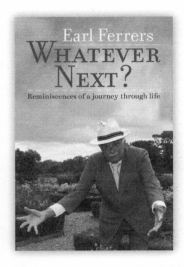

In this charming and poignant memoir, the 13th Earl Ferrers – Robert Washington Shirley, farmer, businessman, politician, husband and father – reflects on a life very well lived. Contemplative musings on politics, religion, relationships and the meaning of life are peppered throughout with humorous anecdotes – of an aristocratic upbringing at Staunton Harold in the 1930s, high jinks at Winchester and Cambridge, national service in the jungle of Malaya with the Coldstream Guards, and his time as a minister in every Conservative Government from Macmillan to Major. *Whatever Next?* recounts captivating tales of the ups and downs of Westminster life from a peer with a real twinkle in his eye.

'Robin Ferrers is one of the most engaging and loved parliamentarians of recent decades. He is a national treasure, and his memoirs are proof-positive that there is humanity in politics.' – Sir John Major

368pp paperback, £8.99

**Available from all good bookshops or order from
www.bitebackpublishing.com**